GENDER, PRACTICE AND FAITH IN NICARAGUA

Gender, Practice and Faith in Nicaragua

Constructing the Popular and Making 'Common Sense'

STEPHANIE LINKOGLE

Avebury

Aldershot · Brookfield USA · Hong Kong · Singapore · Sydney

PU-18 (7) (DL6NO)

Published by
Avebury
Ashgate Publishing Ltd
Gower House
Croft Road
Aldershot
Hants GU11 3HR
England

Ashgate Publishing Company
Old Post Road
Brookfield
Vermont 05036
USA

British Library Cataloguing in Publication Data

Linkogle, Stephanie
    Gender, practice and faith in Nicaragua
    1. Religion and politics – Nicaragua   2. Religion and culture
    – Nicaragua   3. Nicaragua – History – 1990–   4. Nicaragua –
    Politics and government – 1990–
    I. Title
    972.8'5053

    ISBN 1 85972 298 9

Library of Congress Catalog Card Number: 96-83259

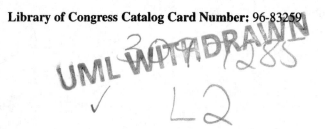

Printed and bound in Great Britain by Ipswich Book Co. Ltd., Ipswich, Suffolk

Contents

Preface

This book examines the structuring of political consciousness through religious discourse in Nicaragua in the period prior to and since the revolutionary FSLN's (Sandinista National Liberation Front) 1990 electoral loss. Focusing in particular on the gendered character of political consciousness, the book seeks to explore the construction of identities and hegemony in Nicaragua through both organised and popular forms of religion. These processes, through which identity and hegemony were built, occurred in all arenas of Nicaraguan society from the national domain to the more micro setting of neighbourhood organisations. On the national level, the book explores how two major blocs competed for hegemonic power: the FSLN/'popular church' bloc, and the Right/hierarchical church bloc. The section of the Nicaraguan church engaged in liberation theology praxis has been called the 'popular church'. The popular church often stood in opposition to the hierarchy or the 'hierarchical church' whose authoritarian vision was accompanied by a conservative, indeed contra-revolutionary, stance.

On the local level, the book looks at women in a communal kitchen or *olla* run under the auspices of San Pablo the Apostle, one of Nicaragua's founding Christian base communities (CEBs). CEBs are small grassroots groups of Catholic laity. The book examines how these women made sense of their lives in terms of their religious faith, political commitment and gender. Yet, revolutionary consciousness was not just created through active participation in religious and political organisations. The 'popular' in Nicaragua was constructed with reference to both religious discourse and imagery. In this way, the book argues that 'everyday' religious common sense has permeated Nicaraguan culture and, as such, both Left and Right have used popular religion and popular religious festivals to bolster their respective causes.

Acknowledgements

My family, in particular my parents Joan and James Linkogle and my grandmother Rose La Doma, deserve much thanks for their love and support. Special thanks should also go to my PhD supervisor Professor Jorge Larrain for his attentive reading of drafts and for his patience, encouragement and keen insight. I would like to thank the women of Olla San Rafael, Juanita Sanchez Villegas, Wilma Sandoval Turcois, Carmen Porto Carrero Narvaez, Flor Nohemí Montoya, Glenda Beteto Perez, Erika de Los Angeles Lopez, for allowing me to interview them and share their "every day life". In addition, I am indebted to Casa CEB in Managua, especially Elba Vasquez for introducing me to Olla San Rafael. Thanks should also go to Lucy from Soy Nica her kind help. Thelma Flores deserves extra-special thanks for her warmth, humour and friendship and more practically for helping me to come to grips with *naulañol*. I am grateful to Kate Corr for her careful reading of Chapter 5. I would also like to thank Yvonne Jacobs and Marie Walsh for support throughout my time as a post-graduate. Beth Humphrys and Sue Gilbert deserve much thanks for their help in the preparation of the manuscript. In addition, thanks should also go to Avebury, in particular to Jo Gooderham, Patricia Marks and Steven Jarman. I would also like to express gratitude to my fellow members of Birmingham Action for the Caribbean and Central America. In addition, the warm support of friends and colleagues at the University of Manchester has been greatly appreciated. I must also express great thanks to the following people: Anahita Razavi, Noemi Rodriguez, Ged Hazelwood, Suki Sanghera, Fausto Ruiz Martinez, Michele Plochere and Kim Pears. Finally, I would like to thank John Gabriel for his careful reading of drafts, his computer detective work and his support and reassurance. He gave me the courage and inspiration to persevere.

Abbreviations

AMNLE	Association of Nicaraguan Women, Luisa Amanda Espinosa
ATC	Rural Workers Association
BANIC	Alliance of Nicaraguan Business people
CAV	Antonio Valdivieso Ecumenical Centre
CDCs	Civilian Defence Committees
CNA	National Literacy Campaign
CDS	Sandinista Defence Committee
CEBs	Christian Base Communities
CELAM	Latin American Episcopal Conference
CEPAD	Evangelical Committee for Aid to Development
CIA	Central Intelligence Agency
CIAV	Commission for Support and Verification
CSE	Supreme Electoral Council
CST	Sandinista Workers Central
DN	National Directorate
DRI	FSLN's International Relations Department
ENABAS	National Foodstuffs Enterprise
ESP	Sandinista People's Army
FNT	National Workers' Front
FSLN	Sandinista National Liberation Front
GPP	Prolonged People's War (pre-1979 FSLN grouping)
IMF	International Monetary Fund
INSSIBI	Nicaraguan Social Security Agency
IRD	Institute on Religion and Democracy
JS19	Sandinista Youth Movement

MO	Mass Organisation
MCN	Nicaraguan Community Movement
NR	Nicaraguan Resistance
NSMs	New Social Movements
PAN	National Nutrition Programme
PLC	Constitutional Liberal Party
PSN	Nicaraguan Socialist Party
TP	Proletarian Tendency (pre-1979 FSLN grouping)
UCA	University of Central America
UNAG	Union of Farmers and Ranchers
UNO	National Opposition Union
USAID	US Agency for International Development
Vatican II	Second Vatican Council

1 Preliminary reflections on themes and methods

1 Introduction

The background against which this book has been researched and written has been importantly, though by no means entirely, shaped by the defeat of the revolutionary FSLN (Sandinista National Liberation Front) government in the elections of 1990 and the victory of Violeta Chamorro's UNO (National Opposition Union) coalition. The post-1990 period has been overshadowed by the extensive implementation of neo-liberal economic policies in Nicaragua at the behest of the World Bank, the IMF and the US donor agency, USAID.[1] The impact of these policies can be assessed through an examination of levels of hardship experienced in Nicaragua in the post-1990 period. In 1993, according to UNICEF, Nicaragua led Central America in rates of infant mortality (83 per 1,000 live births), a key index of living standards (*Barricada Internacional*, November/December 1993). Further, the UN estimated that 75 per cent of Nicaraguan households lived below the poverty line while 44 per cent lived in 'extreme poverty' (*Envio*, January 1995). Poverty, hunger and unemployment (56.6 per cent) were the defining features of Nicaraguan life (Nord, 1994).

While Nicaragua has experienced many changes since 1990, there remain numerous continuities with the period in which the FSLN held state power. While the balance of power has clearly shifted, the victory of the UNO coalition did not signal a final end to the revolutionary process; rather it initiated a period of trenchant battles to undo or preserve aspects of the revolutionary programme such as land and property reform. In cultural terms, the 1990 elections were significant in that they both initiated and reflected a transformation in the way in

1

which Nicaraguans understood themselves and their commitment to the 'rightness' or 'wrongness' of wider social change.

In this book, I am particularly interested in the sources of identification with the revolutionary project and the institutional contexts in which such normative allegiances were both maintained and disrupted. One institutional site of considerable importance in what follows is that of Christian base communities (CEBs), the term used to describe small grassroots groups of Catholic laity. CEB members' commitment to the 'rightness' of the revolution was fractured in a number of ways by post-1990 developments. Firstly, there was much less agreement about the goals and the strategies of the FSLN after 1990. Hence what *Sandinismo*, the philosophy of the FSLN, was and what it meant to be a Sandinista no longer had the focus that it did in the pre-1990 period. Secondly, after its election defeat the FSLN lacked not only the opportunities for articulating and reinforcing its position, but also the wider legitimacy that comes with state power. At the same time, a series of conditions which pre-dated the 1990 defeat served to further undermine the revolutionary consensus. Most important amongst these were the war against the United States-backed *contra* forces, the United States economic embargo and the FSLN's own economic stabilisation programmes.

One of the key continuities between the 'new' Nicaragua and the 'old' revolutionary Nicaragua is the importance of religion and religious blocs. Of particular significance is the part that liberation theology played in the period leading up to the insurrection in July 1979, the revolutionary period itself and post-1990 period. Liberation theology is based on a dialogue, exchange and, to a greater or lesser degree, convergence of Marxism and Christianity. José Miranda neatly states the crux of the issue for many liberation theologians: 'Marx and St. Paul coincide in their [evaluation] of the totality of evil: Sin and injustice form an all pervasive organic structure. Paul calls this totality cosmos. Marx calls it capitalism' (Miranda, 1974, p.250). Developments in Nicaragua were crucially shaped by the emergence of this movement within the Latin American church. Hence analysis of its underlying tenets and its relationship to the Nicaraguan revolution will form an important part of what follows. The section of the Nicaraguan church engaged in liberation theology praxis has been called the 'popular church'. The popular church often stood in opposition to the hierarchy or the 'hierarchical church' whose authoritarian vision of the church was accompanied by a conservative, indeed contra-revolutionary, stance. In an attempt to discredit and undermine the popular church and its philosophy, the hierarchy has sought to equate it with schism or some form of parallel magisterium.[2] The conflicts and allegiances

2

surrounding such debates and their relationship to wider political developments will be discussed more fully in section 3 and taken up again in Chapter 3.

The focus of this book, then, is an examination of the structuring of political consciousness through religious discourse in Nicaragua in the period prior to and since the 1990 change in government, with specific reference to the gendered character of this consciousness. The book focuses in particular on the institutional construction and reshaping of processes of identification as experienced by women participants in the activities of the 'popular church'. It seeks to explore how identification was shaped through the distinct but related discourses of both the popular church and the popular religious festivals of La Purísima and Santo Domingo. It will examine the way in which this identification both transformed and was transformed by existing dominant political blocs.

In evaluating the role of religious discourses in the construction of political consciousness, the book seeks to distinguish the discourse of the popular church from that of popular religion. The basis for this distinction lies in the institutional character of the popular church, with its relatively coherent and well documented underlying philosophy (liberation theology), which sets it apart from the unsystematised set of practices and beliefs that constitutes popular religion. The book examines two key areas. Firstly, it analyses the practice of the popular church with particular reference to the highly gendered phenomenon of participation in CEBs. Secondly, it explores the elements of Nicaraguan popular religion that were constitutive of a religious and often gendered 'common sense' which fostered identification with specific political projects. In making this distinction between the 'popular church' and 'popular religion' I do not wish to imply that they are entirely discrete categories; clearly there is a significant degree of imbrication. However, following the distinction made by Lancaster (1988), I highlight their different functions in the process of religious identification.

The central contributions of the book will be fourfold. Firstly, the book will develop an understanding of the acutely under- researched area of women's participation in the Nicaraguan popular church. How, why and when did women participate in CEBs are amongst the questions I will explore. Secondly, I will argue that political consciousness and identification are formed and recast through the religious discourses of both the popular church and popular religion, particularly as the latter is expressed in popular religious festivals. Part of the argument here will emphasise the significance of gender to this process of identification. Thirdly, religiously structured identification with the Sandinista revolutionary project was a key aspect of the common sense support that underpinned the FSLN's hegemony. The book will argue that the FSLN's attempts to win this hegemony back in the post-1990 period have been based on recapturing this religiously imbued common sense, a task greatly impeded by the disarticulation of the notion of 'moral' or 'right' action from a necessary commitment to the revolution. This was due to the economic crisis and the absence of a politicising state to turn the pragmatic into the political. In post-1990 Nicaragua this process seemed to be working in reverse. Fourthly, the book will emphasise the significance of practice, within the context of CEBs and popular religious festivals, as a site for the contestation, reformulation and in some cases entrenchment of discourses around religion, politics and gender.

2   Themes of the book

In this work, I am concerned to stress the centrality of 'identification' - how people see themselves in relation to a particular national-popular project - through a religious common sense as well as a more structured religious ideology. The revolution called on people 'to do the right thing', in effect defining morality as support for the revolution. Nicaraguans were called upon to identify with the revolution not only out of self-interest but also because there was an ethical mandate to do so. In describing this identity formation, I use the term 'moral identity'. A moral identity, I will argue, is a form of consciousness which structures both rational and common sense understandings of 'morality'. Political, religious and gender identities are part of the process of identification on a 'moral' basis. Although moral identities are not necessarily expressed in a collective fashion, in the context of the Nicaraguan revolution 'the moral' became closely intertwined with 'the collective'. In post-1990 Nicaragua, the consensus on the content and form of moral identification was much more uncertain than in the period which preceded it.

In sum, moral identities combine both a structured and rational commitment to a particular project or programme and a common sense understanding of that programme as 'right'. In this book I will examine how moral identities are constructed in two distinct ways: through the discourses of both the popular church and popular religion. In the case of the popular church I will look at CEBs as an example of how, through active practice, moral identities have been constructed and shaped. In addition, the popular church on its own and in conjunction with the FSLN was responsible for the diffusion of a religio-political discourse which 'moralised' identities. Secondly, I will explore the more fluid and

4

unpredictable ways in which popular religion contributes processes of identity formation.

According to Jorge Larrain, the link between consciousness and moral conviction was made by John Locke, who maintained that 'the continuity or sameness of consciousness allowed identity to exist, and as such an identity was the basis of moral accountability' (Larrain, 1994, p.144). In this formulation, identity and 'morality' were inseparable. Yet in more contemporary explorations of the term, the issue of moral commitment has not figured prominently. Further, the concept of 'morality' has been problematised because it implies a universal standard for belief and behaviour and as such implicitly or explicitly denigrates moralities other than its own western version. In this book the concept of morality is not used universally or prescriptively to defend one political position over another, but in contingent and relative terms, to locate and analyse the transformation of a specific set of allegiances to the revolution in Nicaragua.

Identification with the revolution was based not only on a rational posture of support - that is, out of differently perceived and constructed interests - but also on a more visceral, emotional level. In other words, supporting the revolution came to make common sense insofar as it became seen as doing 'good' or doing the 'right thing'. Identification with the revolution on this level was both cultivated and spontaneous. Religion was one of the primary means by which this identification arose and was shaped.

In exploring this process of identification and 'moral identities' in particular, I draw on a wide range of literature on identity which it would be useful to reflect on at this point. Debates within academia on identity are linked with more general debates which have emerged through and in the wake of what has been called the 'discursive turn' in literature and the social sciences. Derrida's notion that there is no truth outside of texts, in conjunction with the growing influence of the kind of discourse analysis developed by Michel Foucault, turned analytical attention towards the social construction of all aspects of life based on a relativist understanding of knowledge. For some thinkers this discursive turn, the basis of postmodernism, has provided the opportunity to deconstruct previously unchallenged knowledges and has ushered in new possibilities for rethinking the question of identity. As bell hooks argues:

Postmodern critiques of essentialism which challenge notions of universality and static overdetermined identity within mass culture and mass consciousness can open up new possibilities for the construction of self and the assertion of agency (hooks, 1991, p.28).

Categories like identity were 'deconstructed' and explained as the articulation of discourses rather than the expression of any essential personhood or subjectivity. Glenn Jordan and Chris Weedon maintain that discourses are the routes by which we give meaning to the world (Jordan and Weedon, 1995). Moreover, 'they imply forms of social organisation and social practices which structure institutions and constitute individuals as thinking feeling and acting subjects' (Jordan and Weedon, 1995, p.14). In other words, whilst identities articulate with our everyday experience they are constructed and grasped through discourse. This notion of discourse will be drawn upon throughout the book as I examine the shifting processes of identification and identity formation as they are structured through discourse.

Stuart Hall similarly cites the importance of discourses or narratives in the construction of identity. He argues that identity is always at least partly constituted through narratives in which we recognise and represent ourselves (Hall, 1991b). For Hall, identities are always incomplete - never finally formed. In looking at the shifting processes of identification in Nicaragua, it becomes clear that notions of what was right or moral fluctuated and in the process either initiated or reflected changes in the hegemonic configurations. Here the notion of identity as a fluid rather than a static or essential category was borne out.

Although it is fluid, identity is always historically and culturally located. To this end, Hall argues that 'you have to be positioned somewhere in order to speak' (Hall, 1991b, p.51). Significantly, he contends that identity is a process of identification in opposition to 'the other'. Thus identities are from their very inception oppositional. He argues:

> when you know what everybody else is, you know what you are not. Identity is always, in that sense, a structured representation which only achieves its positive through the narrow eye of the negative. It has to go through the eye of the needle of the other before it can construct itself (Hall, 1991a, p.21).

What is significant here is that debates around the formation of identity *vis-à-vis* 'the other' are rarely accompanied by a similarly full discussion of how the identity of 'the other' is constituted (e.g. Said, 1978). Often 'the other' is merely a point of reference rather than a fully theorised human subject. At the same time the notion of identity politics as articulated by Hall, Pratibha Parmar, hooks and Paul Gilroy amongst others has offered a key nub of theorisation addressing the character of political engagement organised around fluid and hybrid identities. As Pratibha Parmar contends:

personal identity is very often tied to the need to articulate a collective identity around race and culture even though as individuals we inhabit a range of positions within our histories and inside our diverse identities (Parmar, 1990, p.116).

Parmar stresses the plurality of identities at the same time as affirming a need for a collective identity. This position is elaborated by Gayatri Spivak, who advances the utility of 'strategic essentialism' whereby subaltern or oppressed people 'choose' a seemingly essential identity in order to pursue a political project wider than merely exploring the multiplicity of identity (Spivak, 1993). If there is not some essential notion of identity, no matter how provisional, tentative or strategic, then the possibility of collective action becomes untenable. Spivak argues that if identities are essentialised in a strategic fashion there can be a productive co-existence of unity and diversity (1993).

My analysis of moral identity formation in both the popular church and popular religion are built around two further concepts; ideology and hegemony. In this book, I aim to use Antonio Gramsci's work as a starting point in order to unpack some of the discourses around the popular church, the FSLN, the hierarchical church and the political Right. In particular, I am concerned to investigate the relationship between political consciousness, religion and politics. It is here that I intend to explore the processes of identity formation, and in particular the moral identities that have emerged from participation in CEBs and the diffusion of popular religious and popular church discourses.

A mapping of these concepts is useful for an analysis of the popular church and popular religion both during the years that the FSLN held state power and in the post-1990 period. Overall the book attempts to examine both periods and contribute to an understanding not only of the particularities of each but also of the continuity between the two. Because the FSLN's 1990 electoral loss was a concrete indication of a 'loss of faith', it is important to explore how and why this arose. Further, since both liberation theology and CEBs were closely intertwined with *Sandinismo* in Nicaragua, a consideration of the post-1990 state of this relationship is a significant focus of this book. The literature reflecting on these changes and continuities is rather patchy, due in good part to the recent character of the change and the uncertainty of the Nicaraguan political scene. I will aim to address this lacuna.

If the 1980s were the pinnacle of Gramscian-inspired theoretical analysis, the Nicaraguan revolution functioned as the exemplar of some key concepts developed within this framework. In particular, interrelated theories of ideology, hegemony and identity featured prominently, not only in academic discourse, but also in common sense understandings of the revolution. I have chosen Gramsci as my starting point for the critical elaboration of these issues because of his uniquely complex and subtle understanding of Marxism, religion and political consciousness.

For Marx, ideology is negative, i.e. a form of distorted consciousness which is produced by a contradictory reality in order to conceal that reality. Capitalism itself assists in this, since it presents itself in a double way, as appearances and as real relations. Marx argued that people do not believe lies but they do believe the lying realities of the experiences that they themselves help to construct through labour or reproductive practice. Ideologies, according to Gramsci, on the other hand, are more neutral and potentially positive. They 'organise human masses, and create the terrain on which men [sic] move, acquire consciousness of their position, struggle, etc.' (Gramsci, 1971, p.377). For him, ideologies do not simply make their influence felt at the superstructural level, they are themselves a superstructure. He maintains that: '"Ideology" itself must be analysed historically, in terms of the philosophy of praxis, as a superstructure' (Gramsci, 1971, p.376). Gramsci explicitly rejects a negative concept of ideology because, for him, such a conceptualisation reduces the meaning of the term to '"pure" appearance' (ibid.). He thus equates all negative conceptualisations of ideology with 'false consciousness', a characterisation which does not do justice to Marx's negative concept of ideology.

Gramsci, not having had access to Marx's negative formulation of ideology in The German Ideology, believed that he was expanding and enriching Marx's concept (Marx, 1970). In fact, what he did was to take the concept of ideology in an entirely new direction from that developed by Marx in The German Ideology. For Gramsci, ideology did not operate against the interests of the working class, preventing them from achieving class consciousness and acting decisively in their own interests (i.e. to become a class for itself). Rather it was a tool, integral to successful praxis, that the working class would have to use if it was to secure political power.

In Gramsci's conceptualisation, intellectuals were the most effective transmitters of ideology. For him intellectuals were not just academics, philosophers or writers; they were also organisers of classes - trade union leaders, priests, teachers, etc. Gramsci defined intellectuals in relation to their ideological function rather than in terms of any intellectual superiority over the masses. His use of the term 'intellectual' is significant because it widened the scope of who is allowed to lead and influence. Moreover, he recognised leadership in a broader and more inclusive sense. However, the intellectual was still posited as having a function distinct from those s/he leads; in this way, a differentiation between the led and the leaders was preserved even as the concept of leadership was deepened and expanded. For him:

> there is no organisation without intellectuals, that is without the theoretical aspect of the theory-practice nexus being distinguished concretely by the existence of a group of people 'specialised' in conceptual and philosophical elaboration of ideas (Gramsci, 1971, p.334).

Gramsci distinguished between two types of intellectuals, the traditional and the organic (Gramsci, 1971, pp. 12-16). The traditional intellectual derives his/her function from an earlier historical period. For Gramsci, the priest was a typical example of the traditional intellectual. Although these intellectuals may derive their power from an earlier epoch, their very presence indicates that the tenacity of older orders should not be underestimated. In contrast, the organic intellectual serves to organise and guide the class to which s/he belongs (Gramsci, 1971, p.6). Both the proletariat and the bourgeoisie have their own organic intellectuals. For the proletariat, organic intellectuals are a key to any successful anti-bourgeois struggle.

In Nicaragua, Ernesto Cardenal would be considered, in Gramscian terms, ironically both a traditional and an organic intellectual; traditional by virtue of his status as a priest and organic through his active participation in the FSLN government. Cardenal is a personification of the radical synthesis of the traditional and the organic intellectual. The power encapsulated in this fusion is an aspect of the progressive church's strength which Gramsci could not have anticipated. However, Cardenal, as a middle-class, 'well-educated' priest, is not the most compelling example of this new intellectual. Rather, it was the recently literate peasants, workers and 'marginals', emerging from the CEB structure to assume positions of prominence and responsibility within the revolutionary government and its organisations, who came to represent the most profound example of this 'new' intellectual. They were traditionally bound in their commitment to the church and organically bound by their participation in the revolutionary process. Thus, the intellectual who develops through the Nicaraguan CEB can be usefully examined through Gramsci's non-hierarchical notion of the intellectual, however much their example may stretch the parameters of this concept.

This new intellectual is part of a wider project which CEBs seem to have taken on: a practical transformation or progressive renewal of their country, their church, and their community. In this process, pre-figurative practice plays a key role. The notion of 'prefigurative practice', although singularly realised in Nicaraguan CEBs, is not original to them. The concept was developed by Gramsci during his involvement with workers' councils in Turin and explored in his articles for the journal *Ordine Nuovo*, but it was not taken up again in the Prison Notebooks (1971). Prefigurative practice, as Jim O'Connor describes it, is characterised by 'attempts to develop co-operative and non-hierarchical practices within and against established bourgeois institutions' (O'Connor, 1987, p.122). The notion of creating effective anti-bourgeois political practices has been 'developed into elaborated forms of criticism/self-criticism and struggles against racism, sexism, national chauvinism, elitism, and individualism in popular movements today' (ibid.).

In Gramscian terms, hegemony is a complex process of securing consent achieved and maintained through struggles on the ideological terrain. In these conflicts, both the bourgeoisie and the proletariat employ distinctive ideologies. However, for Gramsci, hegemony was not merely the dominance of one class over the other, but a situation in which one class had managed to achieve political power through its leadership skills and its willingness to incorporate or co-opt the demands of the allied classes. The hegemonic class cannot merely dominate the allied classes but must also articulate the real 'interests' of these groups, thus constructing a hegemonic bloc. The measure of the hegemonic class's success is the extent to which it secures the consent of the subordinate or subaltern classes. According to Gramsci, consent may be passive and indirect or active and direct, but the latter form of consent is the most successful hegemonic configuration.

The relationship between hegemony and coercion is difficult to conceptualise partly because at some points Gramsci designated them as separate but operating in tandem and at others he posited coercion as one of the functions of hegemony. Expanding on Machiavelli, Gramsci presented the integral state as dictatorship + hegemony (Gramsci, 1971, p.239). Here he indicated that hegemony was the consent factor of the equation while dictatorship was the force component. On another occasion, however, he maintains: 'The normal exercise of hegemony in the area...of the parliamentary regime, is characterised by the combination of force and consensus which vary in their balance of each other, without force exceeding consensus too much' (Gramsci in Joll, 1977, p.99). In this way, Gramsci clearly presented force as a part of hegemony.

Building upon a Gramscian conception of hegemony which incorporates the notion of force and applying it to the Nicaraguan revolution, Doug Brown establishes a polarity between two distinctive types of hegemony at work: democratic and authoritarian (Brown, 1990, p.40). According to Brown, the FSLN built and maintained their hegemonic bloc by both authoritarian and democratic means, although they primarily relied upon the latter strategy. In line with Brown, the 'force + consent equals hegemony' equation could be restated as 'more force + less consent equals authoritarian hegemony' and 'more consent + less force equals democratic hegemony'.

Brown's focus on the distinction between democratic and authoritarian hegemony problematises the latter and implicitly calls into question the validity of coercive state practices even if they serve to buttress hegemony. That coercion is an objective feature of many hegemonic blocs is not in question. Rather what is at issue is the desirability of such a strategy and the tension between the coercive and consenting aspects of hegemony. Not only is there a contradiction between the democratic and authoritarian aspects articulated in *Sandinismo*, there is also the question of how this is expressed in practice. In Nicaragua, the tension was made more taut by the mix of discourse centring on both the 'vanguard' and the 'democratic'.

The importance of democracy to the FSLN was reflected in their ideology, *Sandinismo*. Brown maintained that 'although *Sandinismo* is not a logically consistent set of ideas consciously formulated by reference to current theories of rights discourse, its evolution has been characterised implicitly by this dimension' (Brown, 1990, p.56). The FSLN prioritised the need to create a healthy civil society in Nicaragua and set up the electoral and parliamentary system which facilitated the first ever democratic transfer of state power. The human rights aspect of *Sandinismo* reached its apex when the individual and collective rights of the Nicaraguan 'subject' were enshrined in a constitution, thus making Nicaragua officially a 'law' or 'rights-based' society. The rights-based discourse that the FSLN employed in its struggle to overthrow Somoza also tapped into the 'human rights' discourse highlighted by then US President Jimmy Carter's foreign policy.[3]

Hegemonic struggle is not strictly anti-capitalist struggle because a hegemonic bloc must incorporate more than just one class. Thus coalition and co-operative politics are a key feature of Gramscian-inspired struggle. The idea that the frontiers of struggle have expanded can be very exciting to many who have been locked out of the Marxist framework by its emphasis on industrial struggle. The politics of many Marxists seemed to suggest that anyone who was not a white male industrial worker was somehow peripheral to the struggle against capitalism. The Gramsci-inspired principle that 'my' struggle (as a woman, person of colour or differently-abled person) not only has

11

validity on its own terms but must be incorporated into any successful struggle against bourgeois hegemony has been rightly seen as affirmative, inclusive and liberating politics.

In his analysis of Catholicism, Gramsci illustrates how a form of ideology takes hold of the masses and maintains authority within its own ranks by militating against a split between the intellectuals of the church and the 'simple souls' (Gramsci, 1971, p.331). The Catholic church traditionally preserved its position through alliances with dominant groups, e.g. its support for the Fascist state in Italy. In contrast to religion, Marxism, or the philosophy of praxis, offers a true suture for the split between the intellectuals and the 'simple souls'. Gramsci wrote of the need to form 'an intellectual and moral bloc' which will benefit an entire society. The resulting unity of the intellectuals and the 'masses' would be a true coming together and 'the antithesis of the Catholic' (Gramsci, 1971, pp. 332-3).

The issue of parallel magisterium or the parallel church is one that has been a central preoccupation of the church. Gramsci argued that if debates were carried out amongst an elite of theologians and deviations from church dogma were not widely disseminated, dissension was often tolerated. Liberation theology proper is not widely consumed by the subjects of its theorising, so would see constitute little threat on its own. However, the fact that liberation theology provides the theoretical underpinnings of CEBs and other progressive pastoral programmes constitutes it as a real threat to a hierarchically determined 'unity'. In reflecting on the Catholic church's historical attitude towards unity, Gramsci maintained:

> The strength of religions, and the Catholic church in particular, has lain, and still lies, in the fact that they feel very strongly the need for doctrinal unity of the whole masses of the faithful and strive to ensure that the higher intellectual stratum does not get separated from the lower. The Roman church has always been the most vigorous in the struggle to prevent the 'official' formation of two religions, one for the 'intellectuals' and one for the 'simple souls' (Gramsci, 1971, p.328).

Here Gramsci was arguing that the religion of the 'higher intellectual strata' was not the same as that of the 'masses'. Differences were allowed in order to maintain the support of the former, yet the loyalty of the latter had to be retained. In this conception, the threat to 'unity' springs from the potential of a contradiction ensuing between the 'common sense' religiosity of the masses and the theological debates of the intellectuals. That the 'masses', within the context of CEBs, are now engaging in theological debates of their own means that they are no longer passive recipients of a neutralised 'faith'. In this way, anxieties over 'the official formation of two religions', the *bête noire* of the hierarchical church, are centred around the popular church. Here the 'simple souls' are advancing a provocative theology of liberation and cannot, due to the very character of their deviation and their 'class' position within the church, mask their dissension. The hierarchy's response has been, in addition to more punitive measures, a call for 'unity'. As Andrew Bradstock argues:

> the tendency for some Christians in Latin America to promote a church *of* rather than just *for* the poor, as evidenced by the growing number of CEBs, is responsible at least in part for the Pope's increasing emphasis on the need for unity in the church to be maintained around the hierarchy (Bradstock, 1987, pp. 64-5).

The 'simple souls' might not have the degree of education and theoretical sophistication of the 'higher intellectual stratum', but they have a growing confidence in their ability to biblically contextualise their reality of oppression and to ground their commitment to social justice in specific socio-political activity. Cesar Isaac Gomez, a member of FUNDECI [4], states:

> I believe that there is a similarity between *Sandinismo* and what Christ said, that we must always try to love each other and help our neighbours in their difficulties. *Sandinismo* speaks of this a great deal. I don't know much about communism, isn't there love in it? (cited in Heyck, 1990, p.190).

Here, the objective criterion for accepting 'communism' or 'Marxism' is the degree to which they sincerely incorporate the Christian maxim, 'Love thy neighbour'. What is significant here is not that Gomez has a selective understanding of Marxism or Christianity but that he is taking out of these philosophies what is relevant to his understanding of the world and in this process openly engaging with both. This mode of understanding is a key feature of the *conscientización* [5] process typical of CEBs and it is challenging both to hierarchical Catholicism and to forms of rigid or orthodox Marxism. While Gramsci's Marxism was neither rigid nor orthodox, his understanding of the role of religion was understandable, given his personal and political experiences of pre-Vatican II Catholicism. Given this negative understanding, it is interesting to consider how he envisages that the masses might come to accept Marxism.

Gramsci argues that, if Marxism is to take hold of the masses, it must initially do so through a kind of faith (Gramsci, 1971, p.339). For him, 'everyone is a philosopher' but the tools for systematic and critical reasoning need to be developed (Gramsci, 1971, p.323). Yet the diffusion of Marxism or the philosophy of praxis in a society need not wait until it is understood and accepted in a rigorous manner by 'the masses'. Gramsci argues that people might accept Marxism on faith, as they do Catholicism, believing that if they are not capable of defending it intellectually, someone amongst the ranks of believers must be (Gramsci, 1971, p.339). As the Gomez example demonstrates, revolutionary Christians who are sympathetic to *Sandinismo* and 'communism' might not have a complete or rigorous understanding of Marxism or, for that matter, Catholicism. However, the popular church has attempted to give people the confidence to make decisions and hold beliefs, based not on a 'blind' faith but upon an understanding and consideration of their own circumstances, goals and commitments to their community. Thus, in response to Gramsci's claim that Marxism, or the philosophy of praxis, offers a true suture for the split between the intellectuals and the 'simple souls', one might assert that liberation theology, as lived in base communities, calls upon the intellectuals to recognise that they have much to learn from the 'simple souls'!

This combination of both rational and visceral or emotional sources of identification with the Nicaraguan revolution brings me back to the concept of moral identity. Both Gramsci and José Maríategui wrote of the need for a political project to create a profound and personal identification if it is to be successfully realised (Gramci, 1971; Maríategui, 1958). Ideology must be deeply rooted in the individual as well as the collective. Only then can an ideology and a commitment to a political project make 'sense' both intellectually and emotively. Throughout, I will examine the complex relationship between identity, identification/affiliation, religious faith and political action with particular reference to gender. In the communal kitchen, or *olla*, my aim was to access the factors that motivated the women to participate in the project. Through interviews and the testimonial form, the women conveyed their understanding of politics, religion and gender.

I am also concerned to examine forms of practice and belief that fall outside of the parameters of organised religious activity. In sum, I want to look at how the discourse around religion becomes inscribed in the moral identities of those who do not participate in CEBs or in organised religion. I want to explore how liberation theology shapes their identities, and specifically how it effects the 'moral identities' that generate consciousness, and identification with a specific political project. Yet in Nicaragua, formal participation in CEBs and other organisations of the popular church was limited (as indeed was all formal religious participation). Does this mean that religion was not a significant influence in the construction and support of a revolutionary consciousness? One of my aims is to explore the ways in which popular religion served, in conjunction with liberation theology and *Sandinismo*, to create the moral identities that underlay the national popular consensus of FSLN hegemony.

The significance of popular religion in the creation of a revolutionary identity has been under-recognised within the liberation theology discourse. Liberation theologian Leonardo Boff maintains that one of the defining characteristics of CEBs is the space they offer for the expression of popular religiosity. For him, popular religion enables people to 'keep their faith alive, and nourish their trust while in a society that has denied them their rights, dignity and participation' (Boff, 1985, p.130). Despite the positive role that he ascribes to popular religion, he presents it primarily as a defensive mechanism. He maintains that CEBs provide a space for the expression of popular religiosity and he links popular religion with the popular church. However, he does not consider how popular religion might usefully generate praxis outside of the CEB structure. Nicaraguan theologian Pablo Richard links popular religion and revolutionary consciousness:

> Especially important, in my view, is to make explicit the theological implications of the theology implicit in Nicaraguan popular religiosity, with all its traditions, songs, symbols, orations, myths, etc. Here we can encounter the roots of the spirituality and of the feeling of Nicaraguan popular faith. [We should try] overall, to study the transformation of this religiosity into the interior of the revolutionary process (Richard, 1987, p.254).

The study of this transformation will be a central theme of Chapters 6 and 7. Here, I will examine how popular religious festivals and popular religion in Nicaragua functioned as a cauldron in which moral identities for social change were forged. Here Roger Lancaster's analysis of popular religion in Nicaragua is particularly useful in that he theorises the relationship between liberation theology, popular religious festivals and popular religion (Lancaster, 1988).[6] Yet his analysis of this inter-relationship is bereft of a gender focus, a gap that this book seeks to fill. In Chapters 6 and 7, I will utilise concepts such as sacrifice and martyrdom, exploring their overlapping religious and political meanings. I will also explore the predominance of Marianism, devotion to the 'Virgin Mary', in Nicaraguan popular religious festivals and popular religion, as a means of highlighting the gender dimension of these areas.

Given the history of the Catholic church and its alliance with the Mussolini regime that had imprisoned him, Gramsci could not conceive of a Catholic church actively engaged in socialist praxis. Yet this is just what transpired under the banner of liberation theology and the auspices of the popular church in Nicaragua. The divisions within the church occasioned by liberation theology and the revolutionary praxis that it has generated have implications not only for Gramsci's analysis of the Catholic church but also more generally for his analyses of the role of faith and religion in identity formation and praxis. Throughout this book, my elaboration of the Gramscian framework and use of key concepts such as ideology and hegemony will reflect a critical attempt to address the centrality of a particular form of Catholicism in revolutionary consciousness and practice. Finally, in focusing on the gender aspects of these issues, I will attempt some form of integration between feminist theory and analyses of religiously generated action for social change which have generally neglected the issue of gender.

3   Liberation theology and the popular church

Liberation theology is keenly concerned with processes of social change as achieved through the transformed consciousness of oppressed peoples. It is an action-oriented theology which not only reflects on these processes but also seeks to initiate and sustain them. Liberation theology put forward a competing vision of the church and its role in society and in this way the hegemony of the hierarchy was challenged. The conflicts within the Nicaraguan church reflected larger struggles within the Catholic church as well as the particularities of the Nicaraguan situation. In effect, opposing calls for allegiance and identification were being made, generating tension over what it meant to be a Christian. This section will analyse the emergence of liberation theology and its institutional expression in the Nicaraguan popular church, providing the context for further elaboration of the religiously structured processes of identity, ideology and hegemony.

Liberation theology emerged from the intellectual climate fostered by The Second Vatican Council (Vatican II). Vatican II was a general council of the world's bishops that met in four sessions between 1962 and 1965. The first Vatican Council had taken place more than a century before, so it was highly significant that Pope John XXIII convened this second council with the aim of modernising and reforming the church (Brockman, 1989, p.ix). In addition to the rationalisation and updating that Vatican II initiated, there was a critical attempt to consider 'modern' systems of thought, particularly Marxism (Hebblethwaite, 1978, p.151).

The 1968 Latin American Episcopal Conference (CELAM) held in Medellín, Columbia took this process further, exploring not only how Marxism was tied to modernity, but also how Marxism might be used to analyse issues of poverty and injustice in Latin America. The failure of the Council to sufficiently address third world issues was remedied here by an intellectual openness to Marxism which was translated into a recognition of the need for employing anti-capitalist strategies to redress poverty and oppression in the third world. The Medellín Conference was a deeper manifestation of the church's commitment to social justice and went some way towards rectifying the inherent 'first world' bias of the initial consular documents. Hierarchical support for liberation theology reached its peak at this conference and, despite some conservative opposition, the Latin American church accepted the principle of 'the preferential option for the poor', one of the key tenets of liberation theology. The two CELAM conferences that followed, Puebla (1979) and Santo Domingo (1992) saw a backlash against liberation theology from the conservatives and a defensive posture amongst the progressives.

By the 1979 CELAM conference in Puebla, Mexico, the hand of the conservatives had been strengthened by the investiture of a new Pope, John Paul II, who had both an especially negative experience of state socialism and a desire to reassert the power of the hierarchy, in particular the papacy. Sharp divisions emerged within the Latin American church between conservatives who supported the preservation of hierarchical authority, along with a more cautious approach to social change, and progressives, who favoured a more democratic church fully committed to the 'preferential option for the poor'. In Nicaragua, these divisions were exacerbated by the profound commitment of progressives to the revolution. In many other parts of Latin America, the institutional weight of the Catholic church protected incipient protest movements from oppressive state apparatuses. It also marked out the Catholic church and it personnel, regardless of status,[7] for persecution. This common experience of persecution served to build more cohesive national churches and flatten disputes over status and authority.

However, in Nicaragua progressives within the church saw its project as akin to that of the state. In effect, progressives inside and outside the church had a much stronger benefactor than the hierarchy - the state. In this unity the Nicaraguan progressives were strengthened, leaving the conservatives without one of their two traditional roles - valiant

17

opposition or tacit collusion with a despotic state. The opportunities that the Nicaraguan revolution provided for exercising this preferential option for the poor meant that there was significant involvement of a section of the church in the revolution. The popular church, as it is known, has strong ideological ties with liberation theology and has often stood in opposition to the conservative, contra-revolutionary hierarchical church.

In this context, 'popular' did not attest to any numerical superiority over the hierarchical church. In fact, the size of the 'popular' church was a contentious issue, with the hierarchy contending that the former had marginal support amongst Catholics. Indeed, a 1988 survey found that 18 per cent of the population identified with the popular church compared with 47 per cent who identified with the traditional or hierarchical church, leaving 35 per cent of the population. However, a second survey of the religious beliefs of young people found that only 13 per cent were atheists or unidentified with a religious denomination compared to 20 per cent of the population as a whole, and that 44 per cent identified with the popular church compared to 31 per cent who identified with the hierarchical church (*Envio*, March 1989, p.30). Given the youth of the Nicaraguan population, these figures are suggestive of the future support of the popular church. Moreover, explicit identification with the popular church does not measure its influence within Nicaraguan society. For example, some of those who would be considered part of the 'popular church' reject this term because the hierarchy has equated it with schism or some form of parallel magisterium. So some Nicaraguan proponents of liberation theology sought to distance themselves from the term because of the seditious connotations with which the hierarchy had imbued it. This was not the case in other parts of Central America. As Michael Dodson and Laura Nuzzi O'Shaughnessy maintain: 'the term "popular church" implied a denial of religious authenticity in Nicaragua, while it affirmed that same authenticity in El Salvador' (Dodson and Nuzzi O'Shaughnessy, 1990, p.158). The term 'church of the poor' was often used in Nicaragua.

However, I have chosen to use the term 'popular church' because it aptly captures the real convergence of *Sandinismo*, the philosophy of the revolution, and liberation theology. The notion of the 'popular church' dovetailed with *Sandinismo* because of its focus on the 'the people'. In *Sandinismo*, as Giulio Girardi maintains, 'the People' takes the position that 'the proletariat' holds in more traditional Marxism (Girardi, 1987). For members of the 'popular church', this commitment to 'the people' was similarly central and hence 'popular' encapsulates the centrality of the revolutionary project to supporters of liberation theology in Nicaragua.

Reflecting on the tensions between the popular church and the hierarchy, it becomes clear that while the Sandinistas held state power, the conflicts between the two were played out in a national-political context. However, there is an intrinsic tension between the popular church and the hierarchy which runs deeper than conflicting national-political alliances, although this tension may be expressed through them. In Nicaragua differing visions of the church and the state/society became inextricably linked. For the majority of the Nicaraguan hierarchy, their power and authority was staked upon opposition to the revolution which was grounded in a defence of its particular version of the church. The opposite was true for members of the popular church: for them, service to God was bound to an alternative version of church and society, both of which were linked to active participation in the revolution.

One of the chief practical expressions of liberation theology in Nicaragua and throughout Latin America was CEBs. Although small pastoral groups have been a part of the post-Vatican II Catholic tradition in many parts of the world, it is in Latin America that they have gained the greatest religious and political significance. Nicaragua's first two CEBs, Solentiname and San Pablo the Apostle, were founded in 1968 (Foroohar, 1989, p.68). The San Pablo the Apostle CEB, located in the eastern part of the capital city Managua, had been called the 'mother of all base communities' in Nicaragua. The communal kitchen, or *olla* , run by a section of this CEB was the site of part of my fieldwork. In spite of hierarchical resistance, CEBs grew in response to the unmet practical/political and spiritual needs of many oppressed Nicaraguans. CEBs offered a democratic and somewhat protected 'base' from which communities could oppose Somoza and articulate their demands. In terms of spiritual needs, the belief that 'official' sacraments and rituals were the only means of religious expression available was prevalent and served to engender a passive and disengaged 'congregation'.

CEB participants were encouraged by pastoral agents to make connections between examples of injustice in the Bible and their own experiences of oppression under Somoza. In this way, CEBs often linked 'Christ the liberator' and the modern FSLN and its revolutionary programme. Practically and intuitively, the revolution, and its intellectual project of *Sandinismo*, was 'legitimised' by its perceived similarity to Jesus Christ and the goals of Christianity. The progressive church in Nicaragua, and CEBs in particular, played a key role in the triumph of the revolution. The interplay of the progressive church and the revolution produced a dynamism within each.

In analysing liberation theology, CEBs and popular religion I will draw upon literature that examines both pre- and post-1990 periods. One issue that I will consider in some detail in Chapter 3 and at various points in the book is the prospects for recreating the FSLN's hegemonic bloc. In line with the analysis I will develop throughout, I will consider how the FSLN in conjunction with the popular church generated the identification with its project for social change. Further, I will explore the shifts in this process of identification in the post-1990 climate.

The overwhelmingly female participation in CEBs and the key roles that women played in these groups served as a challenge to the church's deeply ingrained patriarchy. This was particularly evident in the *ollas*, which were run and staffed exclusively by women. *Ollas* were a specific response to the dramatic increase in under- and malnutrition since the Chamorro government's introduction of neo-liberal social and economic policies. In this way, CEBs, and specifically women in CEBs, were reshaping their role in Nicaraguan society.

The Nicaraguan revolution was not only made by 'Sandinistas' and those actively working within the structures of the popular church. It was also made and sustained by a large section of the population for whom the revolution made 'common sense', even if this did not translate into active participation. Supporters of the Nicaraguan revolution came to this position not only by rational choice but also through a profound identification with and self-recognition in the discourse of the revolutionary government and the popular church. The discourse of the revolutionary government and the popular church was reinforced by popular religion: the beliefs and practices outside, although in many ways continuous with, institutional religious customs and credence. Roger Lancaster contends that secular support for the revolution was shaped by liberation theology and popular religion which were expressed in an 'ethical religion' (Lancaster, 1988, p.212). In this way, popular religion often reinforced notions of equality and redistribution that were central to both liberation theology and *Sandinismo*.

4 Some considerations on gender

Throughout this book, I want to examine the popular church and popular religion through a focus on gender. There are four main reasons for this: the lack of research on 'motherist' grassroots organisations; evidence of socially constructed gender role differences; the gendered impact of economic and political developments in Nicaragua, and the contribution of women's studies research to the study of religion.

Meredith Tax highlights the dearth of research on women's participation in grassroots organisations sometimes labelled 'motherist' rather than feminist because the basic underlying identity of the participants is that of the mother and the activities of these organisations are geared at least initially and ostensibly towards the welfare of children. Do these organisations serve simply to valorise and re-entrench the maternal role at the cost of developing a feminist identity? Or do they provide the basis for a politicisation of the 'motherist' programme into a feminist one? As Tax maintains, this is an under-explored area. She contends:

> There is a crux in women's history/women's studies, a knot and a blurry place where various things converge. This place has no name and there is no methodology for studying it. The things that converge there are variously called: community organisations, working class women's organisations, consumer movements, popular mass organizations, housewives' organisations, mothers' movements, strike support movements, bread strikes, revolutions at the base, women's peace movements. Some feminist or protofeminist groups and united front organizations of women may be part of this crux. Or they may be different. There is very little theory, either feminist or Marxist, regarding this crux (Tax in Snitow, 1990, p.20).

In line with the distinction that been made between feminist and 'motherist' movements (Snitow, 1990; Schirmer, 1993), Maxine Molyneux has theorised a key distinction between 'strategic' and 'practical' gender interests that I will use throughout the book (Molyneux, 1984, 1988). My extensive use of this distinction is justified not only because of the distinction's theoretical utility but also because it is widely employed by Latin American feminists (see Acosta, 1994; Villavicencio, 1994). 'Strategic' gender interests are what have traditionally been labelled feminist issues while 'practical' gender interests are interests formulated by women themselves in relation to their everyday lives. In my Nicaragua-based research, a theorisation of practical gender interests is of key importance. As Molyneux argues, it is poor women who most need to have strategic gender issues addressed because they are least able to find individual solutions to problems such as child- care provision or access to abortion as well as being most dependent on provision in a public context, whereas more affluent women are able to make their own domestic arrangements, obtain birth control and abortion and thus exercise control over their bodies.

21

According to Molyneux, the politicisation of practical gender interests and the transformation of these into strategic interests is a central feature of feminist praxis (Molyneux, 1984, p.63). This notion is not only applicable to feminist praxis but can also underlie a general theory of political consciousness and practice. The allegiances that served to generate action for social change in the revolutionary period were rooted not only in an ethical imperative but also in this transformation of the practical to the strategic; hence the articulation of moral and gendered identities. For example, women in the San Pablo the Apostle CEB maintained that their commitment to the revolution began with concern over the effects of the Somoza regime's repressive policies on their own families and neighbourhoods. A commitment to the FSLN and the revolution grew, in part, out of a linkage between these women's practical interests and the strategy proposed by the FSLN.

The work undertaken by Carol Gilligan (1977, 1982) opens up a debate which provides a second important reason for making gender a central category of analysis. Gilligan argues that, due to different social and cultural experiences, moral judgements are approached differently by women and men. Women, she maintains, think in terms of care while men think in terms of justice and these different moral positions may be linked to processes of identity formation. According to Gilligan, women's concerns are centred on caring, often with a tension between caring for themselves and caring for others. When women are unable to meet their own expectations with regard to caring for others, they conceive of their failures to care as failures to be 'good' women. The distinction that Gilligan makes between the modes of moral judgement employed by women and men and the tentative linking of morality and identity is highly pertinent to this book. In the research undertaken in the *olla*, I found that this caring ethic and the way in which it was gendered was the defining feature of the moral identities of the participants in this project.

However, Gilligan's argument, despite her acknowledgement of the social construction of gender differences, has been criticised both on grounds of essentialism and for the limited middle-class, largely white, composition of her longitudinal survey respondents. In terms of the first criticism, she has been linked to the standpoint theory position within feminism (Stacey, 1990, p.538) which is summed up in the following way: 'Provisionally, standpoint theory reflects the view that women (or feminists) occupy a social location that affords them/us a privileged access to social phenomena' (Longino, 1993, p.201).

In developing a unique standpoint position, Sandra Harding writes not of 'being other' but of 'reinventing ourselves as other' and in this way moves away from the relatively undifferentiated category of 'women' that Gilligan employs (Harding, 1992, p.189). Harding writes of the need not only for representing 'the other', but more profoundly of the researcher reinventing her/himself as a number of 'others'. This approach calls upon the researcher to reinvent religion, politics, institutional analysis, etc. from the perspective of 'the other'. Harding's concept of 'strong objectivity' highlights the cultural and temporal location of all knowledge and incorporates the contention that the researcher's thought should be imbued with a whole range of standpoints of subordination (Harding, 1991, p.138). Whilst in terms of my own research in Nicaragua I share Harding's concern to break with an undifferentiated category of women, I also wish to consider Gilligan's concept of a gendered caring ethic and its role in the formation of moral identities.

My third reason for a gender focus follows from Harding's argument for the disaggregation of the category of women. In seeking to develop a gendered focus, I do not wish to utilise any essentialised ideas of 'women's interests'. The diversity of women has been a feature of feminist writings about Latin America (Parpart, 1993; Vargas, 1992; Molyneux, 1984; Blandón, 1994). Further, as I shall explore in more detail in Chapter 3, the attempt to build a broad based women's movement has been a critical task undertaken by Nicaraguan feminists. At the same time, a consideration of practical gender interests means that the feminist movement cannot be neutral on class issues. I will thus argue that a gendered analysis must explore differences between women and further must not be sectioned off from an examination of larger political, economic and religious considerations. My aim is to permeate my research with a gender dimension rather than either to ignore this altogether or to devote a chapter to 'women'. This allows me to incorporate my discussions of gender into the very issues (political, economic, etc.) that so profoundly impact on the lives of women.

In writing this, I do not intend to consider 'gender' as a solely 'women's issue', although clearly women have been made more aware of and arguably reflect more on their gendered selves. In contrast, patriarchy positions men as the universal subject, 'man', and men's particularity often arises from factors other than gender: race, ethnicity, class, etc. This is not to negate the important role that notions of manhood and maleness play in male identity formation. Indeed, essentialised notions of women serve to construct, through binary opposition, what it means to be a 'man'. I aim to move away from the assumption that gender issues are solely 'women's issues' without compromising an analysis of women's oppression.

My objective is to introduce gender into all of the theoretical discourses and approaches to practice that I address. Although gender is both a women's and a men's issue, it is not a neutral concept: it implies a critique of the way in which gender roles and relations are naturalised and 'women' and 'men' essentialised. Further, and of primary importance, a gendered analysis also seeks to make explicit the disempowerment that women experience within patriarchal societies and the role that men play in the maintenance and reproduction of this system. At the same time, I am concerned to address the economic and political issues that are not generally recognised as 'women's issues' but which impact profoundly on women's lives. In sum, I do just want to look at the role of women in CEBs or popular religion, although this is an important project of the book. I also want to consider the broader political, economic and institutional factors that impact on their lives as well as their political commitment and religious faith.

The fourth and final reason for making gender an explicit focus draws on Randi Warne's argument that some of the insights generated through women's studies have invigorated studies of religion by introducing new questions and methods which have helped to destabilise entrenched universalised knowledge claims in the field (Warne, 1989). She contends that women's studies had this influence because it brought more women into the study of religion and relatedly because it grounded research endeavours more firmly in historically and culturally located religious expression. Thus, the book will integrate an understanding of gender into its main questions and themes adding to the overall arguments at three levels; theoretically, substantively and methodologically.

5   Methodology

'Value-free' sociology and the 'value' of social science research

Looking at the culture of others is not a neutral act. The researcher carries with her/him not only a personal history shaped by gender, class, race and a myriad of other factors, but also an institutional location marked by the weight of academic and disciplinary tradition and, not incidentally, her/his own career and professional concerns. In examining the role of the social scientist, Weber contended that while the researcher should have a keen interest in her/his topic, data should be gathered with neither bias nor intention beyond adherence to a professional vocation (Gerth and Mills, 1974, p.135). The research product could then be used to support a particular position or point of view. 'Value judgements', Weber argued, were permissible in the conceptualisation and use of the research product but never in the research itself (Runciman, 1978, pp. 69-70). For Weber, this did not bar the social sciences from considering the values expressed by research subjects. However, here the researcher would reference values rather than engaging in value judgements.

The above notion of objectivity has been vigorously challenged from a number of different perspectives. The corpus of literature that adheres to a the possibility of objectivity stands alongside an equally abiding tradition of social science literature that explicitly rejects the possibility and/or the desirability of 'value-free' research. In addition, there are many positions between and within these two opposing 'poles' and in this sense an opposition between 'value-free' and 'value-full' research can be somewhat artificial. However, in locating themselves and their work, researchers do reference this opposition so it is a useful starting point for an exploration of some essential epistemological questions. In this section I will explore some of the issues surrounding the location of the researcher, the objectives of research and the positioning of the subject/object of research within the ethnographic discourse. Through-out, I will link these discussions to my own experiences as a researcher and to my own research project.

As a middle-class North American woman, doing research amongst working-class Nicaraguan women could be construed as a form of cultural or 'academic' imperialism. In describing some examples of social science 'action' research conducted by middle-class women researchers among 'disenfranchised' women, Deborah A. Gordon notes that a 'troubling "matronization"' can emerge (Gordon 1993, p.438). In looking at action research, Gordon notes that if the research sufficiently involves its subjects it can be both socially transformative and theoretically productive. She maintains:

> We need to understand social processes in a way that does not flatten all research between relatively privileged woman and dis-enfranchised women into images of well-intentioned but naive ethnographers blindly reproducing power inequalities (Gordon 1993, p.436).

Gordon describes a project which seeks to avoid some of the pitfalls of action research. The El Barrio Project, a women's literacy undertaking, brought together researchers, tutors and women seeking to enhance their literacy skills. Literacy in Spanish was prioritised but the project also included conversation classes in English as a second language. Here literacy, perceived as a sort of educational capital, was 'redistributed' from researchers to poor women in a largely Latino New York City neighbourhood. Researchers were interested in how 'shifts in

25

identity empower individuals and communities' (Gordon 1993, p.435). To this end, teaching and research methodologies were designed simultaneously to empower women and to assess that empowerment. For example, initially the women gave oral histories but as literacy skills increased they presented their autobiographies in a written form. In this way the researchers collected the women's 'life histories'' but clearly not as classical ethnographers.

The researchers were in a position to collect autobiographies, conduct interviews, and observe the women both in the classroom and in their daily lives. Because they were providing a highly valued service to the women, the researchers earned their trust, respect and confidence; this fact was evidenced in the women's co-operation with the research aims of the project. Despite the positive response of the participants, the activist character of this research defied the logic of traditional ethnographic work. Here the ethnographer is concerned to 'objectively' observe and record the actions and interactions of fieldwork subjects. The research conducted through the El Barrio Project was an example of ethnography as social action. My own research was designed with the spirit of this project in mind. To this end, my practical work in the *olla* was an attempt at some form of reciprocity, although clearly my contribution was considerably more modest than that made by the El Barrio researchers.

In outlining a set of methodological guidelines for research, Maria Mies lays out a programme for feminist research. In place of 'objective' research, Mies proposes 'conscious partiality', a research mode in which there is a 'partial identification' between researcher and research subject. This form of research 'enables the correction of distortions of perception on both sides and widens the consciousness of both, the researcher and the "researched"' (Mies, 1993, p. 68). Mies posits a praxis-oriented research methodology in which the 'view from below' is given priority and the researcher is actively involved in transforming the status quo.

In this construction, the researcher's 'bias' (here political commitment) is actively expressed in the research process. Although Mies is concerned with expressly feminist research projects, these methodological guidelines are applicable to other types of research. In fact, similar forms of praxis-driven or 'action research' have been advanced by social scientists not necessarily concerned with feminist practice, for example in the community development projects of the 1970s and some forms of anti-racist research. My own research displayed this sense of 'conscious partiality' in that while I was keen to develop my own research interests, I clearly identified with the goal of the *olla* project.

26

The fieldwork component of my research was methodologically significant for the book because it provided a grounding for theoretical insight in addition to the opportunity to record interviews and testimonies in which research subjects were given the space to speak for themselves, albeit within the highly mediated context of an academic text. Too often purely theoretical work about people makes very little effort to engage in empirical research: the theory sits elegantly atop a 'reality' which has become so problematised that its existence outside of the space of discourse is questioned. Empirical research is doubted because it posits that an essential 'truth' can be garnered from fieldwork when in fact this 'truth' is the creation of the researcher. However, as fraught as empirical research is, pure theory can be equally, if not more, presumptive about groups of people. In fact all research experience is mediated and intertwined with other kinds of knowledge. In this regard, I have aimed to employ a strategy of grounded research, in this way letting the theory emerge from the research itself (Glaser and Strauss, 1967).

Fieldwork carries with it a set of assumptions regarding 'the other' and the researcher's relationship to the subject/object of research. As an outsider with a relatively comfortable lifestyle in England, I lived and worked in Nicaragua with the knowledge that whatever difficulties I encountered were temporary; I, for all my commitment to the project, was just 'passing through'. The women who worked in the *olla* and I were separated from each other not only by culture but also by class. Further, I had power not only *vis-à-vis* the relative material differences between the other women in the *olla* and myself but also because of the discrepancy between the status of the women as subjects of research and myself as a researcher. Outside the context of the *olla* I had the power to determine not only how the women and the project were represented to the outside world but if they were represented at all. In effect, in common with almost all forms that utilise ethnography: 'The predominant mode of modern fieldwork authority is signalled: "You are there . . . because I was there"' (Clifford, 1988, p.22). Clifford's cogent discussion of the power imbalances in the research process highlighted the need for sensitivity to these issues in my own practice and were crucial in the formulation of my research strategies.

Although I was very aware of the power that I exercised in the representation of the women who I was interviewing and with whom I was working, this authority was not exercised during the 'everyday life' of the *olla* Here, I was very much in a junior position because I took orders from the other women and regularly performed some of the most menial tasks in the *olla* Further, I was not altogether *au fait* with the 'Nicaraguan way' of mopping and sweeping floors, chopping

27

vegetables, squeezing oranges, etc. and thus the question 'Is this right?' was often on my lips. In workplace relationships, I always deferred to others. This deference was in respect not only to the knowledge and experience of the women and girls with whom I was working but also to my status as an outsider. I was quite conscious of how easy it would be for an outsider's suggestions to be interpreted as a challenge to the existing social organisation or at the very least a sign of disrespect. In addition, I believe that my deferential demeanour and general unobtrusiveness allowed me to fade into the background and observe without making people feel uncomfortable or 'watched'.

At the same time, the work that I was doing required considerable physical exertion which was made worse by my own initial attempts to prove myself a valuable member of the *olla* workforce. More than once, as perspiration dripped down my face and the state of my clothing became increasingly dishevelled, one of the women would admonish me to slow down or to 'take it easy'. This was usually while I was mopping the *olla's* large and extremely muddy floor, a task that became my 'semi-official' responsibility. The intensity of my work was simultaneously impressive and disturbing to the women in the *olla* as it put me out of step with their swift but slightly more tranquil pace. But I had set a standard for myself that was difficult to back down from without appearing to be slacking off. After a few weeks, I relaxed into a more sustainable work routine which allowed me increased time to socialise with the other women.

Research objectives and strategies

My research goals are varied but one of my key aims is to explore the gendered dimension to the role of the popular church and popular religion in the battle over the construction of moral identities in Nicaragua both under the FSLN and, since 1990, under the UNO coalition. Although the book contains a significant block of fieldwork material, its aims are wider than a purely ethnographic monograph could encompass. In a forceful if somewhat polemical critique of anthropology, Stavenhagen takes the discipline to task for failing to locate the groups and communities that it studies in the context of an 'analysis of total social systems', i.e. the national and global frameworks that often condition, limit and shape the communities under study (Stavenhagen, 1993, pp. 53-4). Hence, culture is reified and restricted to the particular social unit taken as the ethnographer's focus.

Subsequent to the 1979 triumph of the Nicaraguan revolution, praxis-oriented research played a key role in both social science and natural science inquiry. Often research was conducted in the context of the researcher's participation in a 'development' or grassroots project directly connected to the revolutionary government. Such research was unambiguously political, often linked to 'defending the revolution' in three crucial ways. Firstly, researchers provided critical technical assistance as well as access to funding through their academic and institutional connections. Secondly, the results of research were often geared towards improving aspects of existing programmes and practices. For example, the McConnell, Pacheco-Anton and Magnotti survey of crop duster aviation mechanics demonstrated the hazards of mixing and loading of pesticides at airports. As a result the government prohibited these practices and introduced protective clothing for mechanics working on crop duster planes (McConnell *et al*, 1990). Thirdly, published research often served to highlight the positive aspects of the revolutionary government's social and economic policies in an international context and to underscore the debilitating effects of the war and the economic embargo on these policies. For example, articles and books reached a professional and academic audience well situated to organise against US aggression.

Since the 1990 change in government, many researchers have continued to work with and support development projects and grassroots organisations in Nicaragua. My own research was clearly sympathetic to the aims of the *olla* as a women's project identifying and responding to the nutritional needs of women and children. While there has been a marked dissipation of 'solidarity' activity in Nicaragua since 1990, it is unclear whether the change in government will precipitate a general decline of research interest in Nicaragua, evident in the decline in the number articles about Nicaragua appearing in mainstream academic journals.

Throughout the book, I will draw upon a number of different aspects of my fieldwork including: the collection and analysis of primary source material in the form of newspaper articles, periodicals and documents unavailable or difficult to find outside Nicaragua; observation through attendance at conferences and popular religious festivals, and participant observation in a CEB project, and in-depth interviews. In the tradition of triangulation and multi-method research, this application of a number of different research strategies provided a wider understanding of the phenomenon under study than the application of a single method. This triangulation underlies the methodology of the book. If epistemologies emerge from ontologies (Stanley and Wise, 1993), and it is difficult to see how these can be fully disengaged, then the overall methodology of this book emerged from a combination of my own background as a researcher in combination

29

with the lived experiences of the people who were the focus of this research.

In analysing religious (and 'religiously imbued') icons and images, it is necessary to locate these in the semantic field from which they emerge and in which they are received. This is equally true of the religious and political discourses that I will examine. In other words, the meaning of a discourse or indeed an image or an icon is not fully present in the icon, image or discourse itself but additionally and dialectically realised in the way in which it is understood and received. As P.N. Medvedev and Mikhail Bakhtin maintain:

> Every ideological product and all its "ideal meaning" is not in the soul, not in the inner world, and not in the detached world of ideas and pure thoughts, but in the objectively accessible ideological material - in the word, in sound, in gesture, in combination or masses, lines, colors, living bodies, and so on (Medvedev and Bakhtin, 1978, p.8).

If Barthes's notion of the denotative and connotative aspect of a sign (the signifier and the signified), is taken as the starting point in the examination of religious and political icons and images, it is clear that an examination of images and icons in and of itself is only one strand of the analytical process (Barthes, 1967). A second key strand is the analysis of these icons and images in the process of their reception and further, asking participants what they understand to be the meanings of the icons and images under analysis. In this manner, a highly textured understanding of icons and images in their specific historical, cultural and temporal locations emerges. It is in this way that I conducted the analysis of icons, images and discourse throughout the book.

Fieldwork design

The fieldwork consisted of three case studies. In the first case study, I explored the struggle between the Left/FSLN/popular church bloc and the Right/traditional church and the way that the relationships between as well as within the two blocs have changed as a result of the FSLN's 1990 electoral loss. I analysed the way in which both sides were competing for the right to define the popular and influence the construction of moral identities. In this effort, I used primary source material including interviews, meetings, conferences and articles from the three main daily newspapers gathered in the course of my fieldwork and numerous secondary sources. In the second case study of the book, I explored the construction of moral identities on a smaller scale, within the confines of a communal kitchen operated by a section of the historically significant CEB, San Pablo the Apostle. Here I employed the techniques of participant observation and in-depth interviews with the women who worked here.

In the third case study, also concerned with the creation of moral identities, I examine the phenomenon as it is manifest in popular religion and popular religious festivals. To this end, as an 'observer-participant', I attended a number of events connected to the religious festivals of Santo Domingo and La Purísima, conducted formal interviews and made extensive use of newspaper articles and radio programmes reporting these festivals. Further, my general understanding of a number of the book's preoccupations was enhanced by my attendance at the eighth annual 'Theological Week' sponsored by the Antonio Valdivieso Ecumenical Centre and the 500 Years of Resistance Campaign Conference, both of which were held in Managua in 1992.

Whilst the research for this book draws primarily on qualitative methods, this is not to the exclusion or pre-emption of quantitative data. Toby Epstein Jayaratne argues forcefully that when feminists abandon traditional research methods, and in particular quantitative research, they leave unchallenged the authority of these forms of research. She argues: 'There is an "objective" aura about traditional research which makes it convincing and influential. Thus findings which are often products of poor methodology and sexist bias are interpreted by the public as fact' (Epstein Jayaratne, 1993, p.110). Epstein Jayaratne contends that feminists should realise the shortcomings of traditional research methods but should reinvigorate them rather than dispensing with them altogether. Even if researchers have a commitment to qualitative forms of research, quantitative methodologies can be employed as a complement. To this end I have not shied away from using quantitative research as secondary sources. For example, neo-liberal economic and social policies have created the conditions which *ollas* seek to address. The effects of these policies are starkly measured by quantitative data on nutrition, unemployment levels, infant mortality, etc. and studies of this order were invaluable for gaining an overall understanding of the difficulties faced by large sections of the Nicaraguan population.

Overall, I employed a range of social research methods. In looking at the women in the *olla* and popular religious festivals I used techniques most closely linked with ethnography. As such, it was necessary for me to consider the benefits and difficulties of these techniques. This continuous evaluation of methods is a common feature of ethnographic fieldwork: the title of this section is misleading because it suggests too much of a causal relationship between research design and execution.

The process is more complicated in that research design is subject to the reality of the field and hence subject to change.

In the research, I employed a threefold strategy for addressing the limitations of the methods that I have chosen. Firstly, I engaged in multi-method research or triangulation which posits that social phenomena should be approached and understood through the application of a variety of research methods (Fielding and Fielding, 1986; Denzin, 1978). The research picture which emerges is not necessarily more 'objective' but it is certainly fuller. As Rosaldo argues, social scientists should look at their subjects from a 'number of positions, rather than being locked into any particular one' (Rosaldo, 1993, p.169). Secondly, I aimed to make myself explicitly present in the research process rather than maintaining a strictly 'objective' or 'detached' stance, in this way making my role plain. Thirdly and finally, while I was sensitive to power differentials between myself and the subjects of my research, I acknowledged the irresolvable character of the power differentials involved not only in cross-cultural research, but in all research. In looking specifically at some of the methodological dangers of the research process, I have aimed to make difficulties more explicit and to acknowledge the power imbalances and problems of representation.

Participant observation

Of all of the research strategies that I employed, the two most complex and potentially fraught were the in-depth interviews I conducted and the participant observation that I carried out. I will discuss some of the issues around in-depth interviews and their relationship to *testimonio* in the next section of the chapter. Here I will address methodological and ethical questions surrounding participant observation. Participant observation is considered by many anthropologists as 'basic to carrying out naturalistic research' (Ely *et al.*, 1991, p.42). In this form of inquiry, the researcher seeks to operate within the 'natural' or 'unaltered' world of her/his subjects. In the past naturalistic research has often staked a claim to objectivity based on its ability to blend into the 'natural' surroundings of subjects, hence avoiding the disruptive and obtrusive strategies of positivist research. In this context, bias is associated not just with the bias of the researcher but also with the effect that the researcher has on the subjects of her/his study. In both the positivist and the naturalist tradition, there has been a notion of the 'uncon-taminated' research project that has prevented an engagement with the issue of reflexivity (Hammersley and Atkinson, 1983, p.18).

Yet as physicists working in the field of quantum mechanics demonstrated so elegantly, the very act of observing a phenomenon alters it (March, 1978, p. 230). This is also true in the social sciences where the presence of the researcher and the methods that s/he employs similarly impact on the research environment. As Gordon's analysis of the El Barrio Project demonstrates, social scientists working within the framework of action research actually embrace this opportunity to alter the research environment because this impact is fundamental to the cause of social transformation. Even amongst social scientists who do not engage in action research, there are few who would claim to produce absolutely 'bias-free' research (Ely*et al.*, 1991, p.47). Thus, although participant observation is defined as an activity which can range from complete participant to complete observer, even the complete observer is in this sense participant (Babbie, 1983, p.247).

My own participant observation, within the context of the *olla* and the Santo Domingo and La Purísima events that I attended, was marked by a shifting relationship between participant and observer roles. This shift was effected at different times by both myself and my 'research subjects'. In the four months that I worked in the *olla* , when I became engrossed in a task such as mopping the floor, I was acting more as a participant than an observer. However, at other times I focused more intently on the activity of others. Thus sometimes I was accepted as an honorary 'insider' and full participant while at others I was viewed as more of an 'outsider' and observer. My participant observation at events surrounding Santo Domingo and La Purísima was somewhat different in that I functioned primarily as an observer. However, particularly with the different Santo Domingo festival events, a large proportion of those present stood on the sidelines rather than fully participating in the revelry. In this sense I 'participated' as a fellow spectator. Yet I was observing not only the 'participants' but also the spectators. In a sense, part of my observations involved looking at those who looked. For those both observing and participating my obvious status as a foreigner marked me as an outsider. However, in the midst of the general confusion and boisterous activity, my prominence as an outsider varied in significance.

James Clifford defines participant observation as an 'amalgam' of 'intense personal experience and scientific analysis'. In his conception, the participant observer is constantly moving between the 'inside' and the 'outside' of events (Clifford, 1988, p.34). As I learned through my own experiences as a participant observer, the process of entering into another environment with the intention of belonging yet remaining apart is a fraught and challenging endeavour. This dialectic of experience and analysis is a part of both the actual fieldwork and the latter documentation and theorising, and it is this tension which is often so theoretically productive. My participant observation allowed me unique access to the lived experience of a popular church project and popular religious practices. Yet my status as an outsider helped me to retain at key moments a critical distance from the thinking of my research subjects. At the same time, participant observation in the *olla* and the in-depth interviews that it facilitated, gave me the scope to hear and understand what the women in the *olla* actually thought about religion, politics and gender issues. Further, within this context I was able to realise that my priorities around these issues were not necessarily those of the women with whom I worked. Thus, in my own research experience, participant observation, was a fruitful technique both in generating observational data and testing research hypotheses as well as in allowing space for the contentions of the researcher to be contradicted or challenged.

In my case study of the *olla*, I was concerned to explore in some depth the functioning of a CEB project and the role that religion, politics and gender played in the attitudes and motivations of the women who participated in the project. If I had expanded my area of focus to include, for example, a number of *ollas*, the character of my participation and the quality of my observational and interview material would have been altered. Further, my book would have been more about *ollas per se* rather than the overarching theme of the creation of moral identities. This concern also dominated the case studies of the national political polarisation and of popular religious festivals. From what I have already argued, the triangulation techniques adopted for the three case studies do not themselves guarantee greater objectivity. The diverse methods and sources of data and analysis including documentary, observational, participant observational and interviews do, on the other hand, provide a 'thicker' analysis of processes of identification and thus help meet the overall research objectives.

In-depth interviews

In addition to my 'participant observation' in the *olla*, I chose to do interviews for a number of reasons. I wanted there to be a counter-weight to my voice as the author of this book, and one means of achieving this was to allow space for the women to 'speak for themselves'. However, this process was not as straightforward as it may seem because regardless of how open and non-directional interviews are the basic power relationship cannot be side-stepped. Despite my friendship with the women and my efforts to accurately record their understandings of themselves and their participation in the project, the fact that I have recorded the interviews, organised and selected from them and commented upon them in the context of a piece of academic work suggests a power relationship which should not be downplayed. It is possible and moreover necessary for analyses of structures such as the *olla* to be framed around the words of those who are responsible for it. Yet it remains a delicate balance between giving women the platform to 'speak for themselves' and contextualising the interviews and drawing out more general points about the *olla* .

While my participant observation in the *olla* provided me with a significant insight into the motivations of the women participants, my understanding of the construction of moral identities in post-1990 Nicaragua was greatly enriched by the in-depth interviews that I conducted. As Renato Rosaldo suggests: 'Rather than being merely ornamental, a dab of local colour, protagonists' narratives about their own conduct merit serious attention as forms of social analysis' (Rosaldo, 1993, p.143). In this way, I used the interviews to test the validity not only of the assumptions that I brought to the *olla,* but also of the thinking that I developed through my observations. Thus the interviews themselves, particularly when juxtaposed with the material that I gathered when working in the *olla* and observing the events of daily life, generated a richly textured understanding of the women's motivations.

The interviews helped to 'validate' or challenge elements of existing theoretical material and my own suppositions, but their validity rested on the women being 'interviewed in sufficient detail for the results to be taken as true, correct, complete and believable reports of their views and experiences' (Hakim, 1987, p.27). After three months of working in the *olla* , I had built up relationships of trust with most of the women. Hence I was able to obtain interviews that were detailed and complete and thus 'valid'.

The 'testimonial' character of some of the interviews became evident only after I had completed the interview process and realised that the women had given me life histories which reflected both a personal and a collective sensibility. This was a surprise to me, as I had originally considered taking testimonies as part of my research but had decided that this particular form was incompatible with the format of the research I had believed that *testimonios* would not necessarily address the issues with which I was directly concerned.

It would be propitious to consider in more detail the features that define *testimonio*. Georg Gugelberger and Michael Kearney make a distinction between autobiography and *testimonio* (Gugelberger and Kearney, 1991). In the former, an individual writes or speaks out of a sense of her/his own uniqueness. In this way s/he seeks to designate

35

what sets them apart from others. In the latter, the *testimonialista* , or testimony giver, makes sense of herself/himself and the events of her/his life in terms of collective experience and struggle. In this sense the 'I' that designates the *testimonialista* functions as a 'we' (Sommer, 1991, p.39). Lynda Marín extends the definition of *testimonio* to address its intention in addition to its form. For Marín, Latin American women's *testimonio* is intended to 'speak in a unified way for a people in struggle' (Marín, 1991, p.55). According to Marín, such women's testimonials speak for both men and women but do so from a 'woman-centred experience' (Marín, 1991, p.61).

The emergence of the testimonial form also owes much to the advent of liberation theology in Latin America. Like the Christianity proffered by many fundamentalist sects, liberation theology stressed the importance of the individual by prioritising a personal relationship with God over ritualised or strictly formal religious observance. Yet unlike the former, liberation theology saw this personal relationship with God as inextricably bound to a relationship with and responsibility to the larger community. In reflecting on the Bible, participants in CEBs and other liberation theology-oriented groups were encouraged through the process of *conscientización* to make connections between passages that they had read and their own lives in both a personal and a political sense. Within this context, people often gave *testimonios* about their lives and their struggles. These were made in a group context, and sometimes recorded for a wider audience.

I would posit that *testimonio* is a form of expression which is particularly appropriate to certain historical circumstances. In societies that undergo great changes and upheavals, there is a heightened sense of connection between the personal and the collective. In Nicaragua, the insurrection and the subsequent struggle to deepen and defend the revolution encouraged people to make connections between their own lives and a wider socio-political project. Because these events often shaped their lives, it was difficult for many Nicaraguans to have a purely individual understanding of their personal histories. The suitability of *testimonio* to recording the experiences of Nicaraguans is reflected in the amount of testimonial literature which has appeared in the years subsequent to the 1979 revolution. For example, Omar Cabezas's *Fire from the Mountain* (1985), a recollection of the time that he spent fighting in the mountains during the insurrection, was a *testimonio* that spent weeks on the Nicaraguan best-sellers list.[8]

According to Jean Franco, *testimonio* 'implies a subject as witness to and participant in public events'. Here the term 'embraces a corpus of texts that range from fragments embedded in other texts to full-length life stories' (Franco, in Yúdice *et al.*, 1992, p.71). This 'catholic' view of *testimonio* would incorporate all of the above forms of artistic expression and most others that captured, no matter how briefly, participation in a collective struggle. If it is true that 'fragments embedded in other texts' can be considered *testimonio*, what separates this version of *testimonio* from mere quotations which are 'always staged by the quoter and tend to serve merely as examples or confirming testimonies' (Clifford, 1988, p.50)? Can a *testimonio* retain its integrity and its impact if it is not presented as a complete and seamless narrative?

These questions are of particular significance to this book because some of the interviews that I conducted 'became' *testimonios*. However, within the context of this book, I did not present them as uninterrupted life stories. Rather, I utilised fragments of *testimonios* in the way that Franco describes. I contend that if pieces of *testimonios* are used in the spirit in which they were given and are not misrepresented or manipulated, then it is possible to utilise segments of *testimonios* and still retain the probity of this form. Indeed, in the case of full-length *testimonios*, a transcriber is usually involved in recording and putting the work into a publishable form. What may appear as the verbatim utterances of the *testimonialista* have often been translated, edited and organised by the testimony taker. In this book, I have tried to acknowledge my role as an interviewer and testimony taker and to recognise the difficulties of using this material while remaining true to the spirit in which it was given.

Chapter 2 focuses on liberation theology, feminist liberation theology and CEBs. Here I aim to explore the literature that deals with the evolution and functioning of CEBs as distinctive organisations. I argue that there has been a significant gap with respect to the analysis of the gender dimension of CEB participation, a gap which this book aims to address. The book also aims to contribute to an analysis of the more oppositional role that is emerging for CEBs in the post-1990 context, a role which has yet to be substantively theorised.

The analysis of popular religion and popular church requires a related but quite distinct framework of analysis. In this literature review section, I survey literature that addresses CEBs and, in particular, women in these organisations. In contrast to the popular church and CEBs, popular religion in Nicaragua is not realised in anything like such a concrete fashion, as it is more diffuse and less tangible. This lack of organisation and high level of diffusion are what make it so hard to analyse yet so necessary to examine. How was the faith-praxis network, so extensively theorised in liberation theology, manifest amongst the politically uncommitted, i.e. the majority of Nicaraguans? I maintain that this link between the politically committed and the 'unpoliticised' majority was an identification with the revolutionary project that was built through faith. Yet analysing organised groups with explicit and somewhat systematised activating and sustaining discourses is quite a different exercise from exploring how or if an amorphous and unstructured phenomenon such as popular religion served a particular role in the overarching hegemonic configurations of Nicaragua in the past twenty years. In other words, if not in the dialogical crucible of the CEB, how did religious faith engender loyalty to and identification with a particular political project? This is a question to be explored in Chapters 6 and 7.

In Chapter 3, I explore the battle for hegemony in Nicaragua prior to and following the FSLN's 1990 electoral defeat. Despite factionalism, inter-class conflicts and family alliances the two major blocs competing for hegemonic power have continued to be the FSLN/popular church bloc and the Right/hierarchical church bloc. Both attempted to control the space of 'the popular'. The chapter argues that hegemonic strategies were premised on a claim to a moral high ground and that affiliation to particular blocs was constructed around this point of identification. Sacrifice was a key theme in this construction and women were called upon to sacrifice/suppress their strategic gender interests in deference to the 'larger' struggle to 'defend the revolution'. The chapter argues, however, that the revolutionary government's strategy of reinforcing traditional maternal roles may actually have heightened the impression that the revolutionary government was proving increasingly unable to meet women's practical gender interests. The focus on maternal roles as evidenced in the FSLN's rejection of gender-neutral conscription meant that women were poorly integrated into the war effort in any way other than as sacrificing mothers.

The hardships of conscription and economic deprivation became a feature of everyday life for the very young in Nicaragua at a time when the maternal role was reinforced at every turn. The result was that many Nicaraguan women took their protective role to its logical conclusion by voting against a government which was seen as unable to meet their interests as mothers. Chapter 3, in exploring issues of hegemony, common sense and the popular, sets the framework for the following three chapters, which examine these issues on a more micro level.

Chapter 4 considers the San Pablo the Apostle CEB through an analysis of the way in which the organisational practices and forms of religious expression pioneered by the CEB served to challenge the power of the hierarchical church. Thus this chapter presents a more micro example of the conflicts examined in the previous chapter. I argue that CEBs strove to change the "common sense" relating to the power of the hierarchy and the role of the laity within the Catholic church by a restructuring of religious practice and a reinterpretation of the central meaning of the church's function and mission. I further argue that 1990 proved a decisive turning point in the changing balance of hegemonic religious/political forces and relationships.

Chapter 5 is based on my participation in the San Rafael communal kitchen, a project of the San Pablo the Apostle CEB. Here I was particularly concerned with ascertaining the motivations of the women who worked in the communal kitchen. I examine how the women made sense of their commitment to the community in terms of their religious faith, their political commitment, their gender roles. What emerges is a multi-layered portrait of the communal kitchen, the women who ran it and the factors that underlay their participation and shaped their understanding of it.

I argue that the communal kitchen was a site for the reproduction of traditional values, especially around gender, as well as a space for resistance. In other words, the kitchen was an 'ideological terrain' on which conflicting interests, desires and goals were constructed, reinforced, challenged and recast. I maintain that in this way the moral identities of the women who participated in the project emerged. I argue that this was a local process, in terms of the 'everyday' practice of the project as well as a global process, in relation to the socio-economic factors that underlie poverty and malnutrition.

In Chapter 6, I address in some detail the role of popular religion in Nicaragua with an exploration of some of the general points of debate that characterise analyses of this area of religious expression. In this chapter I explore the involvement of the FSLN and the popular church in some of the activities around the commemoration of the 500 years of resistance to the conquest. Here, I maintain that both the popular church and the FSLN attempted to use indigenous identity and reformulations of indigenous religious beliefs and practices as a tool of politicisation and motivation.

In Chapter 7, I examine popular religious festivals looking in particular at La Purísima and Santo Domingo, the two most 'popular' and well attended festivals. I uncover and analyse some of the vestiges of indigenous religious beliefs and practices in contemporary popular religious festivals. I argue that the 'popular church', the 'traditional church' and their respective political allies all struggled to control and contain the fluid and unstable 'common sense' which these religious practices generated. Following this analysis of popular religious festivals, I move to an investigation of the 'construction' of the 'popular' in Nicaragua. Here I maintain that the notion of the 'popular' has been used by opposing forces competing for hegemony in Nicaragua. The FSLN used religious imagery to construct the 'popular': through its engagement with the popular church and popular religion, the FSLN was able to establish not only an intellectual rationale for the revolution but also an ethical-religious paradigm in which the revolution made 'common sense'.

Notes

1   The FSLN implemented its own more limited structural adjustment policies in the late 1980s in order to correct some serious distortions of the economy, in particular the spiralling rate of inflation. Although the effects and necessity of these policies have been debated, they were to quite a large extent disarticulated from the wider premises and goals of neo-liberalism (Gonzalez, 1990).

2   Parallel magisterium can be defined as a situation in which a section of the church gains theological and/or practical autonomy from the main body of the church, as represented by the hierarchy.

3   Although Carter's emphasis on "human rights" set his administration apart from those that preceded and followed it, there were a number of glaring inconsistencies in his policy towards Nicaragua. As late as 1978, President Carter sent Somoza a letter congratulating him on "human rights gestures". In addition, military aid to the Somoza regime continued almost to the end of his regime and after its cut-off Israel took over this role with tacit US endorsement (Chomsky, 1985:128).

4   Nicaraguan Foundation for Integral Community Development, a CEB movement founded in León in 1973 by Miguel D'Escoto.

5   *Conscientización* is pedagogical strategy developed and elaborated by Brazilian educator Paulo Freire (Freire, 1972,1985). Here, through a dialectical process, people become conscious of the factors that shape their world and their power to affect change. Yet this process is vastly different from politicisation or 'consciousness-raising'. As Freire maintains: 'no one conscientizes anyone else. The educator and the people together conscientize themselves, thanks to the dialectical movement that relates critical reflection on past action to the continuing struggle' (Freire, 1985:125).

6   See also Gismondi (1990) for an examination of the connection between religious faith and political consciousness in the decades prior to the 1979 overthrow of the Somoza regime; Holler (1992) for an analysis of Marian devotion in Latin American popular

religion from Vatican II to 1979; and Recinos (1993) for an analysis of Salvadoran refugee popular religion.

7   The 1980 assassination of Salvadoran archbishop Oscar Romero by a death squad is evidence of the boldness of the political Right in seeking to neutralise any resistance put forward by the church.

8   The title in Spanish is somewhat longer and more descriptive: *La Montaña es algo mas que una imensa estepa verde*, or the mountain is something more than an immense green steppe.

2 The theory and practice of CEBs and the popular church in Nicaragua

1 Introduction

My starting point, in trawling in the divergent sources that contribute to an understanding of the popular church in Nicaragua, addressed one of the primary aims of this work: examining how moral identities for social change were created through religious and political 'faith'. Given the heady brew of religion and politics of liberation theology in Nicaragua during the years of revolutionary government and in the post-1990 period, I made this my point of departure. Yet looking at the work of liberation theologians is not enough. Leonardo Boff contends that liberation theology is the theory and CEBs the practice (Boff, 1986). Indeed he maintains that 'reflection' should follow 'action'. Some feminist liberation theologians have developed the concept of 'doing theology' whereby active participation in organisations like CEBs is considered a form of theological activity.

However the relationship between liberation theology and CEBs is conceived, an analysis of the popular church in Nicaragua needs to be deepened by an examination of the literature that analyses organisational structure and composition of CEBs. Most liberation theologians do not write from an empirical perspective; even if their analyses stressed praxis, their writing was not able to look at the lived culture of CEBs or to adequately access the attitudes, motivations and beliefs of participants. Feminist theologians, many of whom were involved in pastoral activities with CEBs, did not generally adopt an empirical approach, although clearly a more active engagement with CEBs and popular church organisations informed their work.

CEBs have been conceptualised as part of a larger institution (the Catholic church), as part of a quasi-parallel institution, (the popular church) and as unique institutional forms in and of themselves. A further level of empirical and ethnographic work recognises the diversity in the organisations that are placed under the CEB rubric. These differing levels of analysis both converged and diverged with the more theoretical and theological approaches of liberation theologians. An empirical analysis of CEBs is a vital complement to and useful point of discussion for both theological treatments of CEBs and more general conceptions of praxis within the field of liberation theology. Women liberation theologians were more frequently involved in active pastoral praxis than their male counterparts, in effect implementing and reshaping the theory/ideology of liberation. Thus, in feminist liberation theology, a wedding of theory and practice is particularly pronounced. In unpacking liberation theology, I aim to show how it served to activate particular moral identities in changing political and economic conditions. I will examine how the literature has addressed the implications of the overwhelmingly female participation in these organisations.

2 Liberation theology

Liberation theology has provided one of the most important corpuses of work exploring the emergence and practice of CEBs. Yet liberation theology did not just examine CEBs but also furnished a blueprint for their emergence. It is a rich and varied field ranging from the cogent class analysis of Leonardo Boff to the feminist woman-centred contributions of Elsa Tamez (Boff, 1985, 1986; Tamez, 1989). These studies are linked by a vision of the liberating potentials of spiritually motivated communities and the need to use this power to challenge poverty and oppression. In addition, they usually share some class-based analysis and the belief that praxis is central to eradication of oppression.

In this section I will explore the praxis orientation of liberation theology and in particular its relationship to Marxism. I will begin with an analysis of how liberation theology's engagement with Marxism developed and the course of this relationship and will then move to a brief consideration of the way in which divisions within the church have been conceived of by liberation theologians. I will return to the issue of conflict within the church throughout the book. In the following section I will consider the field of feminist liberation theology, examining how the oppression of women both within the church and in society is conceptualised within the framework of liberation theology.

Any reflection on liberation theology and its relationship with Marxism must first explore the links between the former and dependency theory. Liberation theologians have often used a dependency theory framework in their analysis of economic and political issues and indeed the two bodies of thought developed in Latin America during the 1960s. David Ormrod maintains that in Nicaragua liberation theologians who embraced a 'non-dogmatic Marxism' were in reality drawing upon dependency theory (Ormrod, 1988, p.7). I would contest this assertion inasmuch as liberation theologians in Nicaragua as elsewhere in Latin America worked with concepts of both Marxism and dependency theory, concepts that were often overlapping. However, Ormrod is correct in identifying the importance that dependency theory has played. Indeed Franz Hinkelammert, one of the leading proponents of dependency theory, also works closely within the field of liberation theology. In discussing the interrelationship of the two, he maintains: 'One assumes that theology offers a judgement upon the economy and one discovers inside the [economic sphere] - be it economic activity or theory - a theological vision' (Hinkelammert, 1987, p.257).

In *Theories of Development*, Jorge Larrain maps out the field of dependency theory, highlighting the importance of the 'centre-periphery' economic model. He groups theoretical approaches according to the emphasis that they place on either the global or the national aspects of this model. In the first case, analyses are focused on the relative prosperity of 'centre' countries at the expense of 'peripheral' or dependent countries. The work of Frank, Wallerstein, Emmanuel and Amin typifies this first approach (Frank, 1970; Wallerstein, 1974; Emmanuel, 1972; Amin, 1974). In the second case, theories take into account the global character of capitalism but tend to concentrate on the national relations of production and class conflict. Cardoso, Faletto, Palma and Hinkelammert work primarily in this second tendency (Larrain, 1989; Cardoso and Faletto, 1969; Palma, 1981; Hinkelammert, 1972).

Although liberation theologians use both the global and the national strands of dependency analysis, in that the intersection between the global and the national is often highlighted, it is in the national and the local that praxis-oriented strategies are most often developed. Because the 'preferential option for the poor' is a strategy that involves the creation of a church not only *for* the poor but also a church *of* the politicised poor (rather like Marx's 'class for itself'), liberation theologians have often focused on the more tangible national and local factors that shape the circumstances of the poor. Further, because consciousness is the antecedent of praxis, liberation theologians' focus on the local and the national has also been based on an assessment of the most immediate sphere of praxis - the community, the region, the nation. So a political programme that utilises a dependency analysis would most fruitfully concentrate on the local aspects of dependency rather than the global facets, although these must form a part of any broader analysis.

In his ground-breaking book, *The Theology of Liberation*, Gustavo Gutiérrez explores the notion of the 'sin of societies', which he distinguishes from personal sin (Gutiérrez, 1973). It was not enough for a Christian to seek liberation from personal sin, s/he must also challenge the 'sin of societies' which manifests itself on both a national and a global level. Gutiérrez pays particular attention to the activities of both the Peruvian oligarchy and the United States who have worked in tandem to create the poverty and oppression experienced by many Peruvians. It was Gutiérrez who, through *The Theology of Liberation*, provided the framework for discussions at the CELAM conference at Medellín in 1968. At this conference notions such as the preferential option for the poor, unjust structures of social sin and institutionalised violence received institutional validation and emerged as 'legitimate' and as categories of analysis (Lernoux, 1989, p.94).

Another significant figure in the development of liberation theology was Leonardo Boff. According to Penny Lernoux: 'If Gutiérrez is the intellectual "father" of liberation theology, Boff is the leading proponent of its pastoral application among impoverished Latin Americans' (Lernoux, 1989, p.103). For his pains, Boff often came into conflict with the Vatican and conservative factions of the Brazilian hierarchy. At one point he was even sentenced to an indefinite period of silence for promoting, according to Cardinal Ratzinger, 'revolutionary utopianism foreign to the church' (Lernoux, 1989, p.109). After years of constraint on his teaching and his writing Boff, left the Franciscan order in 1992. According to Boff, his decision has freed him to peruse the theology of liberation in a more radical and ecumenical way (Ferrari, 1992).

For Boff, Marxism as a literal discipline is for all practical purposes untenable. In maintaining so emphatically that liberation theology is 'gospel' rather than 'Marxism' (Boff, 1986, p.42), he proposes an opposition which collapses many of the categories that he utilises with such skill and sophistication elsewhere. A recurring theme in the work of Boff and other liberation theologians is the need for a synthesis of religion and a radical anti-capitalist politics involving some recon-struction or incorporation of Marx's ideas in order to dislodge the status quo. The maintenance of this status quo is largely attributed to capitalism and the social relations that it engenders. Yet many of the reflections on the Christian/Marxist debate were written in response to a dogmatic form of Marxism and within the context of a struggle within the Latin American Left over which particular Marxist 'line' was valid (see Segundo, 1975; Bonino, 1975; Comblin, 1989; Sobrino, 1984; Betto, 1987).

Approaches to overarching belief systems are often in practice much more partial and flexible than the theological debates around Christianity and Marxism. As Rigoberta Menchú maintains, the Bible is one 'weapon' in the revolutionary struggle; for her 'the whole truth is not found in the Bible, but neither is the whole truth in Marxism' (Burgos-Debray, 1984, p.246). This flexible approach is echoed in the practice of CEBs in that they set out to provide members with the means of discovering which 'weapons' are appropriate for their struggle.

However, this is still a proscriptive position: there is an effort to contain 'the people's' understanding of reality within a particular discourse. Marxists, for their part, have a lot to answer for in this area, and perhaps the fear of losing the uniqueness of 'liberation theology' to a set of rigid 'Marxist' categories is partly behind Boff's rejection of 'Marxism'. In addition, due to the literal death sentence that the label 'communist' has been in many of the countries in which CEBs operate, a clear separation between the Gospel and Marxism may be prudent. However, as any belief system which challenges capitalism has often been labelled 'communist', this measure has not assured the safety of liberation theology practitioners. The distinction between 'Christian' and 'Marxist' seems a false one in that both categories are open to varying definitions, so that at any given moment in the debate it must be established which Christianity and which Marxism are being discussed. The inability of both to fulfil the needs of the 'poor' whose interests they champion has led to a greater flexibility within these discourses as both seek to retain their viability.

In the last twenty years the Catholic church in Latin America has been experiencing a membership drain as large numbers of nominal Catholics join evangelical sects and other Protestant churches. Similarly, 'Marxism' appears, due in part to the failure of East European versions of socialism, to be a discourse in retreat. In many ways the Christian vs. Marxist debate may in many ways be superfluous, given the current crisis in Marxism.

Still, Boff's work stands out for its willingness to challenge all social relations within the framework of a class analysis, including those of the church itself. In fact, as Alistair Kee (1990) suggests, the class analysis of the church contained in *Church Charism and Power*, and not the use of Marxist language per se, was the reason why Boff was silenced by the Vatican. This willingness to challenge the institution is one of the key strengths of Boff's work. In maintaining that capitalism is the major source of oppression in the lives of the poor, he prioritises the struggle against capitalism and the social relations that characterise it.

José Porfirio Miranda has a unique view of the Christian vs. Marxism debate that concerned Boff and other liberation theologians. In *Marx and the Bible*, he equates the Christian belief that faith will produce a just society to the Marxist conviction that this can be achieved through dialectics. For Miranda, there is no contradiction between Christianity and Marxism; for him both have the same aims and both operate in the realm of faith and belief - Christians in God and the Bible and Marxists in dialectics and *Das Kapital*. However, Miranda is clear that Marx's thinking is part of a continuum that began in biblical times. He maintains:

> What is clear is that the totality and organicity of injustice structured into civilization was pointed out by Paul eighteen centuries before Marx, and ...those who think that the totality called capitalism grew up like a mushroom without roots or precedents in history betray Marx's dialectical thought (Miranda, 1974, p.254).

For Miranda, capitalism's co-optation of Christianity can only be uncovered through Marxist dialectics; thus any choice between the two is a false one. While Marxism may save Christianity from the 'dulling' effects of capitalism (Miranda, 1974, p.254), ultimately it is up to a rejuvenated Christianity to combat the structural sin of oppression. Here Miranda's work reflects a greater willingness to engage sympathetically with Marxism than many of his theological counter-parts. He expresses a suspicion of those who reject Marxism in favour of Christianity because, he contends, their motives are often based on a desire to preserve the status quo of capitalism (Kee, 1990, p.209). Boff, for example, presents a clear choice between 'Marxism' and 'Gospel'. For Miranda, there is no need to choose: both 'Marxism' and 'Gospel' are part of the same struggle against oppression.

In *Marx and the Bible*, Miranda has an advantage over other liberation theologians in that he does not address any existing examples of the preferential option for the poor in operation. Miranda was unable to comment on the CEB movement owing to its inchoate state at the time he wrote *Marx and the Bible*. The work is very much a theological and theoretical text unfettered by the sometimes contradictory character of praxis. Praxis itself, however, is a key concept for Miranda, who maintains that God can *only* be approached through the struggle for justice (Kee, 1990, p.205).

Elsa Tamez's *Bible of the Oppressed* is similarly a theological text that provides a systematic analysis of biblical references to oppression. Tamez, a Mexican evangelical, examines all the passages in which the Hebrew roots meaning oppression are found or in which oppressive situations are described. The nine Hebrew roots she uses all provide a different nuance of the term: pressure, degradation, oppression which provokes a 'cry out for liberation', etc. Her analysis is enriched by the distinction she makes between oppression at an international level and oppression that operates at a national level. She explores the profile of both the oppressors and those that they oppress and draws out the paradoxical condition in which the oppressed find themselves: 'they are the oppressed because they are poor...they are the poor because they are oppressed' (Tamez, 1982, p.37).

For Tamez, oppression is a multi-faceted entity, and part of the struggle against it is to become conscious of these facets and those responsible for cutting them. The first step in the process of liberation is to recognise oppression and the system that sustains it. Yet for Tamez this is not easy because oppression is made to appear 'natural'. As she explains:

> The oppressor conceals the fact of any responsibility, and the oppression simply happens, as it were. Psalm 55 explains: "His speech was smoother than butter, yet war was in his heart; his words were softer than oil, yet they were drawn swords" (Tamez, 1982, p.51).

Here, without making explicit reference to 'ideology' or the body of work that addresses it, Tamez maintains that oppression is perpetrated not just through brute force but also through the finesse and deception of the oppressor. Tamez does not explore how the oppressed come to see their oppression as 'natural'. However, she does utilise an implicit theory of class consciousness and ideology: the oppressed cannot oppose their condition unless they recognise it but recognition is impeded by the deception of the oppressor. Indeed, distilled to its most basic rendering, Marx's concept of ideology posits 'a consciousness which conceals contradictions in the interest of the dominant class' (Larrain, 1979, p.61). Tamez, unlike Marx, does not explore the mechanisms by which this consciousness is constructed and potentially deconstructed or reconstructed, issues that I will touch on in section 4 of this chapter. The strength of Tamez's analysis is that she Biblically contextualises the experience of the oppressed as a 'class' striving for the consciousness to act for 'itself'.

According to Tamez, in fighting against oppression, people do not struggle alone: God is with them. But although the people have God 'on their side', they cannot wait passively for their liberation. As Tamez asserts:

It is not to be thought that Yahweh literally takes the place of the oppressed in their historical struggle. Such a view could have negative consequences such as the abandonment of all human effort, in the expectation that Yahweh, when called upon will "intervene". All this means is that in our present historical situation of oppression/liberation, our faith in the God of the bible does not excuse us from taking part in the struggle for liberation (Tamez, 1982, pp. 61-2).

It is interesting to note here the similarity between this tension and the dialectic of class struggle/human agency and the inevitability of revolution/progress present in Marx's work. God, in a liberation theology context, or progress, in a Marxist context, is posited as an all-pervasive force on the side of the people/ proletariat. 'Consciousness' as a precursor to praxis is a concern of both Marxists and liberation theologians. This faith/praxis dialectic fuels the transformative power of liberation theology and is a strong feature of Marxism. Throughout this work, I will examine how revolutionary consciousness both precedes and generates praxis.

Liberation theology has attempted to sponsor a critical engagement between Christianity and Marxism. As the above discussion demonstrates, there are many points of convergence between the thinking of liberation theologians and Marxism, some of them unacknowledged. However, in addition to academic engagements of Christianity and Marxism, the praxis of liberation theology in the popular church and CEBs has often produced a much more whole-hearted alliance. This was particularly the case in Nicaragua where Sandinismo was a fusion of versions of both Marxism and Christianity. So neither Marxism nor Christianity could be described in monolithic terms: there were competing versions of both discourses. As Giulio Girardi contends:

'Marxism' and 'Christianity' do not exist, neither one nor the other. In reality only Marxisms and Christianities exist. It is evident that there are Marxisms and Christianities that are radically incompatible; this is the case, in particular, of the orthodox tendencies of one or the other movement. Such mutual incompatibility is evidence of their similarities. (Girardi, 1987, p. 280.)

This open attitude towards Marxism reflected the willingness of liberation theologians to pursue a line of inquiry that conflicted with the priorities of the official church. The multi-disciplinary approach taken by liberation theologians (often encompassing sociology, economics, anthropology, etc.) has led to claims by some sectors of the church that liberation theology was leading the church away from its fundamentally spiritual project. Often this was expressed in complaints aired by the Vatican and sections of the hierarchy that the analyses employed by the liberation theologians were 'too political'. Of course, the Catholic church has always been 'political' in its institutional form, but it has often been slow to challenge 'structural sin'. Vatican II, while providing the basis for the emergence of liberation theology, seemed in large part based on an attempt to modernise the church rather than to transform it. As the hierarchical church drew back from the enthusiastic commitment to liberation theology made at Medellín, liberation theologians became more critical of the institution and its practices.

Thus, divisions within the Catholic church have been considered by most liberation theologians (see Segundo 1975; Gutiérrez, 1973; Castillo, 1976; Cabestero, 1983). In *Church, Charism and Power,* Boff applies the Marxist-influenced analysis of class society (which has so irked conservative sectors of the church) to an examination of the structures of the church itself. Boff describes a church in which there is a ruling class composed of the Pope, cardinals and bishops and an oppressed class of religious and laity (Boff, 1985). Women, because of their marginal status within the church, are always in this oppressed class. Sandwiched between these two classes is a middle class of priests who may have their roots in the oppressed class but who usually identify with and aspire to be part of the ruling class. According to Boff, the hierarchy validates the existing class structure of the church by their interpretation of the will of God. As he observes:

The system of power within the Church believes itself to come directly from God, and believers must accept it in faith. Socialization through catechises, theology, and the accepted exercise of power guarantees the preservation of the structure from generation to generation (Boff, 1985, p.40).

In attempting to counter the myth that the present hierarchical structure of the church is divinely mandated, Boff provides a history of the institutional church demonstrating the way in which the present authority structure was constructed. Although it is clear that both the authoritarian and counter-authoritarian tendencies within the church did not develop in isolation from the outside world, the 'official' position is that the church influences the outside world but is itself impervious to outside influences. This view is manifest in the encyclical *Gaudium et Spes* which, according to Boff, takes the position that 'the Church is in the world and not the world within the Church' (Boff, 1985, p.109).

The tension between what is 'God given' and what is human made is discernible in discourse not only concerning the church's power structure but also in regard to the content of Catholic belief. Boff's analysis of the debate around syncretism (eclecticism, fusion of two or more beliefs) in Catholicism is a keen illustration of this point. The 'official' position denies its existence because Catholicism is said to be a 'revealed' religion (Boff, 1985, p.92). However, as Boff observes, syncretism is 'a universal phenomenon constitutive of all religious expression' (Boff, 1985, p.93). I will return to some of the debates around syncretism in Chapters 6 and 7, where I explore popular religion and popular religious festivals. Here the church's official denial of syncretism is germane because it is the theological justification for a resistance to changes in dogma and to internal reform.

3 Feminist liberation theology

The belief that the church is impervious to the influences of the outside world is particularly evident in its official position on the status of women. According to Boff, one of the key divisions within the church centres around the marginalisation and exclusion of women both in the church and outside of it. The attitudes and activities of the hierarchical church have effectively constrained women in both. Women theologians have often worked from their position within the church to their position within the larger society in order to theorise the oppression of women and envisage the liberating strategies to combat it. I will examine some of the work produced by women seeking to carve out a 'woman-centred' or feminist liberation theology.

To his credit, Boff has been one of the few male liberation theologians to make more than a cursory analysis of women's oppression. He takes a strong stand against the marginalisation of women from positions of power and leadership. In both *Church Charism and Power* and *Ecclesiogenesis*, Boff is quite adamant that the exclusionary treatment of women is a grave fault of the traditional church and that any church which follows the 'People of God' model must make amends. In addition, as Boff notes, women numerically dominate in the church:

51

Discrimination against women in the Church is one of the most clear examples of the violation of human rights. Women make up at least half the faithful and women religious are ten times the number of their male counterparts.(Boff, 1985, p.35).

Boff is critical of many attempts to rectify the apartheid-like structure that marginalises women. Yet he does not believe that the situation can be alleviated simply by inserting women in the hierarchical structure. Not only are women locked out of positions of institutional power, but they have no control over the forms the institution takes or the priorities that it sets. As Boff maintains on the issue of women entering the priesthood:

All official faith institutions are male in tone. It would be a sad mistake for women to seek the concrete historical image of the priest as it has been lived by men....Women neither can nor should simply replace male priests. They should articulate their priesthood in their own way (Boff, 1986, p.89).

Except for a section on the 'sexual violation of women', Tamez does not specifically address the oppression of women in the *Bible of the Oppressed*. In contrast, the focus of her next book, *Through Her Eyes: Women's Theology from Latin America* attempts to mesh feminist and liberation theologies within a Latin American context. This edited volume was the result of a 1985 meeting of Latin American women involved in progressive church work. The contributions in *Through Her Eyes* are specifically concerned with the marginalisation of women as a form of oppression. Many of the contributors also attempt to explain what distinguishes the theological contributions of women from those of their male counterparts.

Uruguayan theologian Ana María Bidegain maintains that when liberation theology was first being theorised it was within a Latin American intellectual framework which sought to resist North American imperialism (Bidegain, 1989). Within this context, feminism was often located amongst the products of imperialism to be resisted. As liberation theology developed and became more rooted in the 'popular reality', i.e. more of a praxis and less of a theory, women were marginalised in a different fashion. According to Bidegain, 'although women religious had been the first to intuit and assume this radically new way of being Christian, once again it was clerical males who wrote the books' (Bidegain, 1989, p.28).

While male liberation theologians 'wrote the books', women liberation theologians generally contributed to the anthologies. Indeed, in addition to the Tamez anthology, Latin American women working within the liberation theology tradition have been represented in a number of other publications: see Kwok Pui-lan and Letty Russell (1988), Virginia Fabella and Mercy Amba Oduyoye (1988) and Ursula King (1994). The relative dearth of single-authored books by women liberation theologians is due to a number of factors. Unlike their male counterparts, women often do not have the support of an academic institution that encourages and enables them to publish. In addition, and relatedly, women liberation theologians are often engaged in work with an active pastoral dimension, so their literary contributions are shaped by a more praxis-oriented approach to theology.

This distinct approach to 'doing theology' is, therefore, based on women's different positioning within the church and the larger society. However, there is a tension between this contention and the suggestion that women are somehow more essentially committed to a particular form of theological practice. The church's location of sex and sensuality exclusively in women further complicates the matter. Women liberation theologians often speak of a theology that emerges from the reality of women's lives. Here there is a convergence between the discourse around women's *testimonios* explored in the previous chapter and the notion of women doing theology. In describing the emergence of a distinct feminist liberation theology, Ivone Gebara states:

> It is as though we were discovering, very powerfully and starting from our own situation, the mystery of the incarnation of the divine in the human, not just because "we have been told", but because we experience it in the confines of our lives as women (Gebara, 1994, p.52).

Gebara argues that women religious[1] have been at the forefront of enabling theological praxis among CEB members, thus extending liberation theology beyond its academic bounds. While male liberation theologians have been active in this redefinition of theological practice,[2] women have generally played more a robust and innovative role. Further, given their positioning within the church and the larger society, theological reflection based on experience is qualitatively different for women. As María Clara Bingemer contends: 'A woman who does theology is called to bear witness to this God with her body, her actions, her life' (Bingemer, 1994, p.316). Women liberation theologians maintain that because of their social positioning, they 'do theology' differently. At times, however, essentialised notions of men

53

and woman creep into the discourse: women are said to be more patient, physical, spiritual and creative/procreative while men are more rational and less in tune with their spirituality.

Although she does not address the issue of essentialism within the discourse of feminist liberation theology, Ana María Bidegain does contribute to an understanding of it through her examination of the way that women and sexuality are positioned in official Catholic dogma. She links the fear of sexuality in general, and women's sexuality in particular, to women's marginalisation in the church. In order to remedy this, she maintains that a break needs to be made 'with the traditional notion that reduces sexuality to an isolated area of the social relationship and an expression of sin, the latter being embodied essentially in women' (Bidegain, 1989, p.30).

Particular notions of womanhood are constructed around devalued attributes. In this way women simultaneously are devalued by and devalue certain ascribed characteristics. Bidegain argues that until the church develops a healthier view of sexuality, women will never be able to fully participate in the life of the church. Although Bidegain confines her comments to women and sexuality, a broader insight can be gained from her work. Namely, the essentialisation of particular characteristics as female may be rejected while retaining or rehabilitating the integrity of the characteristics that women themselves value.

So far I have examined how feminist liberation theology has been a response to the oppression of women. Yet theological reflections are mediated not only by gender but also by class, race, ethnicity, age and status within the church. Even women from similar backgrounds can have different attitudes, experiences and opinions, and this diversity must be accommodated within the framework of feminist liberation theology. The preoccupation of many feminist liberation theologians with women's oppression inside the church is understandable, given that many are church personnel. Yet oppression outside the confines of the institutional church is often a more critical feature of women's everyday lives. The two are not unconnected: the institutional church, as the arbiter of 'morality', directly and indirectly, shapes the legal and cultural limitations imposed upon women and thus impedes the pursuit of strategic gender interests. Patriarchy and papacy operate in tandem.

Writing before the 1990 change in government, Luz Beatriz Arellano maintains that in Nicaragua it is impossible to divorce the fight against women's oppression from the struggle for revolutionary transformation. For her, the revolution had and would continue to improve women's lot (Arellano, 1994). Hence defending the revolution against US aggression was conceptualised as a form of feminist praxis. In an article entitled 'The Role of Women in the Transformation of Society and the Church in

Nicaragua', Arellano addresses the issue of strategic gender interests in a footnote to a section called 'A Revolution Against Machismo':

> There exist other particular problems for women that need to be elaborated such as social issues, abortion, sexual education, and physical and psychological mistreatment ... [however these] are not covered in this work (Arellano, 1987, p.142).

Arellano's acknowledged omission is not remedied elsewhere in the work of Nicaraguan liberation theologians. There are numerous reasons why the Nicaraguan popular church in general, and women liberation theologians in particular, have not engaged in a consideration of the issues Arellano mentions. Firstly, in Nicaragua as well as elsewhere in Latin America, the relative strength of the Catholic church has made it a powerful opponent to reforms that would address gender specific interests (see Molyneux, 1988 and Wessel, 1991). Secondly, while the church's social doctrine was relatively more amenable to interpretation, prohibitions on abortion and contraception, for example, were absolute and dissenters risked excommunication. Thirdly, many popular church personnel, male and female alike, were suspicious of birth control and abortion because these had been championed within the framework of foreign-imposed 'population control' policies perceived as racist and imperialist (Altman, 1991; Teles, 1994). Finally, there was a deeply rooted resistance amongst many Nicaraguans to open discussion of abortion, contraception and domestic violence.

All of these factors underlie the popular church's failure to take up strategic gender interests. In my research I aim to consider how or if women participating in CEBs, the chief grassroots structures of the popular church, position themselves with regard to these interests. In my analysis of the San Pablo CEB I will focus on women CEB members, considering issues around the 'everyday life' of an *olla* or communal kitchen that they run.

4 Conscientización and faith: CEBs

In addressing the role of women in CEBs, Ivone Gebara looks at women as pastoral agents[3] rather than as participants in these organisations (Gebara, 1989). She maintains that by taking an active role in CEBs lay women and women religious are 'prefiguring within the Christian churches a new way of organizing ministries'. That these ministries are often not approved by church officials does not diminish their impact because they are legitimised by those who are their beneficiaries.

According to Gebara, this 'service' is essentially different from that which has traditionally been provided. As she maintains:

> The new element in this service is found in the way it responds to a certain number of the community's vital needs and in the fear that it is generating in those who are in charge of the church and who are gradually losing their former prestige (Gebara, 1989, p.48).

Here Gebara sees the work of CEBs very much as a new service which is being 'provided' to members of these communities by women pastoral agents. On this basis, she contends, women's ministry is 'shaking up' men's ministry (Gebara, 1989, p.48), which she associates with more traditional and less responsive 'service'. Gebara criticises the church's gender stratification whereby women are relegated by a male hierarchy to a lower status than their male counterparts. Women have superseded this through their innovative new service to communities, which take the place of the hierarchy in legitimising these women's ministries as well as their status. However, in some CEBs, for example the ones studied by Madeline Adriance, gender divisions are actually reinforced by the communities themselves. In these cases, women religious do most of the work in the community, yet the priest who has much less frequent and more formal contact with the community is the one who legitimises the CEB in the eyes of its members. While women's ministries may be challenging men's within the institutional structure of the church, in some cases people still cling to the belief that the old forms of service (for example consecrating the Eucharist) are somehow more valid.

It is interesting to note that in the more idealised representations of CEBs, such as those found in the work of Boff and Gutiérrez, the relationship between community and pastoral agent is represented as a dialogue between the two rather than a service provided by the latter. While Gebara does provide ample evidence in her essay of the pivotal role that women CEB members play in their communities, she views the woman pastoral agent's role as one of 'server' rather than the 'co-worker' role that Boff and Gutiérrez might envisage. It is an open question whether Gebara's assessment represents a more restricted conception of the role of the pastoral agent or perhaps just a more realistic and less academic one than that offered by other theologians.

In a study of rural Brazilian CEBs, Madeline Adriance examines the role of pastoral agents in these communities (Adriance, 1991). Adriance found that priests, women religious and lay people all performed different functions and had varying degrees of authority in the eyes of CEB members and potential CEB members. While women religious formed the bulk of pastoral agents and had more practical and direct contact with communities, it was the priest who was endowed with the ability to legitimise the CEB. This legitimacy was greater than that of the local bishop. In fact, her research demonstrated that the number and strength of CEBs did not necessarily depend on the actions or attitudes of the bishop, but was contingent upon the degree of legitimacy accorded to them by the local priest. According to Adriance:

> The priest is perceived by CEB members as having authority over pastoral agents. Three sisters (out of a total of eight interviewed) told me that they would have little influence with the majority of the laity if they ever appeared to be in opposition to the pastor. On the other hand lay people will support both sisters and priests against a bishop (Adriance, 1991, p.300).

Through the process of *conscientización*, CEB members are encouraged to locate the source of their oppression. In large measure the blame for oppression is attributed to the capitalist system. As Boff observes, 'When it comes to identifying the causes of the miseries they suffer, the members of the basic communities see the main one - not the only one, but the main one - as the capitalist system (Boff, 1986, p.42).

Boff has a particular conception of what a CEB is and the under-standing of reality that it will develop through the *conscientización* process. However, because this is not instruction or indoctrination, people may draw conclusions about their 'reality' which do not coincide with the line that Boff or any other liberation theologians may prefer. There is a tension here between the idea that people are able to gain awareness and the role that the pastoral agent plays in determining the content of that consciousness. As Johannes Van Vught notes: 'Perhaps the greatest criticism that can be levelled at the CEBs is that the analysis of the social situation does not come from the people themselves' (1989, p.83).

Here the tension between the concepts of 'popular' and vanguard struggles reappears. People are 'conscientized' and given a voice but this is a process which is most often initially prompted from without the community. But does this mean that, left to their own devices, these communities would not have been able to organise in their own interests? Further, as most CEBs are initiated by pastoral agents who are resigned at least to respecting the authority of the church hierarchy, the radical potential of these communities may ultimately be stymied. As Van Vught observes: 'The very deference to religious leadership and their need for legitimation is a limitation of the CEBs' functioning as an independent democratic organization' (1989, p.83).

For Boff, CEBs are a major part of the solution to the problem of an institutional church which, in its pursuit of a monarchical power structure, has moved away from the source of its spirituality. Boff maintains that the traditional conception of the church is based on a monarchical model whereby power is distributed as such: God--> Christ-->Apostles-->bishops--> priests-->faithful. Here, Boff observes, 'The bishops and priests receive all religious "capital", produce all religious "goods" and the people consume them' (Boff, 1985, p.133). In contrast, Boff's conception of 'Church as the People of God' challenges the monarchical model. In this configuration, authority is structured in the following way: Christ/Holy Spirit--> community/people of God-->bishop-->priest-->co-ordinator. CEBs, Boff contends, are a key vehicle for the full realisation of the church as the 'People of God'.

Of particular interest is the way in which Van Vught considers the crucial question of authority. Here he takes up issues of leadership and control both within the CEB and outside of it by looking at the way the larger church structure and the Sandinista government impacted upon the CEBs. Within the CEB a division of labour of sorts tends to develop; certain individuals assume specific tasks. Although this is necessary in order to accomplish the practical work that CEBs set out to do, it can also serve to reproduce and reinforce roles which the 'ideology' of the CEB seeks to challenge. Drawing on the work of Dominique Barbie, Van Vught cautions that 'the CEB must militate against those with specialised tasks becoming the new authorities rather than facilitating consensus' (Van Vught, 1989, p.142).

Here Van Vught touches upon the tension between authority and consensus that is echoed in a number of other 'oppositions', including the masses vs. the vanguard which has been of significance to the FSLN's internal debate. He compares the Nicaraguan CEBs to the mass organisations which worked closely with the Sandinista government. In this way he is able to look specifically at Nicaraguan CEBs, a micro-level analysis, within the context of a macro-level analysis of other 'democratic organizations for social transformation'. What this analysis elicits is a complex articulation of authority and co-ordination between the organisations, the 'outsiders' who may have supplied the initial impetus for their formation, and the institutional structures such as the Catholic church and the revolutionary government. Van Vught's key concern is to establish a framework within which the existence and functioning of democracy in Nicaraguan CEBs can be evaluated.

In a wider social context, CEBs have been hailed as prefiguring a new society which, as Betto contends, will be 'popular, democratic, [and] socialist' (in Hewitt, 1988, p.165). Similarly, Boff calls the CEB a 'miniature model of a new society' and Gustavo Gutiérrez sees them as part of the people's emergent struggle for liberation (Gutiérrez, 1983). Nico Vink reflects on the prefigurative character of religious rituals conducted within the space of the CEB. With regard to the Eucharist, Vink argues that, 'through sharing the bread together people anticipate a society without shortage of food' (Vink, 1985, p.102).

Still, Boff's project is not only to define what the church is not, but also to examine what it is and imagine what it could be. As Boff himself maintains: 'Practice precedes theoretical systematizing; always reality first and reflection latter' (Boff, 1985, p.131). And it is in the CEBs that the potential for a more democratic church and a more egalitarian society is being prefigured.

5   Disharmony in the Nicaraguan Catholic church

The conflicts within the Nicaraguan church can be attributed at the most fundamental level to a struggle over authenticity and authority. In effect, both the hierarchy and the popular church claimed to be the authentic voice of Christianity in Nicaragua. As discussed in the previous chapter , liberation theology grew out of a critique of poverty. Soon the analytical focus was turned on the church itself (see Boff, 1985, 1986; Gebara, 1989). Here the validity of the hierarchy and the traditional organisational structure of the church were called into question by some liberation theologians.

The differences between the 'progressives' and the 'conservatives' (as they have been labelled in discussions of divisions within the Catholic church: see McDonagh, 1991; Linden, 1993) have centred around a number of features. The conservative position, which has valorised hierarchical power and authority, has generally been identified with an 'anti-communist' position. Theologically, questions of personal sin have been of primary importance. In contrast, the progressive position has been characterised by a dialogical Freirean mode of interaction between the religious and the laity. It has generally been characterised by an open, although critical, relationship to Marxist/socialist discourses. Theologically, questions of 'structural sin' have been of primary importance. In contrast, the 'progressives' have been associated with liberation theology and the sections of the church which have to a greater or lesser degree (greatest in Nicaragua) developed an autonomous agenda.

This aspect of the struggle within the larger Catholic church between advocates of liberation theology and the church hierarchy, provides the background to understanding the conflicts that emerged within the Nicaraguan Catholic church. In Nicaragua, a section of the church was allied with the revolutionary government, with the significant entrée into political power and the platform that this provided (Lernoux, 1989, p.369). The 'popular church' as a distinctive and oppostional entity was constructed by the alliance between on the one hand, the progressive church personnel and the laity and, on the other hand, the FSLN (Dodson and Nuzzi O'Shaughnessy, 1990, p.147). In other words, Ernesto Cardenal, as Minister of Culture, had the resources of the state to proffer his theoretical vision. His status was determined by his relationship to the revolutionary state rather than by his positioning within the hierarchical structure of the Catholic church.

Thus, while the popular church was a key ally of the FSLN in the struggle for national hegemony, this was not the only hegemonic struggle that the popular church was engaged in during the 1980s. During this decade, it was involved in a struggle with the Nicaraguan hierarchy and to some degree the larger Catholic church. Yet the struggle for national-popular Sandinista consensus was closely linked with the struggle for hegemony within the Nicaraguan Catholic church. As Giulio Girardi maintains:

> the internal ecclesial conflict unites with the struggle for hegemony within the society. The ecclesial hierarchy objectively supports the hegemony of the bourgeois opposition; the popular church supports the hegemony of the Sandinista Front. But at the same time these sectors of the church are struggling for their own hegemony in the society and in the church (Girardi, 1987, p.414).

Nowhere in Latin America are the divisions within the Catholic church more pronounced than they are in Nicaragua (Mainwaring and Wilde, 1989, p.20). The relative success of progressive church personnel and laity in creating create a 'grassroots' church has met with complaints from the hierarchy that a 'popular church' was in fact a 'parallel' church which posed a threat to Catholic unity and authority. The oft-heard claim that the popular church was 'too political' belied the fact that conservative sectors of the hierarchy had been as prominent in right-wing political activities against the Sandinista government, as 'radical' Catholics had been in efforts to support it. Further, while progressive church members were sanctioned for their efforts, the conservative church was validated by the Archbishop of Managua, Miguel Obando y Bravo, the Latin American bishops' conference, and Pope John Paul II. The battles between the 'grassroots church' and the 'hierarchical church' have taken place both within in the church itself and outside it in the sphere of national politics.

In looking at conflicts within the Latin America church Mainwaring and Wilde use the term 'progressive church' to denote what in Nicaragua, as elsewhere in Latin America, has been called the popular church. For them, the progressive church has three important elements: an emphasis on CEBs, a commitment to liberation theology and a belief that the church must have a political project for achieving social justice (Mainwaring and Wilde, 1989, p.5). Implicit in this configuration of the progressive church is the very real potential for conflict between the top-up strategies of the progressives and top-down authority structure they confront. This conflict has often been realised around the issue of CEBs, which practically embody and influence the theology of liberation.

It is difficult to disentangle the hierarchy's objections to the popular church in Nicaragua. Its claim to oppose the latter's activities because they were 'too political' seems at the very least disingenuous given the hierarchy's well documented support for the *contras*. [4] It is pertinent to question if the church worried solely about a Marxist government or if they were more profoundly troubled by the implications of *Sandinismo's* fusion of Marxism and Christianity and its enshrinement of Sandino and other revolutionary 'martyrs'. Clearly, in Nicaragua, the rhetoric (and practical and material support for the *contras*) seemed to be geared towards an attack on the Sandinista revolution, and moves against the popular church were taken on this basis. However, the deeper issue, perhaps, is the challenge that the progressives presented to the status quo of the Catholic church itself. As Andrew Bradstock observes:

The emergence of liberation theology, for example, has increasingly worried the Vatican, not only because it makes political commitment *a priori* and uses Marxist categories of social analysis and the language of class struggle, but because it also leads very often to a rejection of the whole hierarchical structure of the church (Bradstock, 1987, p.64).

In Nicaragua, the popular church from its inception challenged the Somoza dictatorship and in this it was grudgingly supported by the hierarchy.[5] Their stated objectives were the end to dictatorship and the creation of a 'just' society. It was only when these goals were concretised into revolutionary programmes that the most virulent attacks from the hierarchy arose. The Nicaraguan hierarchy, spearheaded by Managua's Archbishop Miguel Obando y Bravo, protested against the 'Marxism' of the revolutionary government and in this objection they received the full support of the Vatican.[6] The popular church, in broad agreement with the FSLN's policies, openly rejected the stance of the hierarchy. As Crahan observes:

> The unity forged within the Catholic church during periods of right-wing repression tends to disintegrate when it is ended, with old ideological divisions re-emerging in the context of the generalized societal conflict and tensions generated by the revolutionary process (Crahan, 1989, p.57).

The hand of the popular church was greatly strengthened by its collaborative relationship with the FSLN. In many ways, personnel of the popular church were able to bypass the authority of the hierarchy because they received institutional support from the state. The independence accorded to the popular church undercut the power of the hierarchy and gave rise to claims of parallel magisterium from the hierarchy.

But can the Catholic church be transformed into a progressive or popular church and still maintain its spiritual or 'non-political' character? Revolutionary slogans such as 'With the Virgin Mary on our side, we'll smash the bourgeoisie!' illustrate this tension (Bradstock, 1987, p.39). Here there was an attempt to reconfigure 'Mary' from a passive and reactionary figure into a revolutionary one. But is the figure of Mary elastic enough to be both 'Mother of God' and 'smasher of the bourgeoisie'? Is it really possible for liberation to be the primary focus of the Catholicism given that there are other themes which have scriptural justification? In no way am I posing a theological question; rather, I maintain that it is a practical question which is fundamental to the problematic of liberation theology and the project of base communities. This tension is expressed by Enzo Bianchi, a critic of liberation theology, who asserts:

> This approach represents a neo-Marcionist[7] choice of some Biblical texts and rejection of others, the criterion being the liberation of the oppressed. In this case the word no longer judges the community, but the community judges the word (Bianchi, 1987, p.135).

The progressive church had the pragmatic goal of using the institutional framework of the church in order to protect and legitimise its attempts to create alternative justice-seeking structures (i.e. CEBs, Delegates of the Word, human rights commissions, etc.) in response to repressive governments. The Nicaraguan example was unique in that the Sandinista government not only tolerated the popular church, but actually incorporated many of its goals and personnel. Witness the large participation of priests, religious and members of base communities in Sandinista organisations and leadership positions.

'No matter how conflictual their relationship with the institution as a whole may be, progressive Church people generally want to remain part of the institution' (Mainwaring and Wilde, 1989, p.16). The changing argument about the merits of working within the system *vis-à-vis* changing the system from without has a strong resonance for those active in oppositional politics. However, I maintain that the essential religious elements which the church encapsulates make the former strategy the overwhelming choice of those who wish to transform the structure of the church. The CEBs represented an attempt by the progressive church to circumvent direct conflict with the hierarchy over issues of class position within the church. Thus, instead of campaigning for the ordination of women, for example, many women assumed leadership roles in CEBs, in this way challenging hierarchical positions themselves. In the same way, members of the progressive church who participated in the revolutionary process stressed their loyalty to the church while simultaneously positing a new understanding of loyalty and obedience. As Ernesto Cardenal maintains: 'My obedience to the revolution is my obedience to God. And this does not imply any disobedience to the Church' (Williams, 1989b, p.69).

Many discussions of liberation theology have focused on its ability to merge elements of both Marxism and Christianity into an effective formula for social change. In addition to providing compelling philosophical support for liberation struggles, groups of Christians have formed practical political alliances with Marxists and socialists under the auspices of liberation theology, notably in Nicaragua where the 'ideology' of *Sandinismo* served to support the reality of Sandinista state power. In fact, the diverse character of liberation theology has been lauded as one of its primary strengths (Boff and Boff, 1985). However, most considerations of the unity of Christians and Marxists have, understandably, been undertaken at a pragmatic level: how and why co-operation is necessary/possible, etc. Discussions which attempt to preclude co-operation are often based on either a reactionary Christian position or a dogmatic, blinkered Marxist one.

In the context of its participation in the Nicaraguan revolutionary process, the popular or grassroots church has often been considered as a body separate from the Catholic church. This is understandable, given the authoritarian practices and traditional alliances of the latter. However, this assumption is contrary to the stated intentions of members of the popular church, who have consistently rejected the suggestion that they are, or aspire to be, an institution parallel to the main body of the Catholic church. The popular church sees its project of 'liberation' as inclusive of the goal of transforming the larger Catholic church *by working within its existing structures*. In sum, the popular church views its future as inseparable from that of the Catholic church and sees its mission as seeking 'liberation', whether from repressive governments or oppressive church structures.

Certainly, the very existence of the popular church is a threat to the hierarchy which, in Gramscian terms, has always worked against 'the "official" formation of two religions, one for the "intellectuals" and the other for the "simple souls"' (Gramsci, 1971, p.328). As Gramsci contends, the Catholic church has worked tirelessly to maintain 'doctrinal unity' (ideological hegemony?). Liberation theology, and its exemplar the popular church, have constituted themselves as a threat to this unity. However, the struggle in the Catholic church has not only been about the 'official' formation of two religions; it is also about the aspirations of growing numbers of Catholics to challenge the hierarchy's hegemony within the church.

Clearly then, liberation theology saw its project as preceding Marxism and ultimately surpassing it. It is relevant to consider how within a hegemonic configuration Christianity and Marxism might fit together. In Nicaragua, the popular church became a part of the FSLN's hegemonic bloc. This has significant implications for coalitions between Christians and Marxists because it raises the question: can the popular church ever really be a part of a hegemonic socialist project or will their alliance always be merely tactical and subject to the concerns of the larger Catholic church?

Gramsci's analysis of the church is in many ways like Marx's analysis of capital - its power to combat and/or absorb any potential 'enemy' is so well delineated that it is often difficult to imagine any realistic possibility of its transformation. Indeed, the Catholic church has acted decisively in Latin America to undercut initiatives of the popular church, particularly in Nicaragua where the conflicts between the two have been most pronounced.

6 Conclusion

In this literature review I have attempted to locate and contextualise my work within a number of different theoretical frameworks. I have tried to demonstrate not only my critical engagement with the literature but also some of the connections between seemingly disparate approaches to consciousness and praxis. As I will go on to explore, Nicaragua has been a testing ground for the active collaboration between Christians and Marxists. Of primary importance is the way theory and the praxis have been interwoven around both discourses.

In Nicaragua, theological writings have been cast in the crucible of revolutionary praxis. Luz Beatriz Arellano highlights the importance of women's *testimonios* within the context of CEBs. Here women giving *testimonios* were in effect engaging in, and redefining, theological practice. The consideration of gender issues within liberation theology has been brought to the fore by women liberation theologians seeking to introduce a feminist perspective into the discourse. Here, especially within the Catholic tradition, there is a marked lack of consideration of 'strategic' gender interests, particularly as they relate to issues of reproduction and sexuality.

As this review of the literature has demonstrated, the links between liberation theology and Marxism have been exhaustively debated within the former. In Nicaragua the defeat of the FSLN and the enactment of neo-liberal political and economic policies have given rise to a new set of theoretical preoccupations for liberation theology, suggesting that engagements with Marxism may diminish. Liberation theologians have been much bolder in addressing issues of poverty and class than they have been in grappling with issues of gender.

CEBs, the practical expression of liberation theology, have been examined by both liberation theologians and social scientists. Yet for all the cogent and informative reflections on the character of grassroots democracy, prefigurative practice and non-hierarchical practice, there is a dearth of literature addressing women's participation. In Chapters 4 and 5, I explore the specific character of women's participation in CEBs through an examination of Managua's San Pablo the Apostle CEB and the communal kitchen or *olla* run under its auspices. In these chapters I will examine the impact of the change in government and the worsening of the economy on the role of the CEB.

In the next chapter I will explore the FSLN's successful construction of a hegemonic bloc and their subsequent loss of hegemony. In these hegemonic configurations, the popular church and the hierarchy were key players - allies and enemies of the FSLN respectively. Here again the issue of gender comes to the fore. As participants in the insurrection, members of popular church organisations and active and passive supporters of the state, women figured prominently in the building and maintenance of FSLN hegemony. Being amongst the most disaffected voters in the 1990 election, women also participated in the destruction of this hegemony. In considering the past and future prospects of FSLN hegemony, issues of religion and gender have figured prominently and will continue to do so.

Notes

1   Religious is a term denoting a member of a religious order or an individual under monastic vows.

2   Notably Ernesto Cardenal in his dialogues with the members of the Solentiname community in Nicaragua (Cardenal, 1976).

3   A pastoral agent is a lay person or religious usually involved in community development work under the auspices of the Catholic church.   Pastoral agents operate with varying degrees of autonomy.

4   In 1986 Mgr. Pablo Vega, the Bishop of Juligalpa, during a visit to Washington, DC, declared his support for the *contra* and asked the US to continue their financial and material support. Vega's comments were made at a time when the US Congress was considering whether or not to approve an additional $100 million in aid to the *contras* (Williams, 1989b:86). Vega's indifference to *contra* atrocities can be summed up by his response to the *contras* ' murder of a nine-year-old girl. "It is worse to kill the soul than the body" (Lernoux, 1989:385).   The Nicaraguan hierarchy was so involved with the contra project that, according to a <u>Newsweek</u> report, Cardinal Obando y Bravo received $125,000 through a Cayman Island contra bank account set up by Oliver North (Lernoux, 1989:403).

5   On 2 June 1979, a few weeks before the triumph of the revolution, the hierarchy issued a statement supporting the insurrection. The document was welcomed by the FSLN.

6   In 1983, John Paul II, while celebrating mass during a visit to Nicaragua, "lit into the popular church, warning the people to obey their bishops, though for many Nicaraguans the bishops appeared to be allied with the contra opposition. The unity of the church was endangered, by 'unacceptable ideological commitments, temporal options and concepts of the church [i.e. the popular church] which are contrary to the true one'" (Lernoux, 1989:61).

7   Marcionism was a doctrinal system of a second- and third-century sect which advocated a selective adherence to the Bible.

3 Hegemonic configurations in Nicaragua: religion, politics and gender

1 Introduction

In this chapter, I will explore the intersecting loyalties and alliances that characterised national popular hegemony in both the period of revolutionary government and the post-1990 era. As I will demonstrate, the revolution and the 1990 change in government marked great ruptures in the social and political order yet they were not complete breaks with the eras that preceded them. This is particularly the case with the 1990 change in government which has introduced a period of instability and uncertainty, rather than a definitive break with the past. Post-1990 Nicaragua is characterised by a profound lack of hegemonic consensus.

Moreover, there has been a fragmentation within the groups that formed the revolutionary consensus, including the FSLN itself. The popular church, although not 'split', was itself responding to the new situation and redefining its role in Nicaraguan society. Prior to the change in government, the crucial focus of popular church praxis was support for the revolution. In the post-1990 period, the focus of popular church praxis is centred around maintaining the gains of the revolution. Within the FSLN there is no clear consensus on how this might be done. In the popular church, factions have not developed in the same way as they have within the FSLN (although popular church members of the FSLN have been on opposite sides of the ideological divide). Further, while the FSLN lost state power and thus experienced a profound change in its institutional role, the popular church did not experience such a change. In fact, with the revolution, many members of CEBs and popular church organisations left these to work directly with the new government. So the popular church probably underwent a greater transformation in the period subsequent to the triumph than they did after the 1990 electoral loss, although clearly, the latter was more demoralising.

In this chapter, I will begin with a brief examination of how the FSLN achieved hegemony both within its own ranks and in Nicaragua as a whole. I will then explore the FSLN's ideology, *Sandinismo*, and the fusion of Christianity and Marxism that it represents. *Sandinismo* is key to the incorporation of the popular church into the revolutionary hegemony because it is the political articulation of the project of liberation theology. The hegemony achieved by the FSLN through its alliance with the popular church was at the expense of another hegemonic configuration, that of the Nicaraguan Catholic church. I will next examine nationalism, populism and anti-imperialism as aspects of *Sandinismo* and the Nicaraguan revolution and will then analyse some of the issues around the divided Nicaraguan Catholic church. After examining these two interrelated hegemonic configurations, I will explore how the hegemonic relationships that characterised the period of revolutionary government have changed since 1990. To this end, I will analyse the disunity within the FSLN since 1990 and its attempts to achieve internal hegemony in the lead- up to the 1996 general election. I will then analyse how the hierarchical church has been strengthened in the battle for hegemony within the Catholic church. Finally, I will look at how the 1990 change in government has impacted on women's practical and strategic gender interests and how women's organisations have responded to the new economic and political realities.

2   The FSLN: 'internal' and 'external' hegemony

> Revolutionaries can with relative ease take economic power ... But the most difficult task, and one that requires many years, is to take ideological power in this society. To get to the heart of this difficult terrain of ideological struggle is, day by day, one of the fundamental tasks of this revolution (Arce in Girardi, 1987, p.164).

In July 1979, Anastasio Somoza fled Nicaragua and the FSLN seized state power. Somoza's overthrow was almost universally celebrated as his tyranny had isolated him from even the most conservative sectors of Nicaraguan society. In this period, the great achievement of the FSLN was in transforming the various anti-Somoza positions into pro-Sandinista stances. By incorporating an array of anti-Somoza positions into their programme, the FSLN was successful in pushing the national consensus to the revolutionary Left. The FSLN emerged as the only anti-Somoza force with a credible vision for a 'Nicaragua *libre* '.

While the FSLN was able to build a hegemonic consensus against Somoza, the key precursor to this endeavour was the achievement of internal hegemony. Internal contradictions were a feature of the FSLN almost from the moment of its inception. These differences initially turned on disagreements over the appropriate strategy for the seizure of state power, and by 1976 three distinct factions had emerged: (1) the Proletarian Tendency (TP); (2) the Prolonged People's War Tendency (GPP); (3) the *Terceristas* or Insurrectionalists (Vanden, 1982a, p.39). The TP supported a class-based strategy of organising among the urban and rural working class. In contrast, the GPP, drawing upon the Sandinista vision developed by Carlos Fonseca, advanced a strategy of politicising the peasantry for a prolonged 'people's war' in the countryside. The FSLN was deeply riven between these two factions. Yet both the TP and the GPP were linked by the belief that the struggle for power would be a slow and laborious process requiring much preparation and organisation amongst their chosen sectors.

The situation changed in 1976 when a third distinct faction within the FSLN emerged, the *Terceristas* or Insurrectionalists.[1] This 'third way' advocated a more open and less sectorally specific approach to the anti-Somoza struggle. In particular, the *Terceristas* were keen to forge alliances with disgruntled sections of the bourgeoisie and to take advantage of the opening created by the change in US foreign policy. The *Terceristas* saw the struggle for power less in classical Marxist or Maoist terms, as did the TP and GPP respectively, and more in terms of a Gramscian understanding of hegemony. According to Burbach and Nuñéz the *Terceristas* were unique in their ability and willingness to incorporate into their revolutionary project what they have labelled the 'third force'. For Burbach and Nuñéz this third force includes: (1) the middle class, intellectuals, and the petit bourgeoisie; (2) economically marginalised sectors of society: slum dwellers, the unemployed, etc.; and (3) 'social movements' (sometimes referred to as 'new social movements') (Burbach and Nuñéz, 1987, pp. 65-68).

By 1978, these factions reunited and were able to successfully collaborate in the insurrection and the period of state power. According to Burbach and Nuñéz the split and subsequent reconciliation within the FSLN, allowed for the emergence of a 'program that reflected a broader and more open approach to revolutionary struggle' (Burbach and Nuñéz, 1987, p.56). In the final analysis, despite the inclusion and accommodation of the TP and GPP, the *Terceristas* 'won'; the flexible, collaborative *Terceristas* prevailed. Thus through the incorporation of social struggles which did not fit into the traditional parameters of 'working class' or 'peasant', the Sandinistas created a hegemonic block which was able to change the terms of struggle from an anti-dictatorship position to a popular consensus for the Sandinistas, whereby to be anti-Somoza meant to be pro-Sandinista.

Yet many of the mass uprisings and strikes that occurred throughout the country from 1978 onwards were not under the direction or control of the FSLN. In fact, these popular risings dictated the pace of the insurrection by forcing the FSLN into a nationwide armed struggle before it was fully prepared for such an undertaking. For example, the 1978 Matagalpa uprising was principally a spontaneous action that forced the FSLN to seize the initiative and assume the leadership of the Leon and Esteli uprisings it inspired (Gonzalez, 1990, p.40). Many of the popular movements and organisations that emerged through the anti-Somoza struggle were Sandinista identified but not officially part of the FSLN.

Despite the predominance of the open and encompassing *Tercerista* faction, the FSLN has never been a 'mass' party in the sense that its official membership base (about 500 militants at the time of the insurrection) has always been small. This owes as much to the internal structure of the party as it does to the clandestine posture that pre-revolutionary conditions forced them to adopt. Full membership of the party (militant status) is a hard-earned position and requires considerable commitment. The restricted character of full membership is closely related to the idea of vanguards, which is a distinctive feature of the FSLN even as it seeks to create a genuine populist consensus. However, the FSLN through its collaboration with other sectors of Nicaraguan society did function as a typical vanguard party - detached and unresponsive to the interests of its constituents. As Marjorie Woodford Bray and Jennifer Dugan Abbassi assert:

> Uniquely concepts of pluralism and of the vanguard were combined, for although the FSLN emerged as the vanguard party in [the revolutionary] struggle, the leadership saw its role as representing a broad majority in creating a system of popular hegemony (Woodford Bray and Dugan Abbassi, 1990, p.5).

Vanguardism and pluralism are two 'ideologies' that are often identified with the FSLN. These disparate elements are present in *Sandinismo* and the tension between the two remains to some degree unresolved. In its vanguard role, the FSLN provided leadership, direction, and an ideological core to the revolutionary struggle. After the triumph, there was a general acknowledgement amongst the FSLN that the membership needed to be expanded and the party democratised; great strides were made to these ends. The popular organisations were given a key role in the post-1979 state. But whether these organisations *were* the party or whether they were under the direction of the party was a contentious issue. Vanguardism continued to be deeply entrenched in the party structure in that full party membership (or militant status) was restricted and many members of mass organisations are not accorded membership of the party. The FSLN drew its support from broad sectors of the population, yet this diversity was not reflected in its membership or its leadership. At its first congress (the 19 July 1991 'Carlos Nuñéz Téllez' Congress), Humberto Ortega Savedra explained his version of *Sandinismo* as follows:

We could say that we did not invent the fundamental elements of our liberation ourselves. The vanguard gathered these ideas from Sandino, from our own people, and this is what enabled us to lead the people towards their liberty (Vanden, 1982a, p.25).

Without engaging in an extensive theoretical discussion of the problems surrounding vanguardist politics, it is clear that the paternalism inherent in Ortega's statement was partly tied to the suppositions of vanguard-based political programmes. However, his statement does draw out the central issue of leadership and the perceived need to provide guidance and structure to a pluralist configuration in order to retain the goal of realising a socialist project. The presence of pluralism and vanguardism in *Sandinismo* may have served to mediate the worst aspects of each of these programmes. That is to say vanguardism overcame pluralism's failure to give the struggle a coherent voice. The FSLN asserted that *Sandinismo* was 'the truth', even as *Sandinismo* stretched itself to include a number of diverse 'ideologies'.

In discussing *Sandinismo*, the ideology of the FSLN, it is crucial to understand this discourse not just as the ideology of the FSLN but also as the world view that made (common) sense to most Nicaraguans throughout the 1980s. Further, because the aim of the FSLN was to build as wide a revolutionary coalition as possible, *Sandinismo* was similarly open and inclusive. Indeed, *Sandinismo* was forged partially in response to the inappropriate and dogmatic Marxism which was espoused by the Nicaraguan Socialist Party (PSN). Carlos Fonseca explicitly denounced rigid forms of Marxism (although he realised that countries, like Nicaragua, that chose a socialist line of development would see the USSR as an ally). Building on Fonseca's call for a more nationalistic Marxism, the FSLN fashioned its hegemony through incorporating the discourses of the various anti-Somoza factions into

71

Sandinismo. However, this was not a rigid one-way process whereby the FSLN incorporated allies and their discourses. Indeed for its part the anti-Somoza coalition which allied itself to the FSLN tangibly recast *Sandinismo*. In this way, *Sandinismo* was both the governing ideology and the ideology of the governed.

For all its openness and flexibility, there is a definable core to *Sandinismo*. For Giulio Girardi, 'Sandinista Marxism' or *Sandinismo* is characterised by seven distinct elements: (1) the theory of liberating praxis; (2) a Nicaraguan character; (3) nationalism; (4) anti-dogmatism; (5) openness to the contribution of the subjective, the ethical, the utopian, and the cultural; (6) the capacity to recognise and value the revolutionary responsibility of the Christian faith; and 7) a collective fashioning of the aforementioned elements (Girardi, 1987, p.109). Here Girardi presents *Sandinismo* as a diverse collection of revolutionary nationalism, Marxism and liberation theology.

3 Nationalism, populism and anti-imperialism

In light of the definition put forward by Girardi, it would be useful to briefly discuss three discourses which have been linked to *Sandinismo* : nationalism, populism and anti-imperialism. An examination of Sandino's strategy will reveal that he began his armed struggle with an appeal to Nicaraguan nationalism which then came to incorporate more explicitly elements of a populist programme as the first step towards his particular brand of anarcho-communism. According to Hodges: 'Sandino believed that patriotism means nationalism, that nationalism contains elements of populism, and that populism can lead to communism' (Hodges, 1986, pp.79-80). His anti-imperialist stance began as a campaign to expel the US occupation forces from Nicaragua but was eventually presented as a struggle which crossed national boundaries, first within Latin America and then into the whole world. In this latter context anti-imperialism was conceived as part of struggle between an oppressed class and the capitalists or the 'imperialists of the earth' (Hodges, 1986, p.79).

Thus, Sandino saw his struggle not simply in terms of driving out the US occupation forces. For Sandino, patriotism and a commitment to a more equitable society were inextricably linked and he distinguished between authentic and inauthentic patriotism on this basis (Hodges, 1986, p.81). Sandino's philosophy, denuded of its many theosophical elements, was clearly incorporated into the ideology which bears his name, *Sandinismo*. In what Vanden has labelled an 'internationalist vision of revolutionary nationalist', Sandino maintained: 'It would not be strange for me and my army to find ourselves in any country in Latin America where the murderous invader had set his sights on conquest' (Sandino in Vanden, 1982, p.45b).

Yet, *Sandinismo* incorporated not only Sandino's expression of nationalism but also a version shaped through more contemporary anti-imperialist struggles, in particular the Cuban revolution. In working to construct and maintain a hegemonic bloc the FSLN utilised both these complementary versions of nationalism. Combining these versions, the FSLN forged a compelling equalisation of patriotism and support for the revolution. In this way, nationalism played an important role in building FSLN hegemony in the insurrection and the years of revolutionary government. The nationalist character of *Sandinismo* has been noted by many authors (see Walker, 1982, 1985; Vanden, 1982a, 1982b; Brown, 1990; Burbach and Nuñéz, 1987; O'Brien, 1990; Serra, 1985b, Dunkerley, 1988; Gonzalez, 1990; Vilas, 1992-1993; Hodges, 1986).

Populism has also been identified as a feature of *Sandinismo*. However, populism has been used to define widely divergent social movements, giving rise to some confusion over just what phenomena the term encompasses. De la Torre identifies seven distinct usages of the term populism (De la Torre, 1992, pp.366-7). In the first instance, populism is characterised by a situation in which 'demagogic' and 'charismatic' leaders hold sway over 'backward masses' (Germani, 1987; 1978). In the second case, populism is used to designate a situation where middle- or upper-class leaders head multi-class alliances with working-class and/or peasant bases (Di Tella, 1973). In the third instance, populism is said to be primarily an expression of a particular stage in dependent development (Germani, 1971; Malloy, 1977; O'Donnell, 1973). In the fourth case, populism is characterised by state policies which have a redistributive character and which seek to privilege national interests over those of foreign capital (Malloy, 1977). In the fifth instance, populism is posited as a political party sustained by a popular base but led by members of the upper and middle classes. The party lacks a cogent ideology but a leader - usually a charismatic one - utilises a nationalistic discourse (Angell, 1986). In the sixth case, populism functions as a political discourse which seeks to mobilise 'the people' against the state (Laclau, 1977, 1988). Finally in the seventh instance, populism is seen to be a nationalist response on the part of the state to foreign-controlled processes of modernisation (Touraine, 1989).

It is possible to identify three key ways in which the Nicaraguan revolution broke with some of these predominant conceptualisations of populism. Firstly, although hegemony was built by reference to myths and religious faith, there was an equal emphasis on building a 'rational' basis of support for the revolution through popular education programmes. In contrast, Rowe and Schelling note the anti-intellectual character of populism encapsulated in the Peronist slogan 'shoes, yes; books, no' (Rowe and Schelling, 1991).

This could hardly have been further from the discourse of the Nicaraguan revolution, which valorised education and literary expression. They argue that through the 'redistribution of cultural power' the Nicaraguan revolution was at least partly able to break with the populist mould (Rowe and Schelling, 1991, p.183).

Secondly, unlike many populist regimes, there was no single charismatic leader of the Nicaraguan revolution. In fact the notion of many heroes and martyrs dispersed throughout the population was a redistribution of the symbolic power that in populist regimes is often singularly invested in a charismatic leader. The 'martyr' quality that often surrounds such a leader was in the Nicaraguan case based on many instances of genuine hardship and struggle amongst the FSLN leadership which echoed, reinforced and validated the very real sacrifice of many Nicaraguans in the course of the insurrection and then the *contra* war.

Thirdly, populism has often been a middle course between an existing oligarchic structure and a more radical socialist alternative. Populist regimes have served to rechannel popular movements for social change into reformist rather than socialist or revolutionary movements. Steve Stein examines the 1931 Peruvian elections which saw the APRA (Alianza Popular Revolutionaria Americana) as an example of this process (Stein, 1980). Yet, in Nicaragua, although a 'third way' within the FSLN prevailed, the middle classes were unable to create a populist alternative to the revolution. This was in part due to the close and repressive character of the political system prior to the period of the insurrection.

A number of the usages of the term 'populism' as outlined by De la Torre would be inappropriate paradigms for Nicaraguan revolution in general and *Sandinismo* in particular. Due to the different and often inconsistent usages, some theorists have argued for an abandoning of the term altogether (Roxborough, 1984; Quintero, 1980). Yet the notion of populism, particularly as articulated by Laclau, can usefully elucidate some aspects of the hegemony achieved by the FSLN. Laclau maintains that:

> classes cannot assert their hegemony without articulating the people in their discourse; and the specific form of this articulation in the case of a class which seeks to confront the power bloc as a whole, in order to assert its hegemony, will be populism (Laclau, 1977, p.196).

Within this perspective, the Sandinista hegemony was populist because through *Sandinismo*, it articulated 'the people' in its discourse. Certainly, the Nicaraguan revolution was imbued with the notion of the 'the popular', as the central role that 'the people' played in the articulation of the revolutionary project attests. This will be discussed in more detail in Chapter 7, section 5 in the context of a discussion of religious and revolutionary myths. However, here it is important to acknowledge that populism as defined by Laclau can be a useful tool in unpacking the discourse of *Sandinismo*.

Yet Laclau's understanding of populism is not a generalised one and has been criticised within its own terms. Rowe and Schelling critique Laclau's notion that in socialism popular culture will continue to be used in an instrumental way to secure the hegemony of the state (Rowe and Schelling, 1991, p.172). I would argue that aspects of popular culture were indeed 'used' by the FSLN. However, alongside this at times instrumental utilisation of popular culture was the process of *conscientización*, a key strategy for both the popular church and the FSLN. In other words, both rational and non-rational means were used to construct revolutionary hegemony. Although particular forms of thought and discourse could not always be neatly slotted into either the rational or the non-rational category, it was clear that liberation theology generally operated in the realm of the former while popular religion functioned in the realm of the latter.

Patriotism, nationalism, populism and anti-imperialism all seem to be linked by the assertion of the nation-state against some form of foreign encroachment. Yet at the same time they all have, to varying degrees, a component which mandates some form of internal activity. In looking at Iran in the period following the overthrow of the Shah, Valentine Moghadam argues that the Left's almost exclusive reduction of its politics to an anti-imperialist discourse made it vulnerable to hegemonic endeavours of the Shiite fundamentalists (Moghadam, 1987). In other words, by articulating no agenda other than anti-imperialism, the Left was unable to offer a distinctive alternative to the concrete and well articulated domestic agenda put forward by the Shiite fundamentalists. This was clearly not the case with the FSLN, where anti-imperialism, nationalism and populism were features of a wider and more inculturated discourse with a distinctive programme for social change.

In looking at liberation theology and the praxis of the popular church in Nicaragua, as analytically distinct from popular religion, a link between nationalism and liberation theology is somewhat spurious. Liberation theology was a discourse which, although realised distinctly in Nicaragua, was at its core explicitly pan-American in both its theoretical and its practical expressions. One of its distinctive features was that it proposed an overarching analysis of society (poverty as a structural sin), particular forms of social organisation (CEBs, for example), and a specific mode of education and 'conversion' (*conscientización*) which were not determined or tied to any one national experience. In fact, liberation theologians were almost exclusively personnel of the Catholic church, and the institutional structures (conferences, religious orders, etc.) that this provided fostered an extra-national space for theorising and organising. However, the relationship between popular religion as manifest in the festivals of Santo Domingo and La Purísima is a different matter entirely. In section 4 of Chapter 7, where I consider popular religion in Nicaragua in some detail, I will discuss the role that nationalism plays in popular religious practices.

4   Women in revolutionary Nicaragua

How did women fit into the various hegemonic configurations during the insurrection and the years of revolutionary government? Certainly women were differently placed within these configurations and, in this sense, 'women's interests' never were uniform or even definable as such. However, from the outset, women were key participants in the insurrection and in the subsequent structures of the revolutionary government and mass organisations. Yet it is important to consider whether this participation was translated into a greater prioritisation of gender-based, in addition to class-based, struggles.

Despite the fact that a commitment to women's emancipation formed a part of their 1969 party platform, there were serious strains and ambiguities around what such emancipation entailed and the strategy and timing for achieving this goal. To this end, 'elements of the Sandinista bloc were in serious disagreement over some feminist goals' (Lancaster, 1992, p.21), in particular those of a strategic character. Yet there were significant gains for women during the years of revolutionary government.[2] The key gains occurred in two broad areas: changes in the legal system and a greater integration of women into production and political life (Norsworthy, 1990, p.131). Many of the initial ameliorations in living standards and social provision in the areas of health education and housing initially brought about by the revolutionary government particularly benefited women because of their family obligations (Harris, 1987, p.16). Women were not only recipients of social welfare programmes but were the majority of the participants in the early literacy and health care campaigns (Collinson, 1990, pp.97, 124).

In 1979 a law establishing equal rights for all Nicaraguan citizens was passed. Women were guaranteed equal pay for equal work, and this law also stipulated the right to maternity leave (*Envio*, 1987). Between 1980 and 1984, the Council of State passed a series of laws addressing some of the factors underlying gender oppression. The 1979 Provisional Media Law outlawed the exploitative representations of women in the media. In 1980, a law banning advertising for infant formula and promoting breast-feeding came into effect (Lancaster, 1992, p.17).

The 1980 law proposed by AMNLAE, known as the 'Law between Mothers, Fathers and Children', did away with the distinction between children born to legally married couples and those who were not, the practice of *patria potestad*. This law also mandated that men were responsible for the children that they fathered, regardless of their whether or not the children were born within a legal marriage. It was one of a varied group of laws, known collectively as 'the new family laws', which were part of a strategy to improve the legal, social and economic status of women and children. One can see the divergent and often ambiguous attitudes of the FSLN regarding women in the battles over the adoption of these laws. Yet there was greater opposition to these laws and to other progressive legislation from right-wing parties who had no commitment comparable to that of the FSLN with regard to women's emancipation.

With the promulgation of the constitution in January 1987, many of the laws designed to address some of the legislative underpinnings of women's subordination were given the status of fundamental rights. The March 1987 'Proclamation on Women' reiterated and extended the party's commitment to women's emancipation as a key feature of the revolutionary process. The document explicitly addressed the issue of *machismo* in that it problematised the gendered division of domestic labour. Overall, the document gave Nicaraguan women 'a certain moral authority' in organising around gender-specific issues (*Envio*, 1987, p.30).

Despite these gains, the war and the resulting critical economic situation served to constrain AMNLAE's ability to campaign on behalf gender-specific issues. Active support for demands such as contraception and abortion were considered likely to provoke a hostile reaction to the revolutionary government by the Catholic hierarchy and to potentially destabilize the coalition between the FSLN and the popular church. Further, AMNLAE, like all of the other mass organisations, was called upon to defer its own sectoral interests and devote its energies to the war effort. In this respect, AMNLAE proved to be one of the most self-sacrificing mass organisations. So just as its budget was being constricted by the demands of a war economy, so was its field of activism.

Because conscription was an extremely contentious issue during the war, AMNLAE devoted much of its energies to supporting women in their role as the mothers of sons in military service. While this work was undoubtedly worthy, an exclusive focus on women as sacrificing mothers doubtless worked to reinforce traditional women's roles. Here AMNLAE's 'work dovetailed with the very potent role played in Nicaraguan religious and popular culture by the Virgin Mary' (*Envio*, June 1991, p.34).

In the initial stages of the *contra* war, AMNLAE had argued for a more active role for Nicaraguan women by its support for gender-neutral conscription (*Envio*, December 1987, p. 28). During the revolution, over 25 per cent of FSLN guerrilla forces were women and AMNLAE was anxious that women should take an active role in the armed forces. In fact, during the *contra* war, all women volunteer battalions distinguished themselves for their near 'legendary' defence of Nicaragua's northern border with Honduras. However, due in large part to the objections of the church hierarchy and Conservative members of the Council of State[3], women were excluded from conscription (Chinchilla, 1985-86, p.23).

The failure of the FSLN to institute gender-neutral conscription is just one example of the way in which AMNLAE's sectoral demands went unmet. Contraception and abortion were issues that were similarly put on the 'back burner'. Here, too, the fear of offending the church hierarchy played an important and negative role. AMNLAE's acceptance of the lack of priority accorded its demands was due not just to the constraints of the war effort but also to its status as an organ of the state and the party (see Blandón, 1994). As *Envio* observed:

> in a situation repeated in many mass organizations, the party was never willing to give AMNLAE sufficient autonomy to respond to women at the base. The women who most sharply criticize AMNLAE are also very quick to point out that the problem is not, and never has been, one of personalities. It is rather a problem of structure, which created a debilitating level of dependence [on the party] and, sometimes, inertia within AMNLAE (*Envio*, June 1991, p.41).

Further, attempts to sidestep the AMNLAE framework were often looked upon with suspicion:

[An] irony of sorts is that while the party dismissed women's demands outside AMNLAE as "radical" or "petit-bourgeois", those demands were attempting to address the needs of poor women throughout the country. It is the poor women who most desperately need society to address these larger issues. So while the nascent feminist movement in Nicaragua was branded early on as an international import, it has roots deep in Nicaraguan reality (*Envio*, June 1991, p.37).

Middle- and upper-class women had the economic resources to find individual solutions to problems like family planning, legal assistance and abortion. Yet, while the political climate encouraged a collective sensibility based on class - hence the notion of 'the people' - there was not the same imperative for a collective identification along the lines of gender. Thus, gender identities that served to mobilise women in support of the revolution were nurtured and reinforced whilst those that focused on strategic gender interests were often problematised. This pattern has been borne out in other national contexts. For example, in looking at women leaders in Peruvian peasant unions, Sarah Radcliffe concluded that 'women who adopt a more "traditional" view of gender relations in public statements gain greater power than those women who emphasise their gender specific interests' (Radcliffe, 1990, p.231).

One of the key factors that impaired the FSLN's ability to take up contentious issues such as abortion and contraception was the lack of consensus in the party over what women's emancipation as a goal entailed and how and at what speed this project should be undertaken. A second chief factor was the 'entrenched nature of women's subordination' which made rapid and proscriptive change impossible. As Molyneux maintains, revolutionary governments cannot just decree changes of deeply ingrained patterns of behaviour and interaction even if the proposed transformation would mean an objective improvement in the lives of the subordinated. Molyneux argues:

Precisely because [contentious social reforms] challenge existing power relations and widely held ideologies, including ones interjected by the social category subordinated within oppressive power relations, they can only be successful if the ground for the contest is adequately prepared (Molyneux, 1988, p.129).

However, it was this laying of the groundwork for tackling issues around strategic gender interests that neither the FSLN nor AMNLAE could consistently or substantively actualise. In other words, hegemony and a corresponding ideology are necessary for achieving state power but clearly the maintenance of the hegemonic consensus is contingent upon the continued acceptance of the ruling ideology. The ideology must at all times 'make sense', fostering identification and self-recognition. To make changes in the society, this ideology must be stretched and adapted. However, any significant alteration of the governing ideology may imperil hegemony.

Prohibition of pornography was a policy taken up by the revolutionary government and was one of the strategic gender interests behind which the government did put its weight. However, this move was hardly likely to provoke the ire of the conservative Catholic church in the same way that issues of abortion and contraception did. The Catholic church, both in its hierarchical and its popular form, served as a block to the legalisation of abortion and the availability of contraceptive products and advice. The popular church did not deviate from the hierarchical position on these issues, as they had done on so many others, in part because of the repeated and unambiguous stance taken by the Vatican. However, at the same time the popular church played a vital role in helping women to organise around practical gender interests. On a more general level, practical interests for both men and women were translated into strategic interests within the cauldron of the popular church. This process, by which practical interests are 'politicised', already existed in the popular church but has yet to be activated with respect to strategic gender interests.

From 1987 onwards there was an attempt to broaden the women's movement beyond the parameters of the AMNLAE structure (Blandón, 1994). To this end, a wider range of gender issues began to be taken up in the context of other mass organisations. Women's sections were set up in the ATC (Rural Workers Association), and the CST, (Sandinista Workers Central). Here a much more autonomous feminist agenda developed, addressing many of issues that AMNLAE had sidestepped. The Matagalpa Women's Collective was the first women's organisation to declare independence from AMNLAE. In addition, Ixchén, an independent women's clinic offering gynaecological, legal and mental health care, began to operate in January 1989. Further, AMNLAE's 'casas de la mujer', or 'women's centres', often pursued a more radical agenda than the national organisation. Some centres provided gynaecological services as well as support and advice on issues such as domestic violence and family planning. According to Bertha Inés Cabrales, these grassroots initiatives within AMNLAE were not taken up and built upon by the leadership, who were used to 'hand[ing] down from on high' organisational models (*Envio*, June 1991, p.39).

Thus, as the 1980s drew to a close, it was evident that AMNLAE was losing its mandate as the sole representative of the women's movement.

AMNLAE's hegemony within the feminist movement was challenged in part because of the organisation's failure to adequately address strategic gender interests. Had the revolution been allowed to prosper, AMNLAE might have been more autonomous and assertive in its dealings with the revolutionary government. As the revolution was not given this chance, AMNLAE's constrained role limited not only its effectiveness as an organisation but also, ironically, its ability to 'deliver' for the FSLN. Arguably an AMNLAE *modus operandi* more focused on the self-defined and the strategic interests of women might have stemmed the tide of female disaffection from the FSLN.

The FSLN conceived of women's roles as supporting players on the revolutionary stage. The emphasis on women as the caretakers of children or 'the coddled ones of the revolution' coalesced with existing understandings of what women's interests were (practical gender interests on the basis of an unproblematised gendered division of labour). It also served to valorise women as mothers in nurturing and supporting roles, rather than as having a set of interests separate from children. This attitude was reflected in the all-male composition of the nine-member National Directorate during the years of revolutionary government. It is telling that the National Directorate remained an all-male bastion until 1994.

In assessing the FSLN's attitudes and policies towards gender, it is important to recognise that the FSLN was not a monolithic structure and attitudes towards gender varied, as did commitment or resistance to particular policies. Yet there was clearly a disjuncture between the attitudes of some of the leadership and the declaration of equality as enshrined in the Nicaraguan Constitution. It was evident that the goal of 'defending the revolution' served to undercut efforts to organise around strategic gender interests. In both legislation and rhetoric, practical gender interests were given more legitimacy than strategic gender interests.

5 The electoral defeat of 1990: consequences and developments

In retrospect, it is possible to explain the breakdown of the FSLN's hegemonic consensus which resulted in the 1990 electoral loss. However, in the lead-up to the elections the FSLN confidently predicted victory, and this assumption was shared by UNO's chief supporters and financial backers, the United States government (Dunkerley, 1990, p.34). In fact, prior to the declaration of the UNO victory, the US State Department had prepared a statement declaring the elections fraudulent and the FSLN victory a sham. They quickly changed tack when the surprise UNO victory was announced, declaring the elections free and fair and a victory for democracy. Given the years of US military, economic and psychological aggression[4] many commentators maintained that it was more a victory for US policy in the region than for democracy. (see Dunkerley, 1990; Lancaster, 1992; Norsworthy, 1990).

However, within the severely limited framework in which they were forced to operate, the FSLN did make errors that contributed to their electoral loss. Given the likelihood of continuing US hegemony in the region, any assessment of the FSLN defeat undertaken with a view to the 1996 elections must address the failings of the party as well as the conditions that shaped the parameters of the possible. In examining the voting patterns in the 1990 election, it is clear that gender played a significant role in the FSLN's electoral defeat. A 1988 opinion poll revealed that the two sections of the population most discontented with the FSLN government were the female-dominated informal sector and the domestic sector composed of housewives and domestic workers (*Envio*, June 1991, p.35). These two sectors were extremely difficult to organise and, due to their positioning within the division of labour, arguably more conservative. Further, the informal sector was often on the receiving end of government campaigns against speculation and hoarding. Yet women's participation in the informal sector was usually conditioned by the lack of income-earning opportunities available to them in other sectors, a situation caused by the poor state of the economy. It is not difficult to imagine how these factors may have contributed to the FSLN's poor showing amongst voters in the domestic and informal sectors.

Indeed, by the late 1980s, economic hardship - actually made worse by the structural adjustment policies introduced by the FSLN in order to ameliorate a large budget deficit and bring inflation under control (Norsworthy, 1990, p.68) - was negating many of the economic benefits that the revolution's redistributive policies had brought. While AMNLAE avoided organising around strategic gender interests, the precarious state of the economy made mobilisation around practical gender interests a fraught task indeed. Further, in a highly symbolic electoral campaign, Chamorro promised an end to both the war and the economic embargo and an opening of the floodgates of US aid, while Ortega promised somewhat vaguely that 'all will be better'. It is not difficult to understand how many women might have seen that their practical interests would be best served, at least in the short term, by a Chamorro victory. In assessing the FSLN's electoral defeat, Roger Lancaster highlights the role that gender played:

If it is possible to speak of "error" or "miscalculation" in the context of superpower encirclement - then the Sandinistas' "big mistake" might have been their failure to appreciate the gender dimension of politics as defined by their own culture and contextualized by the revolution (Lancaster, 1992, p.292).

While the 'loss' of the women's vote dealt a significant blow to the FSLN's electoral fortunes, class, too, played a role in the party's defeat.[5] Given that the war and economic embargo left the FSLN with very little room for manoeuvre, 'This decade of harsh insecure existence was not the creation of the Sandinistas, but a Sandinista government did administer it' (Vilas, 1990, p.10). The FSLN's 'moral authority' to govern was based in large part on the sacrifice and hardship experienced by the leadership during the insurrection (Lancaster, 1988); on this basis they could justifiably call upon the nation to sacrifice in defence of the revolution. In this context, any unfairness or lack of sacrifice on the part of the leadership or indeed any functionaries of the state was particularly glaring. In discussing the role that inequalities, real and perceived, played in the FSLN's electoral defeat, Vilas argues:

> Such things were not introduced by the Sandinistas, but are part and parcel of the traditional perks of the state and the army in power in most if not all societies, especially underdeveloped ones. But the Sandinistas did little to do away with them, and in many cases encouraged them. To the degree the revolutionary process became ensnarled in its own ambiguities and inability to defend earlier advances, such manifestations became more notorious and reprehensible (Vilas, 1990, p.11).

The disaffection sparked by the FSLN's failure to decline the traditional perks of state power had strong class and gender components. Notions of sacrifice and suffering underpinned the 'moral identities' in support of the revolution; real or perceived deviations from this ethic by the FSLN undermined the basis on which many Nicaraguans internalised *Sandinismo*. It also violated the 'we are the poor' sensibility articulated both by the popular church and in the beliefs and practices of popular religion. The gender aspects of disaffection with FSLN corruption were tied most closely to class interests in that women were hardest hit by economic crisis and thus most called upon to suffer and sacrifice.

The accusation that the FSLN presided over a *piñata* [6] , or 'free-for-all' with the resources of the state, prompted an effort within the party to root out and expose genuine instances of corruption and to distinguish these from the legitimate redistribution of resources within the revolutionary framework. The FSLN also struggled to regain its internal hegemony and to position itself to reconstruct a national consensus culminating in a 1996 electoral victory. Yet the FSLN undertook this task in the context of a changing church/state relationship; in the post-1990 period the conservative church has been greatly strengthened and its involvement in the state immensely expanded. While broadly Sandinista, the women's movement has been coming to terms with both the new political and economic realities and an increase in independence and autonomy from the FSLN. An analysis of these issues will form the core of the second half of this chapter.

First I will explore how the FSLN has come to terms with accusations of corruption and attempted to regain 'moral authority'. I will examine the party's attempts to redefine itself and the differing visions of the FSLN that this has produced and will then analyse the hierarchical church's increased power and authority in the post-1990 hegemonic configuration. Finally I will analyse the rage of women's organisations that have emerged both to challenge and to complement the dominance of AMNLAE.

6   Ethics, 'the piñata ' and the crisis of faith

Arturo Sandino, member of the DRI, the party's international relations section, maintains that the electoral loss was a good thing because the party did not have the solutions to the country's economic problems and because they needed to be humbled. According to Sandino, by the early 1990s there was no longer a party line. In his view, the FSLN was more of a movement than a party and Sandino hoped that this would enable it to find the economic solutions that it had thus far been unable to formulate. Also, and perhaps more importantly, it would fuel the moral regeneration that is desperately needed in *Sandinismo* (Sandino, 1992).

Sandino's comments were a reflection not only upon the FSLN's electoral loss but also on the accusations of corruption that were encompassed in the notion of an FSLN *piñata* with the resources of the state. The issue of the *piñata* continues to linger in Nicaragua not only because it coincides with the party's own internal debates on ethics but also because of the Right's accusation that corruption under the Sandinistas was rampant. There is a number of reasons for these contentions. First of all, there were documented instances of corruption and in some cases an unchallenging attitude regarding the perquisites of leadership amongst some party members. Secondly, the Chamorro government has been plagued by numerous and widely reported instances of corruption, so accusations against the Sandinistas serve to deflect attention from their own misdeeds.[7]   Thirdly land reform, which at times involved the expropriation of land, provoked accusations of corruption and patronage.

Many of the functions of the party and the state coincided during the time in which the FSLN held state power. This changed situation has affected the party in a number of ways, one being the leadership crisis and the emerging divisions within the National Directorate. The other issue has to do with the rank and file. With the change in government, many Sandinistas found themselves without jobs. The distribution of property to poorly paid public sector employees was ostensibly meant to cushion impending redundancy. Whether it was just the low-paid rank and file Sandinistas who benefited from this is debatable.

In an attempt to revitalise the party and to address accusations of corruption during their time in office, the FSLN set up the Ethics Commission. Writing in *La Prensa*, Frederico Dueñas expressed considerable suspicion regarding the FSLN's sincerity in exposing and rooting out corruption within its own ranks. In fact, Dueñas classified the FSLN's Ethics Commission as a 'coarse and infantile trick' designed 'to make us forget eleven years of repression, injustice, domination, blood, robbery and death' (Dueñas, 1992). Dueñas contended that the Ethics Commission was inaugurated with the sacrifice of four of its 'small and filthy rats', who were publicly accused of corruption. Three of the accused subsequently denied membership of the party and thus the authority of the party to sanction them for the infractions of which they were accused.

The Ethics Commission also received criticism from the opposite end of the political spectrum. According to National Directorate member, Bayardo Arce, 'the Ethics Commission transgressed its functions' and thus placed in jeopardy its 'prestige and credibility' (cited in Lacayo, 1992). Arce contends that the Ethics Commission bypassed the Sandinista Assembly and the National Directorate in making public its accusations against the four current and ex-party members. In discussion of the *piñata*, Arce strikes a more combative note. He contends:

> The "Sandinista *piñata*", in any case, existed mainly to return to the people everything the Somoza *piñata* had taken from them. But the difference is that all Nicaraguans were invited to this "party". It began in July 1979....It continued when the government used the budget to teach all Nicaraguans to read and write, not to buy opposition parties (Arce, 1991, p.17).

85

Piñata was a relative term and just what actions constituted the piñata were in dispute. As Arce points out, when it comes to evicting peasants from land so that it may be returned to its pre-revolutionary owners (who most likely obtained it in Somoza's *piñata*), the Right had no qualms. However, the Right does not suggest compensating the state for the subsidised goods and services to which they had access all during the time of the revolutionary government, including liberal credit and flexible loans to businesses and landowners who vilified the revolution. Arce reclaims the term *piñata* and uses it to claim that the resources of the state were at the disposal of all Nicaraguans during the Sandinistas' tenure in government.

Despite his combative tone, Arce acknowledges that the Sandinistas made a major mistake in not legally formalising the ceding of property in both urban and rural areas. Following their electoral defeat, the FSLN attempted to rectify the situation before they left office by passing laws 85 and 86. These laws were designed to give legal title to individuals and co-operatives who currently held land or property. However, the laws have not prevented many people from being evicted from their homes and land since the change in government.

Arce's attitude to the issue of land and property redistribution differs sharply from that of Sergio Ramírez and is yet another example of the rifts within the FSLN. While Arce condemned the Right's efforts to regain confiscated properties, Sergio Ramírez called for the return of as many properties to their original owners as possible. Ramírez maintained that in resolving the property issue: 'The government will have to swallow some things and we will have to swallow others' (*Latin American Weekly Report*, 1993, p.107).

Daniel Ortega's support of the Ethics Commission stems from a conviction that 'in the ranks of *Sandinismo* there is an ethical, moral and ideological crisis' (Alvarez Calero, 1992). Speaking at a public meeting in Masaya, Ortega claimed that *Sandinismo* was 'losing its capacity to sacrifice'. He asserted that the greatest threat to *Sandinismo* does not arise from the far Right or from the 'Yankees' but rather from 'the opportunism that can rise up in our ranks, the shift to the right [and] the proposal of converting the FSLN into a party of the rich' (Alvarez Calero, 1992).

During the time in which the Sandinistas held state power, a significant amount of social labour was performed on a voluntary basis. Good examples of this were the projects which mobilised large numbers of people to build houses, vaccinate children, provide electrification, etc. Most notable was the UNESCO award-winning Gran Cruzada Nacional de Alfabetización (CNA) of 1980 in which 100,000 high school and university students participated. Illiteracy was reduced from 50 per cent to 13 per cent in a matter of months (Collins, 1985, p.249).

In a ceremony to mark the twelfth anniversary of the CNA, Daniel Ortega expressed concern over the policies of the present government which were, he argued, eroding many of the social and economic gains of the revolution. He suggested that university students, flush with their victory in the campaign to secure 6 per cent of the national budget for education, should turn their attention to bringing literacy to the illiterate.[8] Here, for Ortega, the problem of illiteracy, which increased dramatically from 13 per cent to 30 per cent during the war years of the mid- and late 1980s, was not only a matter of changing government policies. The initial war against illiteracy was waged by volunteers or *brigadistas* who gave up several months of their time and their home comforts to live and work in very basic conditions. It was the loss of this order of sacrifice and commitment that Ortega decries when he speaks of an 'ethical and moral crisis in *Sandinismo* ' (Valiverde, 1992).

In response to *La Prensa*'s publication of an internal letter that he had written to the Sandinista Assembly, Father Fernando Cardenal, former Minister of Education, wrote an open 'letter to the Sandinista militants', in order to clarify his position. The original letter had criticised the management of the FSLN's patrimony and made specific suggestions about how its administration could be more rigorous and accountable. In this second letter, published in *Barricada*, Cardenal reiterates and contextualises these points. Here he declares that 'the ethical principles and values that I learned in my Christian formation and strengthened by the example of Carlos Fonseca, Eduardo Contreras and many other Sandinista leaders' were behind his call for an FSLN above moral reproach. For Cardenal, this was a matter of critical importance to the party. He asserts: 'I consider that, in this conjuncture, the fundamental enemy of *Sandinismo* is the lack of ethics and the loss of historic values that so many lost their lives for' (Cardenal, 1992).

It is interesting to note here the fluidity of Cardenal's movement from Christian principles to the sacrifices of Sandinista leaders. For Cardenal, the 'ethics and historic values' of the FSLN are inextricably bound to his Christian faith. It is too crude to say that for Cardenal, Christianity is the belief and the revolution the practice. It is more correct to highlight the way in which the revolution allowed Cardenal and others to make their praxis consistent with their Christian faith. For Cardenal:

> The decade of Sandinista government was characterised by honesty, the delivery of work without conditions and revolutionary mysticism. Of this the people are the witness. All of us used to feel proud to present ourselves as Sandinistas. For this reason responsibility for

abuses committed by individuals in the name of the FSLN should be exposed (Cardenal, 1992).

Here Cardenal is clearly unwilling to allow the legacy of the revolution to be tarnished by individual transgressions. To this end, he argued that the party must refresh its commitment to the fundamental 'values' that motored the revolution. The issue of party ethics is deeply fraught for the FSLN because revolutionary commitment and faith are so closely bound together. If the FSLN is not equal to the revolutionary values it espouses, then a crisis of faith is inevitable. To the degree that accusations of corruption have proven founded or remained unchallenged, the prestige of the party has been diminished. For Cardenal and for other Sandinistas, the FSLN must regain its 'moral authority' and it can do so only when its commitment to its fundamental values is above reproach.

7   The struggle to redefine the FSLN

In the years subsequent to the electoral defeat, the FSLN has been redefining the role of the party *vis-à-vis* institutions of the state that were formerly under its control. The party also struggled to define its new role in Nicaraguan society and its relationship to the Chamorro government. In this section I will briefly explore how two formally Sandinista institutions, the police and the army, have been adapted to the new political climate. I will then move to a consideration of the FSLN's attempts to redefine itself and the differing visions of the party that have emerged in this effort.

A lack of definition between party and government functions affected the police and armed forces during the time in which the FSLN held state power. Since the change in government, there has been a concerted effort to 'professionalise' these organisations. However, as an examination of the 'professionalisation' of the police will suggest, the depoliticising of Sandinista institutions is far from a politically neutral affair. With a new wardrobe consisting of blue uniforms and baseball caps, the national police with much fanfare replaced the Sandinista police. However, it was not just the clothes which had changed but also the personnel of the force, into which former contras were incorporated.

In a society torn apart by the ravages of neo-liberalism, it fell upon the police to make order out of disarray. The frequency and violent character of encounters between police and protesters attested not only to a change in the personnel and tactics of the former but also to a transformation of its role in Nicaraguan society. By 1992 the police were, in effect, presiding over the dismantling of many of the concrete gains of the revolution. A key example of this was its role in carrying out eviction orders against peasants or *campesinos* and in favour of returning landowners. In some cases, they refused to come to the aid of *campesinos* who were being illegally evicted (Vindell Matus, 1992).

The police, although still headed by a Sandinista, have clearly become an instrument of repression. The role of the ESP or Sandinista People's Army is much more ambiguous. The Right and the United States government placed intense pressure on President Chamorro to replace Humberto Ortega as head of the ESP and in February 1995 he retired and was replaced by Joaquin Cuadra (*Guardian*, 21 February 1995). One of the primary aims of the revolution was to eradicate the National Guard, which had for so long served as an instrument of repression and torture; for this reason the ESP was set up. That for so long after the 1990 elections, the army remained the Sandinista Popular Army headed by a man who was tortured at the hands of the National Guard was a sign of the continuing power and influence of the FSLN and a major irritant to both the Right and the United States government.

However, external pressures limited the options of the army and the man who led it. While the army has not been subject to a change in personnel, leadership or uniform, there has been considerable pressure since 1990 to build the army into a neutral organ.[9] The consequences of this have been that in 1992, according to the Nicaraguan Commission for Human Rights, the ESP participated in evicting *campesinos* from land which was, by court order, being returned to former landowners (de Pury, 1992). The sight of the ESP evicting *campesinos* from land which was originally given to them under the provisions of the Sandinista land reform programme is indeed shocking. Yet the army was, by provision of the constitution, a neutral body which took orders from a legally elected government, and as head of that army Humberto Ortega was obliged to oversee this compliance.

Because he was carrying out the policies of the current government and many of those policies were aimed squarely at undermining the achievements of the revolution, Humberto Ortega has been accused by both the Right and sections of the FSLN of placing the Sandinistas in a relationship of 'co-government' with Chamorro (*Caribbean and Central America Report*, 1993; Díaz Lacayo, 1992). This same accusation was made against members of the National Assembly who have voted in line with Chamorro supporters. Humberto Ortega (who renounced his party membership in order to retain his position) explicitly denied the existence of co-government. Nevertheless, the stability of the Chamorro government was seen as preferable to a government of the far Right. Thus, there was a sense in which some Sandinistas were working towards national stability at the cost of the more immediate needs of the rank and file. In fact since the break-up of the UNO coalition in January 1993,[10] the survival of the Chamorro government became even more dependent upon the support in the National Assembly of the Sandinista bench.[11] In a 1993 government reshuffle, Sandinista Fernando Guzman was appointed as head of the newly created Ministry of Tourism (*Caribbean and Central America Report,* 1993, p.2).

This strategy is not the choice of all FSLN members. Gioconda Belli maintained that the FSLN must define itself clearly as an opposition party with a distinctive alternative project for Nicaragua. She maintains that 'this pretension of being at the vanguard of popular struggles and at the same time keeping watch/control over them in the interests of the state [national stability] is the primordial source of the ambiguity' and serves to undermine the FSLN (Belli, 1992). Belli argues that there should be a clear demarcation between the FSLN and the government because the policies of the latter clearly brought poverty and misery. For her, the FSLN must unambiguously dissociate itself from the government and its policies.

The splits within the FSLN over this issue of co-government and others were more evident in the mid-1990s than at any time since its split in the 1970s. The effect these differences have had on the party is debatable. Some commentators believe that such disagreements are a healthy sign of the party's diversity. Others, like Aldo Díaz Lacayo, believe that the existing structures of the party have been greatly undermined. He maintains:

> The current structure of the Sandinista Front, in practice, has collapsed: the Sandinista Assembly does not work; the National Directorate does not work; local department organizations do not work; and the base groups also do not work (Díaz Lacayo, 1992, p.38).

The May 1994 FSLN Extraordinary Party Congress and the build up to it saw two main currents emerge: the orthodox and the social democrat, or as they prefer to call themselves, the 'Democratic Left' and the group 'in favour of a *Sandinismo* that returns to the majority' respectively. The worker and *campesino* centred Democratic Left current wanted to 'guarantee that the FSLN continues to be a leftist party, with revolutionary ideals'. While ostensibly sharing this goal, the reform-oriented 'Majorities' current was concerned to 're-emphasise the multi-class character of the party, renovate its structures and to underline the party's legislative role' (Andersson and Fernández, 1994, pp.4-5).

The leadership elections, held as part of the May 1994 Extraordinary Congress, resulted in a decisive victory for the candidates of the

'Democratic Left', who overall received 65 per cent of the vote to the 35 per cent garnered by the 'Majorities'. Significantly, Sergio Ramírez was not voted on to the National Directorate although Dora María Telléz and Luis Carrión, two prominent supporters of the Majorities current, were. From the Democratic Left current Tomás Borge, Daniel Ortega, Monica Baltodano and Victor Hugo Tinoco were elected to the National Directorate while Daniel Ortega, Tomás Borge and Victor Hugo Tinoco were chosen as General Secretary, Deputy General Secretary and Director of International Relations respectively (Nicaragua Solidarity Campaign, June 1994).

Because of the impending 1996 elections, the 1994 Extraordinary Congress was not nearly as conflictive as it might have been (Buel, 1994). While real differences were expressed, the party was concerned to regroup and to institute necessary reforms. Significantly, for the first time, women were elected to the National Directorate. The statutes of the party were altered to include a 30 per cent quota of women in leadership positions at national, regional and local levels. Thus, five women, Monica Baltodano, Benigna Mendiola, Dora María Telléz, Dorotea Wilson and Mirna Cunningham became part of the party's new fifteen-member governing body (Nicaragua Solidarity Campaign, June 1994). The fact that during more than ten years of revolutionary government no woman had ever been a member of the National Directorate was a telling indication of the party's failure to put into practice its commitment to women's emancipation. The inclusion of women in the National Directorate in the post-1990 period highlighted the increasingly vocal and autonomous character of the women's movement and perhaps a realisation that women are excluded at the party's electoral peril.

Given the consensus within the party on a number of distinct issues, including the systematic incorporation of women into leadership positions, it is worth considering how substantive the policy differences between the Democratic Left and the Majorities currents actually were. Evidently, there were key ideological distinctions between the two, but to what degree were these manifest in the differing strategies put forward by each side? Both factions agreed that the FSLN can only return to power through elections. Significantly, neither faction has developed an economic alternative to neo-liberalism and as such both currents supported Nicaragua's integration into free-trade agreements with the United States (Andersson and Fernández, 1994, pp.4-5). There was very little room to manoeuvre for the FSLN, so some of the disagreements may have been more over style and personality than substance. In this way, Luis Carrión, one of the primary advocates of the Majorities strategy, maintains:

91

It will be interesting to see if there are two major political issues [that separate the two sides] or if it is simply a confrontation between groups and people which are trying to gain leadership positions within the Sandinista Front (Andersson and Fernández, 1994, p.5).

While the FSLN held state power the critical priority of defending the revolution against external aggression was a strong impetus for party unity. Further, such an urgent and clearly delineated project fostered a unifying and integrative praxis amongst the party faithful. Although differences existed, these were blunted by a shared 'common cause' and blurred by pragmatic collaboration. The post-1990 period has provided a radically divergent context for party activism. The activities of the party became fragmented, with some members working in the legislative arena and others participating in the institutions of the state, in particular the army and the police. Other points of activism for FSLN members were municipal government, grassroots organisations, foundations and universities. FSLN activity in these sectors was nothing new, but the lack of a unifying project and state structure definitely was. I would argue that the divisions in the party were a feature of the differing points of insertion into the political sphere and the perspectives that these have engendered as much as fundamental ideological differences.

8 The post-1990 hierarchical church

In this section I will examine the restored prestige of the hierarchical church in Nicaragua and its increased influence in matters of state. Far from retiring shyly into the background, now that the Sandinistas no longer lead the government, Obando has continued to be a vocal force in Nicaraguan politics. During the 1990 election, he actively campaigned for the UNO coalition with Violeta Chamorro. For his efforts he has been richly rewarded. Just a few of his newly awarded perks are: the broadcast of his Sunday mass on state television, just as in the time of Somoza; the allocation of part of the education budget to build a new Catholic university, the existing one (UCA) being too politically progressive for his tastes; and the right to review religious materials of other Christian organisations before they are broadcast (Norsworthy, 1990, p.128).

Far from being appreciative of this preferential treatment, Obando allied himself with the far Right, articulating their anti-Chamorro discourse. The crux of his objections was the tacit alliance between sections of the FSLN and the government. On numerous occasions Obando criticised Chamorro in the same terms employed by the far Right. For example, in a sermon commemorating the anniversary of the death of her husband, Obando explicitly criticised President Chamorro, stating: 'it's difficult to have a government in Nicaragua based on honesty and led by those who were really elected' (*Barricada Internacional*, February 1993, p.6). Here, as in other contexts, Obando indicated clear support for the, then, President of the National Assembly and prominent Chamorro opponent Alfredo César in his power struggle with the executive branch (*Barricada Internacional*, November/ December 1992a, p.9). Even more audacious was Obando's support of the far Right's call for UN peacekeeping forces to mediate the political crisis in Nicaragua (*Barricada Internacional*, September 1993, p.7).

Thus it was clear that Obando was intent on remaining a 'player' in the Nicaraguan political scene despite his oft-repeated condemnation of the popular church for being too political. It was similarly evident that he had his own agenda for Nicaragua which was focused on the restoration of the pre-revolutionary order. In their support for the restoration of 'Christian values', Chamorro and Obando were in harmony. In this effort, the sweeping away of the old revolutionary order was as much about cowing the popular church as it was about undermining the FSLN. According to Silvio de Franco, Minister of Economy and Development: 'The fundamental task for the reconstruction of Nicaragua's social bases is above all a spiritual task: the re-Christianization of each and every Nicaraguan' (Norsworthy, 1990, p.107).

The brand of conservative Catholicism favoured by many in the Chamorro government was that of the 'City of God', a Nicaraguan charismatic Catholic group founded in the mid-1970s. In 1992, this offshoot of the Michigan-based Word of God had approximately 800 members in Nicaragua. A prominent member of the US organisation was pizza mogul Thomas Monaghan, who donated one million dollars towards the cost of building the new Catholic cathedral in Managua. Prominent Nicaraguan members included Minister of External Co-operation, Erwin Krüger and Minister of Education, Humberto Belli (Norsworthy, 1990; Friedman, 1992).

Since becoming Minister of Education, Humberto Belli has implemented his version of Christian principles.[12] Belli claimed that, in contrast to education under the Sandinistas, Nicaraguan education under the present government would be 'permeated with Christian-inspired values' (Norsworthy, 1990, p.107). To this end, primary school teachers in parts of Nicaragua were compelled to attend talks and seminars presented by Catholic clergy and funded by the state

(*Barricada Internacional*, June 1994, p.15). Belli also introduced tuition fees for state primary and secondary schools, a measure that has forced many children out of the educational system and placed a heavy financial burden on the families of many others. This action represents a violation of the Nicaraguan constitution and was the first time since 1979 that universal free education became unavailable (*Barricada Internacional*, March 1993a, p.9; Ramírez, 1992).

In this period of backlash, the popular church as well as the concrete gains of the revolution were under attack. Attacks on the popular church were carried out by the hierarchy rather than by conservative Catholics within the government as was the case with educational reforms. Yet the goal of a particular kind of 're-Christianisation' was the common cause. One of the key weapons in the hierarchy's arsenal in their battle with the popular church was the former's ability to transfer many popular church personnel at will. In this way, the hierarchy was able to undermine projects and isolate personnel whom they believed to be too political (read too supportive of the revolution). The continuation of this practice, begun during the revolution, demonstrated that the relationship between the popular church and the hierarchy remained a fraught one. There continued to be a remarkable degree of co-operation between the FSLN and the popular church, although because neither had the resources of the state behind them, projects had been scaled down. So because it was bereft of the institutional support it had received under the Sandinistas, the popular church was weakened to a degree. Yet, as I will demonstrate, it has continued to be a vital and significant presence in Nicaragua.

9   Women's organisations in the post-1990 period

In this section, I will examine how practical and strategic gender interests are being articulated in the post-1990 period. Here I will examine AMNLAE, the programmes advanced by the Chamorro government and autonomous women's organisations. As I explored earlier in this chapter, prior to the 1990 change in government some sections of the women's movement began to organise independently of AMNLAE and to place greater emphasis on gender-specific interests. This process has accelerated in the post-1990 period. However, the possibilities of the state responding to both practical and strategic gender interests have diminished in the Conservative and neo-liberal climate.

Subsequent to the 1990 elections and a change in its leadership, AMNLAE set about developing a degree of independence from the

FSLN. Since the change in government, AMNLAE has organised primarily around economic issues, placing a strong emphasis on the class-based interests of women. In the face of an ever deteriorating economic situation, AMNLAE prioritised work with women, who have been hardest hit by the economic policies of the present government. To this end, in 1992 it operated fifty-six 'casas de la mujer', twenty-eight medical clinics, and two 'casas maternas' (*Barricada*, 28 September 1992).

Trade unions have also become a key site of feminist organisation and most have established women's secretariats. Yet, a strong focus on class can serve to limit the diversity of the women's movement and to downplay the importance of strategic gender interests. According to Ruth Herrera, labour policy adviser to the National Workers' Front (FNT) the relationship between class and gender is a complex one. She argues:

> There is obviously a contradiction between having political-ideological plurality and being able to represent the class-based demands of the majority of Nicaraguan women. If we were talking about women in a society where economic difficulties aren't an issue, the analysis would be different: perhaps we could agree on environmental issues, on given cultural values and artistic perspectives or on how to better organize our work. But this isn't the case. Our demands as women are meshed with class demands, so it's terribly difficult for women of different ideologies and political affiliations to unite around a common cause (Herrera, 1992, p.28).

Some of the divisions in the women's movement have resulted not only from diverse class positions and priorities but also from a distinct vision of how women's organisations should be structured and led. For a number of women, the leadership style of AMNLAE was too top-down and authoritarian. In an open letter to Gladys Báez, twelve women criticised AMNLAE's attempts to 'discredit' and smear women who chose to organise outside of the AMNLAE framework as 'libertines and lesbians'. The alternative women's organisations objected to the way in which issues outside of AMNLAE's focus were branded as individualistic and selfish. For the signatories of the letter: [13]

> To reflect on the persistence of these methods and authoritarian styles, we see that AMNLAE National insists on its exclusive [right to] represent the women's movement, to try to annul divergent expression. We believe that the moment has come to strip ourselves of the sectarianism and the styles that we have inherited from patriarchy (*Barricada*, 4 Nov. 1992).

In the post-1990 period, the women's movement has sought not only to deal with its own internal contradictions but also to address the new political realities. Since 1990, a number of new initiatives directed at women have emerged. On 4 December 1992, Radio Mujer, a station dedicated exclusively to issues of concern to women began broadcasting. Programmes on the schedule included: Gynaecological Consultation, a question-and-answer phone-in; Law Consultation; and SOS, a call-in programme in which missing persons, as well as cases of physical abuse were reported. Radio Mujer's opening ceremony was attended by President Chamorro, who expressed her support for the initiative (Sánchez, 1992). In 1992, President Chamorro set up the Nicaraguan Women's Institute to address problems facing women. In early 1993 she set up a council which draws its membership from a cross-section of governmental institutions, political parties and non-governmental organisations working with women, to advise the institute. In 1993, President Chamorro also announced the establishment of a 'Women's Commission', under the supervision of the police department, to give legal and counselling services to women who have been raped or victims of physical or mental abuse. The commission was a response to the demands of women's collectives struggling to provide these services to women (*Barricada Internacional*, April 1993c, p.7).

President Chamorro has endorsed or initiated a number of programmes which address women's gender-specific interests. Given the conservative values that her government endorses, it is illuminating to consider how these programmes came about. It seems likely that women's organisations, freed from the responsibility of 'defending the revolution', feel no pressure to suppress their gender-specific demands. Thus, Chamorro's attentiveness to women's issues can be read as, at least partially, a response to increased pressure from women's organisations. Further, as the restoration of 'Christian' values was the stated programme of the government, there has been a critical impact on issues such as abortion rights, access to contraception and lesbian rights.

Not only has the present government not supported these rights, but there have been significant reverses. For example, while therapeutic abortions were available on a limited basis from one Managua hospital (Bertha Calderon), this policy has been curtailed since the change in government (Wessel, 1991, p.544). While the FSLN backed away from these issues for fear of rupturing already strained relations with the hierarchy, the Chamorro government was in basic agreement with the prohibition on abortion. In 1992, legislation was passed which criminalised sexual relations between persons of the same sex (Barberena, 1992). Greater open hostility to issues of abortion, contraception, and lesbian rights have been the mainstay of Chamorro policies. The government has used its resources and legislative power to advance the Catholic hierarchy's moral vision, much of which seems focused on practices and policies that impact negatively on women's strategic gender interests.

Ironically, the greater platform accorded to the hierarchical church has not paid ideological dividends with regard to popular attitudes to artificial contraception.[14] In fact, according to a 1993 survey carried out by the Association for the Welfare of the Nicaraguan Family, Nicaraguan women's views of contraception have become more liberal. The survey reported that 53 per cent of Nicaraguan women used contraception, preferring artificial means by a wide margin. These figures reflect a significant change in attitude from similar surveys conducted in 1988 and 1989 where only 23 per cent of women used contraception.[15] In the 1993 survey, two-thirds of the women who did not have access to contraception would use it if they could and a minuscule 1.2 per cent of respondents cited religious reasons for not using birth control (*Barricada Internacional*, January 1994, p.25).

The survey attributes the change in attitudes to the severity of the economic crisis. Economic issues, while not specifically women's issues, often form the mainstay of practical gender interests. As the majority of women will spend a part of their lives as single parents, the Chamorro government's neo-liberal policies (and indeed the structural adjustment policies initiated by the FSLN in the late 1980s) hit women especially hard. The intersection of class and gender issues is crucial here. The devastating effects of Chamorro's economic policies coupled with the virtual dismantling of the social welfare system placed the majority of Nicaraguan women at the margins of economic survival.

Yet the changes in attitude toward contraception cannot be attributed solely to worsening economic conditions; this formulation assumes a functional relationship between economic necessity and ideological transformation. Rather, the change in attitude must be tied to the proliferation of women's heath centres where family planning and contraception were readily available. However, it was not the mere availability of contraception in these clinics that was significant but the fact that the clinic provided a space where the prevailing notions around women's bodies could be effectively challenged. In discussing the work of the Mulukukú Women's Clinic, Dorothy Granada describes helping women to overcome the shame and sinfulness that many associate with their bodies (Granada, 1992). In clinics throughout Nicaragua, the slogan 'Free Body or Death' employed by some Nicaraguan feminists (a play on the revolutionary slogan 'Free Fatherland or Death') was put into practice.

According to Molyneux: 'it is the politicisation of these practical interests and their transformation into strategic interests which constitutes a central aspect of feminist political practice' (Molyneux, 1984, p.63). In women's health centres this politicisation gave women the 'tools' to make connections between their practical and their strategic gender interests. Thus, women's changing attitudes to contraception demonstrated the success of feminist organising around health care provision for women.

Since 1991, in the northern department of Nueva Segovia, there has been a women's organisation which pursues a gender-specific class-based strategy. The Nora Astorga Front was one of the most remarkable women's organisations in Nicaragua. Taking their name from a Sandinista guerrilla fighter, the women are a diverse group composed of young and old women, former ESP members and even a few ex-contras. The women call themselves 'Noras' and claim amongst their membership a few male collaborators called 'Noros'.

The front, though founded in 1991, first came to prominence in April 1992 when it took over the post office in Ocotal by armed force. Perhaps its most spectacular action to date was the take-over of a section of the Pan-American highway. Its two primary demands have been housing and the payment of promised compensation for ex-members of the ESP. Following in a line of armed 're' groups (e.g. *recontra*, *recompas*, *revueltos*) the members of the front have been dubbed 'rewomen'. Although members have gone into the mountains for forty days of military training, their most sustained project to date has been a non-military one (Castillo, 1993, p.140).

Since early 1992, the Noras have been building houses on twenty-two acres of land that they 'expropriated'. They have secured promises for building materials from the government and for a health centre and school from the Committee for Support and Verification of the Organization of American States. Another major task for the front has been the pursuit of promised compensation for ex-ESP members. Wading through the bureaucracy was tedious, time consuming and a drain on the meagre resources of very poor women. Yet the burdens of pursuing these claims were shouldered collectively by the front. Through its willingness to tackle fundamental problems, the Nora Astorga Front has made a critical difference in the lives of its members. It has further demonstrated its resolve to achieve its goals by taking up arms when necessary.

10 Conclusion

Gladys Ramírez de Espinosa, Minister of Culture in the Chamorro government, stated that a 'new balance of power' was in effect, now that the Sandinistas had been 'abolished and pulverized by history' (Kattenberg, 1991, p.2). While there was indeed a sharp change between pre- and post-1990 Nicaragua, there was still a visible Sandinista presence. Many murals, lovingly and painstakingly painted during the revolutionary years, had been covered with grey paint, and shiny new cars, many with Florida licence plates, clogged the streets but the silhouette statue of Sandino still dominated the Managua skyline and 65,000 people turned up to celebrate the fifteenth anniversary of the revolution.

When the Sandinistas left office in 1990, the first ever democratic transfer of power in Nicaraguan history was achieved. This was no aberration; the Sandinistas had spent the previous ten years building and nurturing the institutions of civil society. For example, under the stewardship of the late Carlos Nuñez Téllez, the National Assembly, the country's governing body, was established. Another important contribution to the landscape of Nicaraguan civil society was the constitution, which enshrined the rights and responsibilities of the Nicaraguan people as well as formalising the system of representative democracy which had already been set up. In 1987, after extensive consultations with the mass organisations, church groups, unions, and other sectors of society plus numerous town hall meetings, this constitution was passed by the National Assembly.

As significant as these achievements were, they did not signal the wholesale uncritical acceptance of Western-style representative democracy to the exclusion of other forms of political expression. There was always a tension between the need to create a civil society and the desire to preserve the grassroots power invested in groups such as the mass organisations. Further, the functioning of these organisations was not untouched by the tension within *Sandinismo* between 'popular' and 'vanguard' conceptualisations of power.

All of these tensions are related to a further difficulty experienced by the FSLN during its time in government: distinguishing between state and party functions. Were the mass organisations a part of the mechanisms of the state, were they a section of the party or were they autonomous organisations representing the interests of their members? This was never clarified and, given the imperative of 'protecting and defending the revolution' in the face of a decade of US-sponsored war, this clarification was an extremely fraught task. The mass organisations were constantly called upon to suppress their sectoral interests in

99

deference to the war effort, but since the electoral loss they have been freed of obligations to the state and have operated much more independently of the party. As Kent Norsworthy describes it: 'Suddenly, a large segment of the popular movement was no longer tied to the government and was freer to organise and militate for its particular demands' (Norsworthy, 1990, p.96).

Freed from the critical priority of 'defending the revolution', sectors of Nicaraguan society that had formerly subordinated their sectoral demands felt no compulsion to remain silent. This was healthy in terms of the autonomy of these movements. Yet the FSLN, for all its failings and ambiguities, constituted a framework for the fundamental transformation of Nicaraguan society. When asked whether it was better to have a *machista* revolutionary in power or a woman of the Right, Sofía Montenegro replied that the former was most definitely preferable: 'At least we could negotiate with him, convince, persuade him, politicise him and make him more aware; there was a space for discussion' (Montenegro, 1994, p.177).

Notes

1   The *Terceristas* were known as 'insurrectionalists' because they advocated a strategy of immediate action to overthrow Somoza rather than the more cautious and sustained campaigns advanced by the GPP and the TP.

2   See Collinson, 1990 and Stephens, 1988 for a more extensive discussion of the legal reforms with a gender dimension.

3   A provisional legislative body between 1980 and 1984.

4   For an analysis of the role of propaganda in destabilisation campaigns in Nicaragua and Mozambique see Thompson, 1988: 28-31.

5   See Gonzalez, 1990 for a fuller discussion of the dimensions of the FSLN's defeat.

6   A *piñata* a is clay or *papier mâché* figure decorated and usually filled with candy and small gifts that features at parties. It is struck with a stick by blindfolded people, generally children, until it breaks open and its contents spill out. At this point, a scramble usually ensues as people come forward to grab the treats. In post-1990 Nicaragua, 'the *piñata* ' is used as a metaphor for the irregular and unregulated distribution of the resources of the state. The term has been used inconsistently by the Nicaraguan Right, which

has failed to distinguish between instances of genuine corruption during the years of the revolutionary government and redistributive policies themselves. The term *piñata* was first used by the right to describe the period between when the FSLN lost and when they actually left government. In this period there was an attempt to codify some of the concrete gains of the revolution, primarily land reform. Laws were passed to legalise property and land, cars, office supplies, etc. which had been given to state employees who were soon to be made redundant. In these efforts there were instances of corruption but in the discourse of the Right all attempts to codify land and property reform and to cushion redundancy were corrupt. The Right construed all these efforts as unlawful distribution of the state's resources. The term then came to be used more generally to refer to all redistributive programmes as well as all instances of FSLN corruption both before and after the electoral loss.

7   There have been a number of scandals involving financial impropriety since the 1990 change in government generally involving embezzlement, the awarding contracts for government services and privatisation programmes. *Barricada Internacional*, 12 (345), January 1992:24-25 and 13(358), February 1993:19

8   According to Maria Ramírez, the entire budget for adult education which the government allocated for 1993 was to have been US$500 (Ramírez, 1992).

9   The war is officially over so the size of the army has been drastically cut. According to Col. Oswaldo Lacayo, in 1990 the ESP had 90,000 members, 2,700 officers and 350 military bases. By 1993 the ESP had been reduced to only 15,250 members, 2,700 officers and 60 military bases (*Barricada Internacional*, April 1993b:7).

10   In January 1993 the far Right parties of UNO officially withdrew their support for the Chamorro government, which subsequently became dependent upon the support of the Sandinista bench in the National Assembly.

11   There were 39 members of the Sandinista Bench in the 82-seat National Assembly.

12   During his "exile" in the United States, Belli renounced his Nicaraguan citizenship to became a US citizen. Thus, according to the Nicaraguan constitution, which prevents non-citizens holding office, Belli's position as Minister of Education was unlawful.

13   The signatories of the letter were María Dolores Ocón, Magaly Quintana and Eva Molina Chow of the Matagalpa Women's

4 Nicaraguan CEBs: An analysis of San Pablo the Apostle

1 Introduction

In the previous chapter, I explored the manner in which the FSLN was able to construct a hegemonic block which allowed it to hold state power for over a decade. This hegemony, hard won and tenaciously tended, was due in no small part to the participation of the popular church in the 'tasks' of the revolution. Further, liberation theology, and the popular church which grew out of it, provided the language in which the Sandinista project was often articulated.

Yet the relationship between the popular church and the FSLN was not as mechanical as the above might imply. The FSLN did not just pilfer religious language and dole out jobs from a position of absolute authority. There was a genuine convergence of interests, goals and, in many cases, personnel between the FSLN and the popular church. However, the collaboration between the popular church and the FSLN did not mean that the former was without a unique history or project. In this chapter, I will examine the concept of prefigurative practice and the manner in which this has been realised in Nicaraguan CEBs. Perhaps the most influential of Nicaragua's CEBs was the Managua-based San Pablo the Apostle (Molina, 1987, p.57).

In locating San Pablo in the broader context of Nicaraguan society, it is important to assess the relative size and influence of the CEB movement in Nicaragua. There are no exact figures on the numbers of participants in Nicaragua as a whole. However, a useful place to begin with an assessment of the significance of CEBs would be with an examination of the religious affiliations of Nicaraguans more generally. Lernoux estimates that 80 per cent of Nicaragua's population is Catholic (Lernoux, 1989, p.367), whereas Crahan put the figure at between 80 per cent and 90 per cent (Crahan, 1989, p.50). The remaining 10 per cent to 20 per cent of the population identify themselves primarily as Protestant, with a small percentage claiming a non-Christian affiliation. These figures do not measure active participation or even formal attendance of religious services. Rather they encompass the spectrum of religious activity from nominal identification to active participation. Further, participation in popular religious festivals such as La Purísima and Santo Domingo is identified by participants and observers as a 'Catholic' activity. Thus a variety of participation, religious expression, identification and affiliation link Nicaraguans to a Catholic identity.

In 1990, the Catholic church had 178 parishes in 143 municipalities, making it the sole Nicaraguan organisation with an institutional presence throughout the country (Norsworthy, 1990, p.120). The membership of CEBs was constituted initially from those already active in a particular parish in more traditional church activities. Due to the large gap between affiliation and formal participation, the field of potential CEB members was much wider than those who attended church services, and CEBs also drew their numbers from those who might not previously have had much formal participation in the church. The success of a CEB is often contingent on the approval given to it by the local priest. In this way, the efforts of the pastoral agent, often a woman religious or lay person, is validated by the approval of the priest, who may play a less active part in the day to day activities of the community (Adriance, 1991).

Despite the large numbers of potential participants, the actual numbers of CEBs is unquantified yet undeniably low. Even within those who are classed as CEB members, levels of active participation vary (Houtart and Lemercinier, 1989). Figures about more general participation in the popular church are similarly inexact, but Lernoux has estimated the number of 'committed followers' at approximately 50,000 (Lernoux, 1989, pp.390-1). She also calculated that no more than a quarter of clergy and religious in Nicaragua identified themselves with the popular church (ibid., p.390).

Williams identified five 'ideal-type' attitudes held by clergy and religious with regard to the revolutionary process. Types one and two were 'direct participation' and 'active collaboration' respectively. He estimated that 15 to 20 per cent of clergy and religious could be located in these two categories. In the third category, 'passive collaboration', 20 per cent of clergy and religious could be placed. In group four, 'passive opposition', Williams located between 40 and 45 per cent of clergy and religious. In the fifth and final category, 'active opposition', Williams placed 20 per cent of clergy and religious (Williams, 1989b, pp.69-75). Thus, clearly, during the years of revolutionary government, clergy and religious affiliated with the popular church were in a minority. In 1979, Crahan maintains, 85 per cent of the 120 priests in Nicaragua and the majority of the women religious were 'strongly opposed to Somoza' (Crahan, 1989, p.43). However, this did not translate into a similar level of support for the revolutionary process, in part at least because of the oppositional line taken by the hierarchy.

Quantitative data on how CEB membership itself was constituted is not available for the years prior to 1989. In this year, a nationwide survey of the CEB population was carried out by François Houtart and Geneviève Lemercinier. Out of this survey of 487 CEB members, 71.4 per cent of the population surveyed was female. 78.03 per cent of the population was over the age of 25, with 59.41 per cent over the age of 35. 16.16 per cent were illiterate while the remainder of the participants had educational levels ranging from basic literacy (14.44 per cent) to academic post-secondary education (1.94 per cent). The largest concentration of the population had an incomplete primary education (30.39 per cent) (Houtart and Lemercinier, 1989, p.7). In Managua specifically, the rate of female participation was somewhat higher than in the country as a whole, with 78 per cent of the survey respondents being female. In addition the population was slightly younger with 63.5 per cent of the population being over the age of 35 (Houtart and Lemercinier, 1989, p.93).

CEBs played a distinct role in Nicaragua in three different historical periods. Beginning in the late 1960s, they formed an important part of the revolutionary struggle at the level both of practice and of ideology. On the practical level many CEBs were actively involved in the insurrection. On an ideological level, CEBs served to raise political consciousness within their own ranks and in the population more generally. In the second period, the years of revolutionary government, the CEBs experienced an identity crisis on the one hand but on the other provided a base of support for the revolution. In the third period, in the years after the FSLN lost state power, the CEBs along with other former mass organisations (MOs) began to assume an oppositional character *vis-à-vis* the state and to attempt to fill the gaps of rapidly diminishing state provision of social services. In this third period CEBs, although generally in an oppositional role were not, as they had been prior to the triumph, 'the only channels for political expression and grass-roots organization' (Williams 1989b, p.91).

Even after the triumph of the revolution and the opening up of new spaces for grassroots organisations, CEBs still maintained an importance in Nicaraguan society beyond their numerical strength. This significance was twofold. Firstly, as the practical manifestation of liberation theology, CEBs nurtured this discourse. In other words, if liberation theology was a key component in the ideology of *Sandinismo* upon which FSLN hegemony was constructed, it could not be a moribund ideology: it must have some concrete expression. Secondly, CEBs in their support of the revolutionary government were given a platform beyond their numbers. As I will detail in this chapter, CEBs and San Pablo in particular were particularly supportive of the revolution; in fact, their emergence and growth as a social phenomenon was inextricably linked with the anti-Somoza struggle.

The significance of CEBs was not in their size but in their influence. In 1979 there were an estimated 300 CEBs scattered throughout Nicaragua (Williams, 1989a, p.52; Serra, 1985a, p.152). It is generally acknowledged that in subsequent years the CEBs experienced a membership drain due in part to the integration of many of their members into the institutions of the revolutionary state (Lernoux, 1989, Williams, 1989a, 1989b; Crahan, 1989; Serra, 1995; Dodson and Nuzzi O'Shaughnessy, 1990). The religiously inspired discourse of the FSLN government, which will be explored in some detail in Chapter 7, heightened the platform and influence of religious groups which supported the revolutionary process. Further, as well organised and tightly knit communities with local, regional and national bodies co-ordinating their activities, CEBs had a well integrated institutional structure. In the context of a relatively underdeveloped civil society, this comparative institutional and organisational sophistication heightened their importance. As Dodson and Nuzzi O'Shaughnessy maintain:

> In the much smaller scale of the Nicaraguan political arena, crises at the local level could have immediate repercussions at the national level, and CEBs had an exaggerated impact far out of proportion to the relative size and sophistication of the CEB experiment as compared to that of Brazil (Dodson and Nuzzi O'Shaughnessy, 1990, p.151).

They go on to argue that in Nicaragua the revolution heightened the impact of organised groups, including CEBs. CEBs provided a space for *concientización* and reinforcement of a particular form of religious and revolutionary consciousness. Due to the institutional setting and the elaborate process of *concientización* which occurred in CEBs, moral identities in support of the revolution emerged in a more 'rational' and structured fashion than religiously inspired revolutionary consciousness in the population more generally. So the emergence of a revolutionary consciousness from within CEBs was distinctive from the revolutionary consciousness which was inculcated by popular religion and the diffusion of the discourse of liberation theology.

2   CEBs and gender

As the figures for the gender composition of CEBs delineated above indicate, significantly more women than men participated in CEB activities. Yet this feature of CEB participation has been largely ignored in analyses of Nicaragua CEBs, most prominently in the study which actually quantified this highly gendered composition of CEBs (Houtart and Lemercinier, 1989). Here I am concerned to discover both how and why women participated in CEBs through an analysis of women's involvement in the historically significant CEB, San Pablo the Apostle. As I will discuss in section 7 of this chapter, the San Pablo CEB, which acted as a catalyst for the emergence of the whole CEB movement in Nicaragua, occurred as a result of a women's meeting in Managua in 1968.

CEBs in Nicaragua began through the activities of women, and their unwavering numerical dominance since this time indicates the value of focusing on women's experiences in CEBs. In the following chapter, I will analyse the functioning of a communal kitchen or *olla* which was a project of the San Pablo CEB. The *olla* project was led and staffed entirely by women and the aim of the project was to provide supplemental nutrition to pregnant and nursing women and to young children. The 'motherist' character of these activities has been under-analysed (Tax in Snitow, 1990).

In looking at moral identities as they are constructed in both the praxis of the popular church and in popular religious expressions such as La Purísima and Santo Domingo, I have sought to demonstrate the convergence of religious and revolutionary identification. This identification played a significant role in the FSLN's efforts to gain and maintain hegemony in Nicaragua, but it began to break down when it could not be sustained in the face of the worsening economic situation. In effect, women, as the primary caretakers of children, began to perceive that their practical interests could not be fulfilled within the context of the beleaguered revolutionary process.

Carol Gilligan's notion of the moral voice may help to explain the basis of women's moral identities in support of the revolution and the defection of many women from the FSLN as the economic crisis began to erode their abilities to provide for their families (Gilligan, 1977, 1982). The sacrifice that was the basis of support for the revolution, and hence the moral identities on which FSLN hegemony was built, may have been different for women than for men. In other words, many women may have made sacrifices for their children, hence supporting the revolution on the basis that it would mean a better life for their children. However, they many ultimately have been unwilling to sacrifice their children (particularly in respect to conscription) for the revolutionary government when its prospects of making 'everything better' seemed increasingly dubious.

Throughout this chapter I will highlight the specific character of women's participation in CEBs. Here gender is a significant category, for three key reasons. Firstly, one of the main innovations of this thesis has been to explore the character of women's participation at the forefront of grassroots struggles as well as the factors that shape their understanding of and identification with a particular project. If the thesis in a broader sense seeks to investigate how 'moral identities' are constructed through organised and institutionalised discourses like liberation theology, a focus on women in CEBs prioritises the gendered aspects of this process. Secondly, gender as a category of analysis within Nicaraguan CEBs has largely been absent in the literature which has taken CEBs as its focus. Thirdly, women are by far the greater number of participants in CEBs and their sheer numbers mandate a specific focus on gender.

3   The fieldwork in San Pablo the Apostle

My involvement with the community was as a volunteer in the *olla* or communal kitchen at San Rafael, one of the four parishes which made up the San Pablo the Apostle CEB. The other parishes in San Pablo the Apostle were la Colonia 14 de Septiembre, la Colonia Nicarao, and Ducualí. In San Rafael, there were about 25 participating members of the community; teams or committees of about five persons each carried out specific responsibilities in the areas of education, 'propaganda', etc. Overall, in the larger community of San Pablo the Apostle, there were between 80 and 100 committed participants.

Through formal interviews, informal conversations and participant observation, I was able to garner an understanding of a number of key issues surrounding not only CEBs but women's collective work in general. In-depth interviews were conducted with Juanita Sanchez Villegas, Wilma Sándoval Turcois and Carmen Porto Carrero Narvaez, all long-standing community members. One of my key research questions concerns the relationship between faith and politics and, through my work in the *olla* I developed a richer comprehension of the network of factors which link the two in the minds of those who participated in the activities of this CEB.

As a volunteer in the San Rafael *olla* located in Barrio Venezuela in eastern Managua and through interviews with many of the women I worked with, I gained insight into a number of issues, including what motivates people to participate in CEBs and in particular what motivated these women to work in the *olla*. In the following chapter I will examine some of these issues in the specific setting of the *olla* Here I will focus on these issues within the context of CEBs in Nicaragua in general, and the San Pablo CEB in particular.

In order to give some background and context to my examination of San Pablo the Apostle, I will explore how and why CEBs have developed in the way they have. I will locate CEBs in relation to other types of organisation for social change, beginning with a brief analysis of the Italian 'little groups', Catholic-socialist organisations that emerged during and after World War II. I will look how these groups emerged and their relationship to the larger Catholic church. I will then examine some of the debates around new social movements and will attempt to contextualise CEBs within the debates. Next I will explore Gramsci's concepts of 'war of manoeuvre' and 'war of position' and locate CEBs within the framework of this analysis. I will also provide the history and context of the emergence of the San Pablo the Apostle CEB, before examining the connection that the San Pablo CEB members made between their religious faith and their political practice. Finally I will explore some of the implications of the post-1990 period for Nicaraguan CEBs and San Pablo in particular.

4   The 'Little Groups' prefigure CEBs and conflicts between the popular church and the hierarchy

CEBs are diametrically opposed to the 'Catholic Action' model of lay participation so vilified by Gramsci. For while Catholic Action proposed a laity faithfully carrying out the instructions of the bishop and priests, and a conceptualisation of the people as the servant of the church, CEBs proposed a bottom-up sense of authority, a manifestation of Vatican II's call to make the church the servant of the people. Gramsci did not live long enough to see the church as anything other than a conservative force in Italian society willing to ally itself with Fascism in order to preserve its power under Mussolini. However, in the early 1940s, sections of the Resistance expressed a kind of liberation theology, fusing their Catholic faith with the goals of national liberation on socialist terms. The most radical of the Italian Catholic resistance organisations was the Catholic Communist Movement. In 1945, in its clandestine publication *La Voca del Lavoratore*, the organisation stated its aims as the desire to:

> lead the Catholic strata of the working classes, and with them all those segments of the population which, although belonging to other social classes, embrace the cause of greater social justice, to a politically constructive position by following the only path that today makes its realization possible....[we seek] the consequent establishment, by means of socialization of the means of production and the creation of new political institutions, of a new order through which the right of all citizens to develop their personalities will be guarantied (Rosengarten, 1968, p.210).

In determining the specifically Catholic character of the movement which distinguished it from other communist organisations, *La Voca del Lavoratore* maintained that the 'metaphysic of integral communism, the utopian ideology with its dangers of false redemption, [and] the whole atheistic and irreligious complex of ideas' (ibid.) were not a part of the Catholic Communist Movement. Although this organisation did not operate according to the principles associated with CEBs, the statements of *La Voca Lavoratore* show that it was addressing many of the problems which have concerned liberation theologians in general and the Nicaraguan CEB movement in particular. A central problem for Christian Marxist groups is how to fully utilise Marxism while maintaining their 'authentic' Christian character. Further, the rapid decline of the Catholic Communist Movement after the liberation of Italy points to the many political factors (the cold war, US pressure, etc.) which served to undermine the communist elements of the resistance in the post-war period - political factors which play a critical role in the Nicaraguan context.[1]

However, what is perhaps most significant in the scope of this study is the fact that there was no institutional structure within the Catholic church which validated or supported the existence of 'social justice' oriented Catholic movements. Instead, the Italian Catholic church threw its weight behind the Christian Democrat style of 'moderate' and unchallenging politics. Because of the changes in the Catholic church achieved by Vatican II and the absence of any Christian-Democrat-style political alternative, the CEBs in Nicaragua have survived where the once strong Italian Catholic resistance movement was unable to sustain itself.

In post-Vatican II Italy, 'little groups' of working-class Catholics began to emerge more or less outside the initiative of the hierarchy, posing as alternatives to the Catholic Action model. Although these groups claimed that they were attempting to make the 'gospel incarnate in their lives', a goal which was executed with the spirit of Vatican II in mind, they were often perceived as a threat to hierarchical authority. The tension between the desire of working-class 'little groups' to work for social justice and the hierarchy's desire to contain and assimilate these projects is most sharply demonstrated in the incident at Isolotto in 1968. Here a 'little group' near Florence came into conflict with the local bishop over the dismissal of their parish priest. Don Enzo Mazzi was relieved of his duties due to his support for the 'little group's' solidarity campaign for protesters who were occupying the Duomo. For years after his dismissal, Mazzi continued to celebrate mass in the plaza outside his former church while his replacement said mass inside the church (Hebblethwaite, 1978, p.200). This tension between the hierarchy and the 'little groups' presaged similar tensions that were experienced in Nicaragua between the CEBs and the hierarchical church several decades latter.

5 CEBs in the 'War of Position'

For Gramsci, hegemony is never definitive; it can be 'won' but it must also be continually 're-won' if it is to avoid collapse. Two more Gramscian terms can usefully elucidate the struggle to gain and maintain political power: the 'war of manoeuvre' and the 'war of position'. The war of manoeuvre is a direct frontal attack on the state involving a direct challenge to its legitimacy. Conversely, the war of position involves more subtle battles for power waged by differing groups and constituencies for hegemony. In analysing the anti-colonialist struggle in India, Gramsci identifies a third revolutionary strategy: 'underground warfare' or, in post-World War II parlance, guerrilla warfare (Gramsci, 1971, pp.108, 229). The revolutionary insurrection in Nicaragua involved a co-ordination of all three types of 'war'.

Moreover, because Nicaragua's national self-determination was severely compromised by the policies of the US government, the struggle against Somoza and the efforts to pursue a revolutionary project took place in a national as well as an international context. To this end, the FSLN spearheaded a 'war of manoeuvre' against Somoza, 'as a moment in the continuing war of position against the external and internal forces and agents of US imperialism' (Slater, 1985, p.18). CEBs participated in all levels of warfare that Gramsci discusses. In their active support for strikes and political protests, they were at the forefront of the war of manoeuvre. Their involvement in the insurrection, manifested in support for combatants and actual participation in the fighting, placed them squarely as participants in underground warfare. However, it was in the war of position that the CEBs excelled.

Karl Marx described the manner in which people become exhausted from a lengthy endeavour to gain or maintain power. His characterisation encapsulates the way that the FSLN's hegemony was ground down in its wars of manoeuvre and position with the US. He maintained that:

> A resistance too long prolonged in a besieged camp is demoralising in itself. It implies suffering, fatigue, loss of rest, illness and the continual presence not of acute danger which tempers, but chronic danger which destroys (quoted in Gramsci, 1971, p.239).

With UNO's 1990 electoral victory, the collapse of the FSLN's hegemony was confirmed and with it the US victory, at least momentarily, in the war of position. Since the change in government, CEBs have responded to the changed political and economic climate in very pragmatic ways. Yet, if a national popular consensus for a revolutionary project (or at the very least an alternative to neo-liberalism) is to be rebuilt, responding pragmatically to the crisis is only the first volley in the war of position. The strong institutional support provided by the revolutionary government for CEBs may have limited their autonomy but it also helped to give them focus (e.g. defending the revolution) and to protect them from the hierarchy. CEBs, and indeed other popular movements in Nicaragua, will be crucial in the reconstruction of a hegemonic consensus for the FSLN. The re-politicisation of the pragmatic will be a key stage in this process.

6   Old and new social movements: CEBs and the mass organisations

The literature on new social movements (NSMs) is significant to an exploration of Nicaraguan CEBs because it allows CEBs to be considered alongside other types of grassroots organisation which are distinct from more traditional forms of class-based politics. NSMs have been characterised as dynamic, 'democratised' organisations that operate outside the parameters of an exclusively class-based politics (Slater, 1985, p.7). This broader agenda is said to distinguish 'new' social movements from their older counterparts (Melucci, 1980; Castells, 1983).

Although there was a strong class component to CEBs, it is important to view them not just as class organisations. Clearly the centrality of the spiritual dimension militates against them being perceived in this way. Conversely, the praxis orientation of many obviates the understanding of them as merely traditional religious organisations. In looking at CEBs as new and distinctive entities rather than simply recombinant forms of 'old social movements', they may be considered in relation to other organisational forms that similarly transcend the parameters of class. The study of CEBs can be usefully informed by NSM literature because a number of issues germane to the structure and functioning of CEBs are explored within this framework. On a general level, these include the importance of 'class' in political struggles; the relationship between NSMs and the state; and the distinctions and interrelations between NSMs in 'advanced' and 'underdeveloped' capitalist societies. More specifically, considering Nicaraguan CEBs within the NSM framework highlights not only the peculiarity of these groups but also their congruity with other social and political organisations both inside (as with the mass organisations) and outside Nicaragua.

Raymond Williams insisted that a 'new kind of socialist movement' must emerge if the 'broadened' and 'radically changed' interests of late capitalist society are to be addressed (Williams, 1983, p.18). Laclau and Mouffe argue that late capitalism has created more sites of oppression and hence more sites of struggle. As they maintain: 'numerous new struggles have expressed resistance against the new forms of subordination, and this from within the very heart of the new society' (Laclau and Mouffe, 1985, p.161). Further, a highly developed 'civil society' tends to blunt the possibility that the necessary factors will converge to create a revolution let alone a broad-based national movement that would constitute a direct threat to capital.

New social movements can more usefully be seen as an addition to and a critique of traditional class-based politics not a wholesale replacement of them. NSMs often serve to expand redistributive struggles beyond the parameters of a conflict between the bourgeoisie and a rapidly diminishing white industrial workforce. In advanced capitalist states the feminist, peace and ecology movements have usually been viewed as the most significant NSMs. Yet there are 'class' issues relevant to each of these struggles and the weakness of these organisations has often been their failure to address them. For example, sections of the US environmental movement have come into conflict with labour unions (e.g. 'old social movements') over environmental regulations that affect on job prospects. Further, due to the regressive tax structure, the working poor actually pay more for large-scale government-sponsored 'clean-up' programmes (a measure of the success of the environmentalists) than their middle-class counter parts in the environmental movement.

In Latin America, class struggle, envisioned as a battle between the bourgeoisie and an industrial proletariat, has never been the hub of socio-economic conflict. This is attributable, in large part, to a number of convergent structural factors of many Latin American societies including the small size and weakness of the industrial bourgeoisie and proletariat, an overdeveloped state structure, a powerful military and the lack of a fully developed and independent civil society (Larrain, 1989, p.208). NSMs in Latin America emerged out of vastly different socio-economic conditions than those in the US and Western Europe and, as such, have different projects and priorities.

In their work on NSMs in Brazil and Argentina, Mainwaring and Viola identify five distinctive types: CEBs, neighbourhood associations, the feminist movement in Brazil, human rights groups in Argentina, and ecological associations in both Brazil and Argentina. (Mainwaring and Viola, 1984, p.36). Human rights groups and CEBs, while not exclusive to Latin America, generally had a much higher profile there than in advanced capitalist countries. Due to the US policy of funding right-wing military regimes and insurgent groups in Latin America, human rights groups in these countries were almost, by definition, anti-imperialist and opposed to US foreign policy. One notable exception here was Nicaragua during the FSLN's tenure in government when 'human rights' was an implicitly anti-government discourse. In effect, human rights organisations in Latin America campaigned against the government in power. Neighbourhood associations, ecological groups and the feminist movement were all significant in advanced capitalist countries but were realised in a distinct fashion in Latin America.

Roger Burbach and Orlando Nuñéz attempt, amongst other things, to tie NSMs in the United States to those in Latin America (Burbach and Nuñéz, 1987). Although they retain a Marxist outlook, they acknowledge, in line with most NSM theorists, that the most dynamic struggles in the past quarter of a century have not been exclusively class based. Instead, these struggles have been the undertaking of 'the third force' composed of the middle class, intellectuals, the petit bourgeoisie, the economically marginalised sectors of society, and 'the social movements'. In this latter category they locate 'new communities of religious activists ranging from progressive Black churches of the United States to the Catholic *communidades de base* in Latin America' (Burbach and Nuñéz, 1987, p.67).

Burbach and Nuñéz's compelling sense of project and their attempts to link the struggles in countries at both the 'centre' and the 'periphery' of capitalism are unique. They avoid becoming embroiled in a potentially divisive and disempowering exercise in distinguishing between 'old' and 'new' social movements and thus 'old' and 'new' approaches to political struggle. In Nicaragua, the revolutionary experience was both 'old' and 'new' and the discourses utilised by the participants reflected this *mélange*.

I would argue that in Nicaragua, CEBs were not conclusively either 'old' or 'new' social movements. Perhaps, given their increasingly oppositional positioning in post-1990 Nicaragua, their resistance to neo-liberalism, rather than an immediate participation in a transformative social project, may make them easier to locate within the NSM framework. However, they will, by definition, continue to draw explicitly upon both 'old' and universal discourses. For Nicaraguan CEBs the most compelling universalist discourse was liberation theology.

In revolutionary Nicaragua, CEBs worked in tandem with and as a complement to the mass organisations (MOs), the grassroots groups that represented sectoral interests and, like CEBs, worked closely with the state. In fact, after the successful overthrow of Somoza and the consolidation of the revolutionary state, many CEB members left these organisations to work in MOs. In this way, CEBs often generated personnel for the MOs at a cost to their own vitality. Yet the CEBs did continue as distinct and dynamic entities despite the membership drain. Their strength was never solely dependent upon numerical size. Due to the relatively underdeveloped civil society in Nicaragua, Michael Dodson and Laura Nuzzi O'Shaughnessy argue, 'CEBs had an exaggerated impact far out of proportion to the relative size and sophistication of the CEB experiment as compared to that of Brazil' (Dodson and Nuzzi O'Shaughnessy, 1990, p.151). This impact could be measured not only in terms of what these organisations directly accomplished but also, significantly, in their status as exemplars, *par excellence*, of the amalgam of faith and praxis that is liberation theology. In this latter capacity, CEBs, as a key part of the popular church, served to generate moral identities in support of the revolution both amongst their own membership and in the larger society.

As social movements CEBs, together with the MOs, sought to address issues which had never before been on the political agenda. In many analyses of grassroots organisations in Nicaragua the MOs and CEBs were broadly classified as, or examined under the rubric of, new social movements (Serra, 1985a, 1985b; Coraggio, 1985; Ruchwarger, 1985,1987; Luciak, 1990; Cochran and Scott, 1992). According to Gary Ruchwarger, these organisations were one of the three power centres of the revolution, the others being the party and the state (Ruchwarger, 1985, p.93). During the insurrection, the FSLN was involved in the formation

115

of many of the organisations that became the MOs of the revolutionary state. The Rural Workers Association (ATC) was organised secretly with the help of the FSLN and the popular church in 1978. The FSLN was also involved in the creation of Civilian Defence Committees (CDCs), which in the months leading up to the overthrow of Somoza were the only functioning civilian structures in many neighbourhoods. After the FSLN came to power the CDCs were renamed the Sandinista Defence Committees (CDSs). AMNLAE also existed prior to the triumph of the revolution as AMPRONAC, which emerged as a women's response to the 1972 earthquake.

During the years of revolutionary government, CEBs and the MOs differed from NSMs in many other parts of the world in that they had a collaborative, rather than an oppositional, relationship with the state. Their active partnership with the FSLN government clearly did not fit with the conflictive role generally ascribed to NSMs. Yet CEBs and the MOs held they were advancing their particular interests through participating in 'the task of consolidating and giving form to the subject of new Nicaraguan society' (Coraggio, 1985, p.224) rather than exposing the contradictions of the state.

During the 1980s, Nicaraguan grassroots organisations were unique in their lack of oppositional character and in this they differed from NSMs in many other parts of the world. Yet the demands of the state impinged on the ability and willingness of the MOs to defend the sectoral interests of their constituents. As Kent Norsworthy observes: 'The mass organisations were established with the dual function of serving as instruments of the revolutionary state and representing the sectoral interests of their own constituencies' (Norsworthy, 1990, p.92). Some MOs were more successful than others in articulating and realising demands; thus UNAG, the small and medium farmers' union, was much more autonomous and 'self-interested' than AMNLAE, the women's organisation. In fact, UNAG was perhaps the most demanding of all the MOs. The revolutionary government, eager to boost production levels in order to secure desperately needed foreign exchange, acceded to many of UNAG's demands even if these impacted negatively on the interests of ATC, the farmworkers' union.

As I examined in the previous chapter, since the 1990 change in government, AMNLAE and the other MOs were redefining their role. Once integrated into the structures of the revolutionary state, the MOs, bereft of the economic and political support that the FSLN government had provided, moved rapidly into a defensive posture and an oppositional strategy. 'Suddenly a large segment of the popular movement was no longer constrained by its ties to the government and was freer to organize and militate for its particular demands'

(Norsworthy, 1990, p.96). But while the change in government brought opportunities for greater autonomy, it also ended institutional support for the MOs and the CEBs. At the same time, the neo-liberal policies of the Chamorro government created an even greater need for the work of the MOs and the CEBs, as the economic situation worsened and the social service function of the state was wound down.

7 San Pablo the Apostle: the context

From an examination and contextualisation of CEBs in general, I will now move to an analysis of one CEB: San Pablo the Apostle. In this endeavour, I aim to develop a level of understanding of the historical shifts in relation to Nicaraguan CEBs and to this end, I will focus on the emergence of the San Pablo CEB and its role in both the development of the CEB movement and the revolutionary insurrection.

On 12 September 1992 I attended the memorial mass held at San Rafael Church for former priest , José de la Jara who had died of cancer. The church was decorated with vertically hanging yellow banners and huge bunches of fresh red flowers. Every seat was taken and there were many people standing at the back of the church. Friends and family, including de la Jara's children, were in attendance. The mass was celebrated by four priests in festive vestments. It was an emotional experience with many people weeping. Guitars and other traditional instruments were an integral part of the mass and those in attendance clapped and sang along with the music. After the mass time was set aside for people to talk about padre de la Jara.

Twenty-six years before, in 1966, this same man was a young priest working as a professor at the National Seminary. Inspired by a similar community that he had worked with in Panama, San Miguelito, de la Jara obtained permission from the then archbishop González y Robleto for a pilot project of pastoral work in the dioceses (Houtart and Lermercinier, 1989). The result was the parish of San Pablo the Apostle. It is significant to note that San Pablo came into existence and a number of its organisational efforts in Managua and other parts of Nicaragua were carried out prior to the historic Medellín conference which declared the 'preferential option for the poor'.

De la Jara began with a pastoral team composed of 'humble and cordial' Maryknoll Sisters who 'visited homes and gained the heart of the people' (Jiménez, 1987, p.64). Maura Clark, the Maryknoll sister subsequently assassinated by the Salvadoran military, was part of this original team. Since the founding of the original pastoral team, sisters of the Assumption and of the Sacred Heart of Jesus had also worked with the community. Eventually de la Jara was joined by three other Spanish priests, Mariano Velázquez, Félix Jiménez, and later Antonio Esgueva. They formed a parish that would eventually encompass the neighbourhoods of la Colonia 14 de Septiembre, la Colonia Nicarao, Ducualí, a number of other small neighbourhoods or *barrios* and Barrio Venezuela where the San Rafael church was located.

De la Jara and the team were strongly influenced by the organisational structure of San Miguelito community in Panama and in San Pablo's first two years there was close contact between the two communities. On three different occasions, laity from San Miguelito came to San Pablo. The last and most dramatic of these meetings was the January 1968 'Women's Encounter' which was disrupted by a major earthquake. The meeting continued regardless and each of the women of the parish was visited at home by the women who had come from San Miguelito. The visits between the communities of San Pablo and San Miguelito not only enabled a cross-fertilisation of ideas and organisational skills but also established the priority of working with women. This focus also demonstrated a keen awareness of the significance of female participation in religious and neighbourhood organisations. In addition, it seemed to indicate the influence of feminist-inspired discourses on the pastoral agents who prioritised work with women.

The inspiration that the San Pablo community received from their Panamanian counterparts was poured back tenfold into their own national context. San Pablo the Apostle has been called the 'mother of all base communities' and, given the central role that women played in establishing this and other CEBs, the name is particularly apt. This community gave birth to most of Nicaragua's early CEBs. The community as a whole or individual lay members organised encounters or *encuentros* for various parishes in Managua and other parts of the country. In this way the communities of Santo Domingo, and la Tejera emerged. In La Tejera and in the *barrios* on the shore of Lake Xolatlán in Managua, community member Juan Mendoza introduced the 'Course of Christian Initiation'. In addition, San Pablo was involved in the formation of CEBs outside the Managua region in Somoto, Condega, Pueblo Nuevo and Larreynaga.

These direct contacts were not the only way in which San Pablo fostered the development of CEBs in Nicaragua. The 'Misa Popular Nicaragüense', a collection of folkloric religious songs developed by the community, was used extensively by churches and chapels throughout Nicaragua (Foroohar, 1989, p.70). The Vatican's prohibition of it signalled the influence and prominence that it had achieved. According to the Vatican, the line 'Jesus was born of our people' failed to acknowledge that 'Jesus was born of the Virgin Mary'. 'How if the Virgin

118

had not been born of our people!' writes Félix Jiménez, highlighting the absurdity of the Vatican's objections (Jiménez, 1987, p.67). Ironically, or perhaps not, ten years later the 1978 recording of the 'Misa Popular Nicaragüense' was also prohibited by the Somoza regime as subversive. A Nicaraguan friend who played for me her worn but well cared for copy remembered: 'If they [the national guard] found it in your house, they knew that you were with the *compas* [the FSLN]!'

The 'Misa Popular Nicaragüense' was significant not only for its popularity and the controversy that it generated, but also because of the way in which it emerged. This popular mass grew out of new forms of religious expression that stood in contrast to 'traditional' Nicaraguan Catholicism. Of the Sunday religious service, Jiménez recounted, 'The happiness reflected in the songs, jokes, and smiles was the dominant note of the celebration.' However, it was the 'heated homily-dialogues' that caused the greatest 'astonishment' amongst parish priests and 'the people' (Jiménez, 1987, p.67). These homily-dialogues were more like discussion sessions on a given topic which related to the gospel reading. Everyone at the service was encouraged to participate actively.

Obviously, this practice was far removed from the traditional sermon and served to undermine the privilege of the 'official' celebrant of the mass. The homily-dialogue placed 'the people' on a more equal footing with the priest and in this way raised an important challenge to hierarchical divisions between clergy and laity. Although it is clear that the priest retained a special leadership role within this context, this leadership was in many cases contingent on the commitment of the priest to the CEB model. Thus, paradoxically, the authority of the priest was often contingent upon his willingness to share it with the community. This has been demonstrated on numerous occasions when the Nicaraguan hierarchy imposed an unsympathetic priest on a community or removed a sympathetic one. Since 1982 this practice had become prevalent, especially in the Managua diocese.

These impositions and removals were often challenged by the parishioners through church occupations and protest marches (Williams, 1989a, p.59). Some of these protests yielded a reversal from the hierarchy. For example, when parishioners occupied the Parish of the Sacred Heart, they successfully blocked the transfer of Father Manuel Batalla (Dodson and Nuzzi O' Shaughnessy, 1985, p.135). However, more often than not, these protests proved unsuccessful. The case of Mgr. José Arias Caldera, although extreme, demonstrated the level of distrust and animosity that often accompanied the hierarchy's personal decisions. When parishioners protested about the removal of Arias, a priest openly supportive of the Sandinistas, Bishop Bosco Vivas responded to the parishioners' intransigence by personally attempting to remove the ciborium or receptacle for the Eucharist from the church. A scuffle with the bishop ensued, resulting in the excommunication of those involved as well as the interdiction of the church to prevent mass being said there (Dodson and Nuzzi O' Shaughnessy, 1985, p.135).[2]

Conflicts between the CEBs and the hierarchy were based on issues of power and authority not only within the church but also outside of it. The CEBs challenged the authority of the hierarchy within the church as well as their authority to define the church's position in the wider national context. Bishop Bosco Vivas acted as he did because he was defending the absolute right of the hierarchy to remove and appoint priests and religious under its jurisdiction. On another level, he was administering a punishment to Arias and the community for supporting the revolutionary process. As I have already explored, conflict between the popular church and the hierarchy was closely intertwined with attitudes to the revolutionary government. The CEBs and the popular church, through their active participation in the revolution, challenged the authority of the hierarchy to define the 'project' of the Nicaraguan church.

San Pablo's refusal to take the hierarchy's lead was part and parcel of the *conscientización* process whereby CEB members developed the analytical skills which enabled them critically to evaluate the national political situation. In describing the way in which people became members of the San Pablo CEB, Jiménez describes two steps: (1) Initiation, and (2) Christian community. In the initiation stage, the candidate prepares to enter the community. This process usually lasted two to three months and involved weekly study sessions on a particular theme, helping with various community tasks and a three-day retreat held outside the parish. During this time the candidate needed to concentrate on 'the comprehension of the topics [discussed], as well as changes in personal attitudes, family relations, the abandoning of vices, etc.' (Jiménez, 1987, p.70).

In the second stage, the candidate became a full member of the community and was able 'to put into practice what s/he had learned' in the initiation phase (ibid.). In his account, Jiménez mentions the profound effect that the community had on a founding member called Juanita Sanchez Villegas. During the course of my work in the community I had the opportunity to interview Juanita, who spoke movingly about how she experienced the *conscientización* process. She recalled:

> I acquired a lucidity. I didn't know how to speak but through reading the word of God, I acquired a 'taking of consciousness' (*toma de consciencia*), a worth, and it took away my fear. It is in this way that

we return ourselves to Christ. We are not like those who only pray in the churches. The Lord does not want this. He wants us to be active. Thus I gained confidence in myself (Interview, 1992).

Following their initiation into the community, due to the critical national situation, a 'new step' was climbed by members of the San Pablo CEB. Members of the community engaged in political discussions and activities and many became directly involved in the revolutionary struggle (Jiménez, 1987, p.78). During this new phase of activity, beginning at the end of 1974, members hid arms and revolutionary literature and provided safe houses. A number of young people from the community participated directly in the armed struggle and indeed San Pablo's influential *Movimiento Juventil Cristiano* (Christian Youth Movement), founded in 1969, saw the majority of its founding members join the FSLN.

8   The faith-praxis nexus

Before I was only a Christian of the mass but I discovered in the Gospel that it is not enough to pray... and I liked this. I felt like a new woman. Before I didn't do anything, only housework....I have energy. I am an old woman but I have a young heart (Juanita Sanchez; interview, 1992).

It is evident that the praxis-oriented character of CEBs meant that understanding often inspired action. But as I have already explored, the hierarchy's opposition to the revolution was as active as the support that the CEBs accorded to it. In other circumstances dissent within the church has often been ignored or quietly suppressed, but conflict between the hierarchy and the CEBs was played out in a very public way: on the global tapestry provided by the revolution. For the CEBs and the popular church, the revolution became a key point of identification. In addition, the revolutionary government and a highly politicised population provided a measure of institutional support for CEBs and the popular church, preventing 'quiet' hierarchical disciplining.

A few months after the triumph of the revolution, the San Pablo community held a meeting to evaluate the state of the parish and to discuss strategies for the future. In the months immediately preceding and following the triumph, the internal structures of the CEB ceased to function in a consistent and organised fashion. This was due to the significant participation of community members at all levels of the revolutionary struggle as well as the generalised uncertainty throughout the country. Thus this meeting was deemed necessary to determine the role of CEBs in the new revolutionary context as well as to examine 'some of the causes of the stagnation that fell on the communities of the parish' (Jiménez, 1987, p.81).

One of these causes was the efforts of the hierarchy to remove the legitimacy of the CEBs. Jiménez wrote his account of the community in 1987, several years after the meeting that he describes and the acrimony between the popular church and the hierarchy that had passed in the intervening years was palpable in his account of this 1980 meeting. However, the hierarchy and in particular Cardinal Obando y Bravo had always objected to the pastoral line of the parish and this was of concern to the CEB members as they contemplated the future of San Pablo in the light of the hierarchy's anxiety and growing resistance to the revolution.

These fears were proven correct. However, it was evident from my interviews and conversations with community members that while the CEBs were opposed to many of the actions of the hierarchy, they did not altogether reject its authority. One CEB member's assessment of Obando y Bravo is a telling example of this ambiguity. She maintained:

In the time of the Sandinistas, he [Cardinal Obando y Bravo] helped by speaking with the Sandinistas, speaking beautifully on television in favour of the people, of the poor. But at some moments he remained silent and later he spoke against the people, he came to deny [the people]. When the Pope came, he prohibited a mass being said for those who had fallen [been killed by the *contras*].... The hierarchy does not contribute to us the poor. The hierarchy does not see with good eyes. They say that we are communists, that we are Marxists, anti-Christian. We do not read Marxism nor do we read Leninism. We only read the Bible. With the word of Jesus, we nourish ourselves (Interview, 1992).

Here this CEB member spoke with a tangible sense of betrayal and genuine confusion as to why the hierarchy objected to their work. A slightly different view was taken by another San Pablo community member who did not believe that the hierarchy helped or hindered the community. She implied that interaction was minimal. In the second interview, she referred to the Pope's visit to Nicaragua in 1983, and said that his visit was intended as a rebuke to the Sandinistas. 'He came in the time of the Sandinista Front but he did not sympathise with [them]. He came here only to humiliate [them].'

Another factor which affected San Pablo was the departure of two of the CEB's most committed and experienced members. Father de la Jara and another priest, who had been with the community since its inception in the late 1960s, had left the priesthood in order to get married. The loss of these two priests contributed to the 'disorganisation' that the community found themselves in. Further, in the final days of the insurrection the community had devoted the totality of its energies and personnel to the struggle. This was one of the key difficulties that the meeting identified; many of the community's most dynamic and experienced leaders chose to 'dedicate themselves totally to the activities of the revolution', thus leaving little time for work within the community. This was not seen as a necessarily negative situation but it was viewed as one with serious implications for the vitality of the community.

This drain on CEB membership was not a phenomenon limited to San Pablo; immediately following the triumph, CEBs all over Nicaragua experienced a significant loss of personnel to the revolutionary government and the MOs. As the leader of one Managua CEB asserted: 'We realize God is not up in the sky, light years away. God is health, literacy, production. We can find Him by working for those things' (Lernoux, 1989, p.390). For CEB members, working for God became synonymous with working for social change. The revolutionary government was committed to implementing these changes and was willing to put the resources of the state, such as they were, behind them. In this context, it is not difficult to understand why CEB members were drawn away from these communities and into more seemingly 'secular' work.

Yet however understandable, the 'transfer' of personnel from the CEBs to government and MOs was a complicated process with ramifications for both the departing individuals and the CEBs that they left. This was discernible in the Jiménez account of the San Pablo CEB which gives a flavour of the confusion and disorganisation experienced by CEBs all over Nicaragua who lost members. Yet San Pablo, as well as other Nicaraguan CEBs, managed to survive and grow despite losses sustained immediately following the triumph. A 1989 survey found that just over 70 per cent of Nicaraguan CEB members had joined the community after the triumph of the revolution and almost 53 per cent had joined in the previous five years. A solid 30 per cent of the CEB members surveyed had been with their communities prior to the triumph of the revolution (Houtart and Lemercinier, 1989). These results suggest that while there was a membership drain following the triumph, the communities were successful in attracting new members.

These new members chose to join faith-based communities rather than 'secular' revolutionary organisations because they were drawn to a Christian faith-based praxis. But what about the members who left the communities to work with the government or the MOs - were they abandoning their Christian faith? For Christians who left the communities there was the possibility of a 'loss of faith', the roots of which were located partially in the equivalence made by the popular church between serving the revolution and serving God. In this context, the slippage from a faith in God to a 'faith' in the revolution was facilitated. Thus a loss of faith was often more of a redirection of that faith. Revolutionary language, as I shall explore in greater detail in the next chapter, drew upon a base of 'common sense religiosity' and thus there was often a blurring of the distinction between the two.

Despite this convergence, for some within the FSLN religious faith instead of being an 'opiate' was just a stage in political development. Indeed, Monica Baltodano, director of the MOs under the Sandinistas, and National Directorate member Luis Carrión were amongst numerous FSLN members who had lost their faith along the pathway to militancy. Furthermore, community members who chose to work in the state sector not only faced the pull of atheistic currents within the FSLN but were deprived of the refreshment and reinforcement of religious faith that day-to-day involvement with communities had provided. Despite these obstacles, many former CEB members did retain their Christian faith. Perhaps the most famous of these was Ernesto Cardenal, former Minister of Culture, who founded the Solentiname community in southern Nicaragua.

Moreover, CEBs and the popular church worked closely with the revolution and this work was a central part of their identity. CEBs like San Pablo had spent years in an advisory role to the state. With the overthrow of Somoza, the state became the locus of the social changes that CEBs had long been struggling for: land reform, workers' rights, education, etc. In this context, the CEBs were now the allies of the state. For the hierarchy this alliance was more accurately described as domination. And indeed, the hierarchy's contentions that the popular church was dominated by the revolution seemed to be substantiated by some of the statements of the latter's own adherents. For example, Jiménez asserted:

We cannot see the history of our community independent of the march of the people in general, the protagonist of history. The march of the people cannot be unravelled from the march of its vanguard, the FSLN... The people and the FSLN are the ones that pushed the march of the community, accompanied by the spirit of God, that guides the history of our liberation (Jiménez, 1987, p.78).

Much to the ire of the hierarchy, the CEBs and the popular church were more willing to accept the direction of the FSLN than they were to adhere to the leadership of their own church. Here, just as in the case of the priest and the CEB, authority was contingent upon a shared vision and commitment to a social project and not necessarily upon a respect for traditional structures. While Jiménez freely acknowledged the vanguard role of the FSLN, he was also keen to establish the vanguard role of the San Pablo community. In reflecting on the accomplishments of the community, Jiménez cites the two major accomplishments of the San Pablo CEB. He states:

a) In spite of the tensions of the first moments, the Community had advanced and had been able to formulate a new pastoral scheme in the life of the Nicaraguan church, that harmonises Christian faith and compromise in favour of social change. This has been one of the great contributions of San Pablo to the Nicaraguan church and has also a small contribution to the process of Nicaragua's liberation.
b) The other [accomplishment] has been the capacity to be the vanguard of this Pastoral *conscientización*, bringing this message to many other places outside of the parish, this second step being the moment of Community's greatest missionary intensity (Jiménez, 1987, p.77).

The significance of San Pablo was fully appreciated by those who had been with the community since its early days. Wilma Sandoval Turcios, one of the founding members of San Pablo, demonstrated a keen awareness of the significant role that her community had played in recent Nicaraguan history. She spoke of the 'practical theology that we had formed in the CEB' and maintained that 'from San Pablo the Apostle all of the CEBs [in Nicaragua] were born'.

In fact, there was a definite sense in which the members of San Pablo saw themselves as part of the vanguard. The community had made many sacrifices and achieved much and of this the members I spoke with were not unduly proud. The demands that were made on individual members of CEBs were similar to those made of FSLN members. It is interesting to note that in the days of clandestine fighting in the mountains, members of the FSLN referred to their organisation as 'the Church' (Cabezas, 1985). In both the CEBs and the FSLN members needed to demonstrate a commitment to the group through sacrifice and personal transformation before they could actually become full members. Membership of both groups denoted a certain level of 'militancy'.

Both CEB members and FSLN militants became 'new' men and women partly through their reading of, and reflection on, key texts; for the CEB members this was the Bible while for the FSLN members this was the canon of socialist literature ranging from Marx to Mariátegui. Further, the CEBs and the FSLN had in common the ambiguity of their relationship *vis-à-vis* those they hoped to 'conscientize'. On the one hand, both CEBs and the FSLN claimed in a literal sense to be popular movements of 'the people' or the poor. On the other hand their missionary role and their membership selectivity set them apart. They both claimed vanguard status - San Pablo in its relation to other CEBs; the FSLN, at times, in relation to 'the people'. Yet what militated against the perception of elitism was their commitment to social change and economic justice and their use of popular and inclusive language.

In addition, and perhaps more significantly, participation and identification were not limited to membership. Both offered a myriad of opportunities for collaboration and casual participation. In fact, given the relatively small size of 'official' CEB and FSLN membership, the need for alternative forms of involvement was essential to their vitality. Collaboration, for both the FSLN and the CEBs, was a way of bringing people into the party/community who were not willing or able to make the commitment of being 'officially' initiated.

San Pablo was paradoxically both strengthened and weakened by its alliance with the revolutionary government. On the one hand, the insurrection and the revolution gave the community an unambiguous sense of commitment and purpose. The community strongly identified with the revolutionary process and perceived itself as a key participant and innovator in it. Members of the community that I spoke with were keenly aware of their role in Nicaraguan history and this self-esteem was central to the community's identity. On the other hand, as previously discussed, the revolution was responsible for a membership drain on the community and a loss of independence, albeit a consensual one.

It is important to consider what this membership drain actually meant to the community itself. As Jiménez's article and my interviews and conversations attest, members did leave the community and this was viewed as a problem. In addition, the literature on Nicaraguan CEBs often referred to the 'creaming off' of trained and educated CEB leaders by the government and the MOs. But what about those members who remained in the CEBs - who were they and why did they decide to continue working within the community? While the motivations for leaving have been explored, the factors behind the decision to stay have been relatively under-conceptualised.

A number of factors contributed to the members staying with the community. Many of these were bound up with the desire to continue to work within the structure of a specifically Christian community and often within a particular community where bonds of trust and friendship had formed. Age was also a factor in the decision to leave; the women in the *olla* often spoke of the young people or *chavalos* who left to work with the revolution in a more direct way. However, perhaps the most significant factor in the decision to remain was gender. Given the overwhelming majority that women formed within CEBs (Houtart and Lemercinier, 1989), an analysis of the gender dimensions of this phenomenon is propitious.

One reason why many women remained within the community rather than taking a position within the government or a MO was that they had domestic commitments which prevented them from taking on the responsibility that work in the many MOs and government ministries would have necessitated. Further, and indicative of the contradictions of the revolution, men were often, at least for higher-level positions, seen as more 'natural' leaders and thus were more likely to be recruited than women.

In many ways the position of women within CEBs was comparable to that of women in the Committees in Defence of *Sandinismo* or CDSs. Although under-represented at zonal, regional and national levels of the CDS structure, women constituted more than half of all local CDS activists. Further, it is estimated that 80 per cent of those who took part in 'revolutionary vigilance' were women. (Ruchwarger, 1987, p.177). [3] Here women outnumbered men and were responsible for most of the practical work. The situation of women in San Rafael was analogous; here women formed the majority and were similarly responsible for most of the work that was done.

The greater participation of women is one constant in the experiences of CEBs before and after the 1990 elections. However, since the change in government, the concerns and expectations of CEB members have shifted in response to the new political and economic situation. Moreover, new roles and responsibilities have been adopted. In the next section I will consider some of the changes as well as the continuities that characterised Nicaraguan CEBs in general and San Pablo in particular.

9   San Pablo since 1990

In the time of the Sandinistas, I felt that my faith had a connection with the revolution because honour used to be spoken of and there was no fear of anything, including death. The *chavalos* used to say 'Free country or death!' Therefore, we did not have fear of death. I feel that this is natural. My faith gave me cohesion. My faith also had to consider politics. Yes, because as I say to you, the revolution spoke of strength, of honour, of overcoming all difficulties. Christian faith speaks of overcoming difficulties. I think that my faith would not have feeling if I had not taken part in politics (Juanita Sanchez; interview, 1992).

Following the halcyon days of the insurrection and the subsequent years spent struggling to ensure its survival, the 1990 election results produced a sense of despondency in many Nicaraguans, though in others, the many who had voted for the UNO coalition, these same results offered the hope of a better life. The UNO coalition contended that this better life would mean an end to the war, the influx of US economic aid, the lifting of the trade embargo and hence a stabilisation of the economy which would bring an improved standard of living to all Nicaraguans. The election results surprised many, including the Sandinistas themselves who had confidently predicted victory, believing the pull of *Sandinismo* and the promise that 'All will be better' would carry the day.

For the CEBs, whose goals and aspirations were so closely intertwined with those of the FSLN, the election results were a blow. For the members of San Pablo and other CEBs there was a profound sense of loss. So much struggle and sacrifice had ended in defeat and this was a source of disillusionment for the CEBs and the popular church. In addition, despite the long years of war and economic deprivation, the CEBs had maintained a sense of clarity and purpose anchored in their allegiance to the revolution. With the electoral loss, CEBs, in common with many sectors who had supported the revolution, were at pains to navigate their way through the increasingly ambiguous political terrain. Arnaldo Zenteno, a Mexican Jesuit who worked closely with the Managua CEBs, wrote: 'Before, although in the middle of such pain, the struggle against imperialism and for the principal gains of the revolution, health, education, land and housing, was clear. Now the panorama is more confused' (Zenteno, 1992). According to Zenteno, post-1990 Nicaragua could be summarised in three words: hunger, confusion and violence.

On the one hand, the change in government represented not only this uncertainty but also the lack of access to state power that they had enjoyed under the FSLN. On the other hand, having been released from the obligation to defend the revolution at all costs, CEBs had the potential to act more independently and to strengthen their own organisations. It is clear that during the time in which the Sandinistas held state power the 'popular sectors' had been called upon to suppress their own interests in deference to the perceived needs of the revolution as a whole. It is equally evident that the critical priority of 'defending the revolution' was used 'as a comfortable excuse for reformist sector bureaucrats, and reactionaries to delay revolutionary transformations and avoid criticism' (Serra, 1985b, p.82).

Could the Sandinistas' loss have been a boon to the CEBs, in that they were freed to pursue their own agenda independent of the responsibility of 'defending' the revolution? In some respects, CEBs have been freer to agitate around specific neighbourhood and sectoral interests than they were when the Sandinistas were in power. However, the continued armed conflict, the tacit 'co-government' by the Chamorro government and sections of the FSLN and the machinations of the far Right have created considerable confusion. Sections of the FSLN contended that achieving stability would undermine the far Right's chances of gaining power and dismantling even more of the achievements of the revolution. Thus, the emphasis of the CEBs' political activities has shifted from 'defending the revolution' to 'defending the *gains* of the revolution' and in many cases this meant that again, albeit in a transformed national context, they were constrained by the demands of the revolution.

However, because of this greater autonomy and responsibility, the seeds of a different variety of discord were sewn. Leading members and publications of the popular church have openly chided the FSLN leadership for its failure to effectively challenge the Chamorro government's economic policies. At least on this point there was a convergence of the hierarchy and the popular church; both had misgivings about the alliance between the FSLN and the Chamorro government, if from widely divergent perspectives. Many sections of the popular church threw in their lot with the less conciliatory sections of the FSLN which prioritised defending the gains of the revolution over an illusive 'national stability'. These issues were explored and debated in conferences, workshops and informal talks or *charlas* by CEB members.

Arnaldo Zenteno maintained: 'Said in a few words, today there is more hunger than in the hardest times of the war.' In 'hardest times of the war' and the Sandinistas' own economic 'shock' policies, there were rationing, price controls and a system of food distribution organised via the CDSs. Many Nicaraguans with whom I spoke had complaints about the integrity of this system, as well as the quality of food distributed. However, the point is that during the time in which the Sandinistas were in power, making sure that people had enough to eat was considered the province of the state. In contrast, the free market policies of the Chamorro government did not prioritise food provision.

It fell to organisations like the CEBs to attempt to fulfil this role previously taken up by the state. For Wilma Sandoval Turcios, the CEBs have achieved much in a short time. In our interview she informed me that: 'At the level of the thirty-six *barrios* that have CEBs, we have installed twelve *ollas* for the nutrition of children. [There are] only this number because we are lacking in funds.' In fact, organising *ollas* as well as job training workshops and health care provision, was a priority for the CEBs.

Despite the 'new' role that emerged for CEBs within Nicaraguan society, the change in government did not bring with it harmonious relations between the San Pablo community and the hierarchy. This was despite the fact that the hierarchy was no longer being 'persecuted' by a FSLN government that counted the CEBs amongst its key allies. It appeared that the hierarchy had in fact 'won' the battle when Violeta Chamorro, the candidate whom Obando explicitly endorsed, was elected. Yet an undermining and reproachful attitude towards the CEBs and the popular church persisted.

The reasons behind the continued ill-will were rooted in Obando's recognition that the FSLN's electoral defeat was not the end of *Sandinismo* nor of the popular church's identification with it. However, in practical terms, what rankled with the hierarchy most was that the popular church organisations like the CEBs actively demonstrated their commitment to an alternative national project. Projects like the *olla* , although 'read' as apolitical, were confirmation of the negative impact that neo-liberal economic policies were having on the population. Further, more overtly political activities that I witnessed, such as support for hunger strikers and participation in marches and protests, manifested the CEB's unwillingness to return to the institutional fold. I would argue that underlying all of these activities was an unwillingness on the part of the CEBs to submit to the authority of the hierarchy and the hierarchy's inability to suppress or neutralise this dissent.

During the time that I worked with San Pablo, Iglesia San Rafael was experiencing difficulties with a new priest who had been imposed on the community. According to community members, this particular priest was received by the community with 'respect and tenderness' which, to the chagrin of the parishioners was not returned. One of the principal weapons that the hierarchy has against the popular church is its ability to transfer or to impose diocesan priests on parishes.[4] This practice was commonly used during the 1980s to discipline communities that were, in the eyes of the hierarchy, 'too radical'. It was particularly prevalent in the Managua diocese over which Cardinal Obando y Bravo presided. During the months that I spent in Nicaragua, I was made aware of several cases of removals and impositions of priests.

In San Pablo the Apostle, an unsympathetic priest was imposed upon the community by the archdiocese. According to one community member, this priest had attempted to undermine the work of the community by imposing a new, more conservative agenda. For participants who had worked with the community for almost three decades, this was a considerable affront and a negation of what the community had achieved. A meeting was held with the priest in which the community aired their misgivings, but apparently to no avail: his attitude was not changed. This was viewed as an illustration of the way in which the hierarchy impedes the work of the CEBs.

The imposition of priests and the removal of 'unacceptable' ones is not a practice which is restricted to Nicaragua: there are examples of it in other times and national contexts, as my brief analysis of the Italian 'little groups' demonstrated. However, due to the extremely conflictive character of the Nicaraguan church, this practice was particularly widespread, serving as a barometer for conflict between the popular church and the hierarchy. Far from bringing 'radical' communities into line, transferring or imposing priests seemed to engender even greater distrust and disaffection with the hierarchy. As one community member commented:

> Sr. Obando says that he does not accept us [but] we feel tranquil because God accepts us.... It is unique that we have Sr. Obando who is against the Sandinistas and against the government. But we do not change. We are missionaries of Christ. We do not owe him [Obando] anything. On the contrary, he bothers us by sending us a priest, the one that causes a disturbance for us....We owe nothing to him [Obando] (Interview, 1992).

This statement reflects the steadfastness that many CEB members felt in the face of hierarchical disapproval. It suggests a perception of the hierarchy, and Obando in particular, as belligerent and obstructive not only in their relationship with the CEBs but also in their involvement in the national political sphere. Underlying this assessment of the hierarchy was the contention that it not only disregarded the interests of 'the poor' but also actively undermined them.

For a number of the women in San Pablo, the construction of the new Catholic cathedral was a prime example of the hierarchy's lack of concern for the poor. The cathedral, finally completed in mid-1993 after a long series of delays, required considerable fund-raising efforts on the part of the hierarchy. A few hundred yards away from the construction site, the unemployed and children as young as six and seven stood at traffic lights selling fruit, candy and newspapers in an effort to eke out a meagre existence. The contrast between the grand new cathedral taking shape with few expenses spared in its construction and the young children inhaling exhaust fumes and dodging traffic, with scant attention given to their 'construction', was striking. According to one San Pablo member:

> The cathedral should not have been built with such hunger, with such in Nicaragua. They spend this large amount of capital without any interest in the children that die of hunger. I would not be constructing this cathedral. There are parts [of Nicaragua] where in reality there is no land to be had. For this reason, there are so many crimes, so many robberies, so many assaults, and all these things. The people have no way of surviving. I think that there might have been some relief if that cathedral had not been built (Interview, 1992).

Her objections to the construction of the new cathedral reflect those of many of the women that I interviewed and spoke with in the *olla* . Because the cathedral was constructed despite the critical economic situation, it was not perceived as 'belonging' to the women. Many expressed the belief that they would not feel welcome there. Another member of the community, expressed the belief that the cathedral was in some sense a provocation on the part of conservative Catholics and the hierarchy. She contended:

> The new cathedral is [an example of] "low class politics" because there the poor will not be able to participate. This cathedral is for the middle class. The poor will not go there. Here the grand ladies and gentlemen will come. The poor will not fit in. I will not visit it either, because I would not feel good. I am a poor person with a humble point of view. We, the poor, will not fit in there (Interview, 1992).

For yet another, the construction of the cathedral not only indicated the hierarchy's lack of concern for the economic deprivation experienced by the majority of Nicaraguans, but also demonstrated a fundamentally different approach to Christianity. The hierarchy's version of Christianity consisted of a respect for position and authority within the church and the pageantry of ritual and ceremony, both of which were encapsulated in the grandeur of the cathedral. For CEBs, Christianity was invested with a vastly different meaning, of which praxis was a central component. This praxis was, as I have explored, often translated into political involvement which pitted these differing versions of Christianity against each other. As she expressed it:

we are not the same because the cathedral belongs to the hierarchical church. They say that one should not involve oneself in politics. For example, the hierarchical church tells us of a God high in the sky and to the poor, they say that we should not involve ourselves in politics. [But] we do put ourselves in politics (Interview, 1992).

Two major events organised by the CEBs that demonstrated the challenging character of Christianity practised within the communities and the level of interaction of the CEBs in Managua. These were the two-day 500 Years Conference at the University of Central America and the 'Day of the Dead' mass in the Managua neighbourhood of Ciudad Sandino, both organised for CEB members in Managua. The 500 Years Conference was designed primarily to provide space for discussion as well as education on the approaching 500th anniversary of Columbus's 'discovery' of America. The conference was led by Sister Margarita, a religious who worked closely with the community, and Jose Argüello, a theologian who was attached to the Antonio Valdivieso Ecumenical Centre. Sister Margarita convened the meeting in the morning and after lunch and took care of organisational details. Argüello gave several small talks about the conquest, specifically addressing the church's role in it. Both led discussions and helped to organise discussion groups.

Argüello used selections from indigenous religious texts such as the *Popol Vuh* and the *Chilam Balam* to highlight the spirituality of the indigenous people prior to the arrival of the conquerors. The presentations frankly detailed the participation of the Catholic church in the conquest which, Argüello declared, was accomplished by 'the sword and the cross'. However, Argüello emphasised the resistance within the church that was offered by figures such as Fray Bartolomé de las Casas and Antonio Valdivieso. A number of questions emerged in the discussion, including: is it possible to return to the indigenous religion? and how can we call ourselves Catholics when this religion facilitated the murder and conquest of our ancestors? The discussions of these issues were open and at times heated. There was no neat 'wrap-up' at the end which exonerated Catholicism.

The conference itself, attended by about 120 people from CEBs across Managua, was rich with examples of non-hierarchical practice. There were discussion groups in which participants worked with a set of questions relating to material that had been presented to them. Within these small groups the questions were discussed and an individual was selected to report back later to the whole group. Conference participants also broke up into groups of about six and devised a 'socio-drama', drawing, song or poem about some aspect of the conquest. The groups were changed around several times so that conference participants were able to speak with most of their counterparts in the course of the conference.

There were a few elements, however, which did not fit into this non-hierarchical mode. Sister Margarita opened the conference and reconvened it on a number of occasions with a question and answer session in which she asked the group catechism-type questions and individuals were called on to give 'answers'. In this instance the conference took on the form of a traditional classroom with the teacher at the front deciding which answers were 'right' and which were 'wrong'. In addition, in one of the groups in which I participated, two people dominated the conversation and allowed very little space for others to speak. This was despite the best efforts of the conference leaders to ensure that the small discussion groups were a forum for everyone to give their opinion. In general though, my experience of the groups was that they did give space and encouragement for participants to speak.

Another concern was the way in which the discussions in the larger group were dominated by the male participants, despite the presence of a number of articulate and outspoken women, including Juanita, who spoke in the larger group. Although men made up at most 10 per cent of the total participants, they took up at least 50 per cent of discussion time. Moreover, the representative for every group that reported back was a man, either on his own or with a female member of the group. There was a pattern whereby women formed the majority but were visibly under-represented in positions of power and authority.

Another event I attended, the Day of the Dead mass, provided a further example of CEB practice. The mass was celebrated by Padre Arnaldo Zenteno in Ciudad Sandino and attended by CEB members from across Managua. In addition there were a number of young people from the youth groups of the various communities in attendance. Just as with the 500 Years Conference, I attended the mass as part of the San Rafael community and was received with recognition or warm curiosity by members of other communities. There were about a hundred people present, all bearing flowers or foliage for the ceremony. Community members I spoke with described the gathering as a tribute to 'those who have died' and as a 'way of remembering'.

The Day of the Dead or All Souls' Day, unlike All Saints' Day, is not designated on the Catholic church calendar as a 'holy day of obligation'. The selection of All Souls' Day, or Day of the Dead, is significant on a number of different levels. Firstly, it reflects the importance that the day occupies within Nicaraguan culture and is an example of the meshing of popular culture and popular religion that I will explore more fully in Chapters 6 and 7. Secondly, the emphasis of the mass was on remembering those who had died and gaining strength from their examples. Within Catholicism, sainthood has been an individual and narrowly defined concept and the conferring of 'saint' status a long and tightly controlled process. In contrast, as all human beings are reckoned to have a soul, this being the defining feature of humanity, the recognition of 'souls' is a much more open and inclusive undertaking.

Throughout the mass there was copious lay participation, with community members reading from the scripture and bringing bread and wine to the altar for the consecration ceremony. However, the most notable lay involvement came not in these tasks, which could be categorised as assisting the priest, but in the way that the structure of the mass was transformed into a more fully collective experience. To this end, the homily-dialogue, which had been pioneered in the CEBs, took the place of a traditional sermon. This homily-dialogue was loosely based on a discussion of the 'national situation', including how people experienced it and what they thought the CEBs' response should be.

With Sister Margarita carrying a microphone around the church to the many people who wanted to speak, this format seemed oddly reminiscent of a US talk show. Yet the homily-dialogue within the context of the mass not only took the place of the sermon but its presence encouraged a sense of collegiality amongst lay, priest and religious. Everyone was given a chance to speak and members of the congregation addressed each other as much as the priest who stood at the head of the church. What set the homily-dialogue apart from an egalitarian discussion group was that it was conducted within the mass and was clearly an integral part of a religious experience.

Following this homily-dialogue, a number of volunteers made a cross of red flower petals on the ground and candles were lit around it. While the cross was being constructed, two members of the congregation read from a list of people whom the congregation was remembering. The list was several pages long and included, amongst others, those who had died in the insurrection and the *contra* war, the people who were massacred in Guatemala and El Salvador (including the US lay woman and US women religious raped and murdered by the Salvadoran military: Jean Donovan, Dorothy Kazel, Ita Ford and Maura Clark, respectively), the victims of the conquest, José de la Jara, Bartolomé de las Casas and Antonio Valdivieso. After each of these names was read the congregation responded 'Presente!' The same format was used in demonstrations or rallies when people who died in the insurrection or the war were remembered. Here the convergence of political and religious practice was clear.

After the list had been read, everyone walked to the front of the church and one by one laid their flowers or greenery at the base of the cross and stated for whom they were praying. Most people mentioned family members but a number of individuals cited groups of people who had lost their lives. Juanita, for example, presented her posy of geraniums for the indigenous people who were killed by the Spanish. After everyone had laid their flowers, the candles were left burning and the mass continued.

At another point in the mass, a volunteer read out a few 'intentions' which were, in effect, an acknowledgement of living 'souls'. The microphone was then passed around again so that people would have a chance to make their own 'intentions'. As with the homily-dialogue, congregation members spoke freely, and a range of intentions were made ranging from the personal ('Please help my sister to get better') to the more public and political ('Please let the United States release the aid that it promised to Nicaragua'). After the intentions and near the end of the mass, 'the peace' was exchanged, with everyone moving around the church embracing and singing 'La Paz'.

Following the mass, everyone remained in their seats and Father Arnaldo convened a short meeting. He had recently returned from Mexico where he had participated in events commemorating the '500 years of resistance'. The meeting was set up primarily to discuss the events that had taken place in Managua to commemorate the indigenous resistance. After the meeting, a traditional corn and chocolate drink was served and people milled around looking at Father Arnaldo's pictures, which were mounted on large boards.

An important function of the mass was that it provided an opportunity to honour family and friends who had died and the majority of people who laid their flowers at the base of the flower cross took the opportunity to remember someone who had been known to them. However, the mass was also an important forum for publicly recognising people, unknown personally to the congregation, who had lost their lives as a result of the suffering and oppression which liberation theology seeks to address. Here the concept of sainthood was transcended in that the sacrifice and commitment associated with 'sainthood' were recognised as the collective experience of a people. For example, while the Salvadoran people could not be a 'saint' they were, in the context of this mass, given the respect and acknowledgement that has been associated with saints. The constricted framework of 'sainthood' was bypassed, through the selection of the All Souls theme, and at the same time utilised in that individual 'souls', and groups of 'souls', were selected for special recognition.

10 Conclusion

In this chapter I have sought to elaborate an understanding of the factors that impacted upon the growth and development of CEBs in Nicaragua. After the overthrow of Somoza, CEBs became allies not of an insurgent movement but of the state. The alliance between CEBs, other popular organisations and the revolutionary government was a complex one. The perception that all sectoral interests were tied to the survival of the revolution was pervasive. In this way, the autonomy of popular organisations and their ability to agitate on behalf of their constituencies' specific sectoral interests was constrained by the interests of the revolutionary state, i.e. to retain power. The insurrection period and the subsequent years of revolutionary government were characterised by the struggle to build and sustain a hegemonic consensus for the revolutionary project.

For their part, CEBs were involved in this struggle on a number of different levels, but it was in the creation of the moral identities in support of the revolution that they had the greatest impact. In effect, CEBs helped to make 'common sense' of the revolution. In his study of the San Pablo CEB, Jiménez explored the manner in which religious and political consciousness developed in tandem, initially through the intervention of pastoral agents but soon through the practice of community members. In updating and expanding upon Jiménez's examination of the San Pablo CEB, I have focused on the emergence of a political consciousness through religious practice.

Given the central role that women played in the emergence and endurance of these communities, it is notable that their contributions as women have received such scant attention. In attempting to explore the part they played in the Nicaraguan CEB movement, I have focused particularly on the role of women in the San Pablo CEB. In looking specifically at the experiences and beliefs expressed by women participants, I will explore how their political consciousness developed through practice. To this end, I employed a distinctive research methodology by actually participating in the everyday work of a CEB and focusing on women's political values as they are lived in a religious community.

The FSLN's electoral loss was a clear indication of a shift in political consciousness at a national level. CEBs attempted to respond to the changed political and economic situation and the practical problems

137

that this generated. As I will explore in the following chapter, they have begun to assume many of the functions that had been the province of the state. Did this change in practice affect the political consciousness of the CEB participants? I will now go on to examine how women viewed their pragmatic work in relation to their political commitments in order to explore this question.

Activities such as the 500 Years Conference and the All Souls' Day mass provided inspiration and an opportunity for education and critical discourse. However, the Managuan CEBs engaged in a number of more practical projects, including a natural medicine project, sewing and carpentry workshops, and a roof-building project. In addition, members of CEBs in Managua continued to be involved in 'missionary' work in the countryside. However, the *ollas* which emerged as a result of the deteriorated economic conditions were by far the largest and most ambitious in which the communities were engaged. In the next chapter I will examine the work of the *olla* at the San Rafael church, one of the *ollas* in the parish of San Pablo. Here I will explore a number of issues, including the connection between faith and politics and the gender dimension of this woman's project.

Notes

1   Witness the right-wing support for the contras in the US. Justifications for this support usually made reference to 'Soviet aggression' and the 'domino theory'. Conservative Catholic Michael Novak and the IRD (Institute on Religion and Democracy) have singled out the progressive church for attack because they believed that this would fundamentally undermine the Sandinista revolution (Lernoux, 1989).

2   Dodson and Nuzzi O'Shaughnessy also highlight the involvement of CELAM in the transfer of priests sympathetic to the revolution. CELAM made significant funds available to the Nicaraguan hierarchy so that they could 'create new pastoral programs (or restructure old ones) controlled and directed by the hierarchy and priests loyal to them' (Dodson and Nuzzi O'Shaughnessy in Walker, 1985:128). Williams contends that 'In short CELAM's efforts have been directed towards the consolidation of the bishops' authority within the Church and the development of pastoral strategies which will pose an alternative to those of the progressive sector' (Williams, 1989b:60).

3   Revolutionary vigilance consisted of organised walking patrols and generally being alert to possible crimes or contra attacks (Ruchwarger, 1987:163). In neighbourhoods with regular revolutionary vigilance there was a marked reduction in petty crime.

4   Priests of religious orders such as the Jesuits may not be transferred in this way because they are answerable to their order rather than to the local bishop.

5 'Everyday life' in the olla: Local identities, global contexts

1 Introduction

In 1991 a group of women from the San Rafael church, which formed a part of the larger San Pablo the Apostle CEB, decided to set up an *olla*, or communal kitchen, as a means of improving nutrition for women and children in their neighbourhood. To understand the context in which the San Rafael *olla* emerged, it would be useful to consider some social and economic indicators which characterised Nicaragua in the post-1990 period. In 1993, Nicaragua achieved the distinction of leading Central America in the rate of infant mortality (83 per 1000 live births). In addition, analysis of the deaths of children under the age of five found that in 40 per cent of these cases the children suffered from diarrhoea, and in 35 per cent of the cases the children had lacked essential nutrients such as iron, iodine and vitamin A (*Barricada Internacional*, November/December 1993). The UN estimated that in 1994 75 per cent of the Nicaraguan population lived below the poverty line with 44 per cent living in extreme poverty (*Envio*, January 1995). Figures like these give concrete empirical shape to the everyday reality of many Nicaraguan women as they struggle to feed and care for themselves and their families.

Ollas or *ollas comunales* existed not just in Nicaragua but throughout Latin America. In Nicaragua, the San Rafael *olla* and many others throughout the country were *ollas de soya* which received support from Soy Nica, a national organisation which aimed to address hunger and malnutrition by the introduction of a non-traditional foodstuff. To this end, Soy Nica was concerned with the promotion of soya consumption and cultivation. By 1994, there were estimated to be hundreds of *ollas* spread throughout Nicaragua, concentrated in working-class and marginal *barrios* (Cuadra, 1994b, p.13).

In 1992, when the fieldwork in the *olla* was undertaken, there were *ollas de soya* in 27 marginal Managua *barrios* serving a total of 135,000 women and children (Gabriel, 1992). In addition to the assistance that it received from Soy Nica, the San Rafael *olla* obtained support from Casa CEB, a resource centre for the Managua CEBs. The San Rafael *olla* received negligible support from the government, primarily in the form of distributing international food aid. In Nicaragua, *ollas* were generally neighbourhood initiatives run by local women with the assistance of municipal, regional, national and international organisations. The San Rafael *olla* garnered support from Casa CEB, Soy Nica and the Nicaraguan Communal Movement or MCN (a nationwide organisation which emerged from the CDS structure which dissolved in the late 1980s). In addition assistance was received from donor countries in the form of food aid and occasional contributions from international church and solidarity organisations.

In looking at the San Rafael *olla* I was concerned with experiencing and analysing its day-to-day functioning, the way in which it was shaped by the women who participated in it and how it served to reinforce or challenge religious, political and gender conceptions. In effect, I wanted to look at the institutional practices of the *olla* and the way in which it was both a site for the reproduction of traditional values, particularly around gender, and a space for resistance.

As I argued in the previous chapter, it was through faith-generated praxis that the moral identities in support of the revolution were built amongst CEB members. The influence of CEBs and the popular church extended far beyond the confines of active membership. The popular church helped the revolution to make 'common sense' by drawing most powerfully upon elements of Marxist theory, as they coincided with, and reinforced, some of the assumptions of popular religion. In this way, the popular church played a key role in the emergence and maintenance of the FSLN's hegemony.

In this chapter I will contend that the *olla* was a site for the reproduction of traditional values, particularly around gender, as well as a space for resistance. In this way, the *olla* functioned as an 'ideological terrain' where contrasting interests, aspirations, and objectives were constructed, intensified, contested and reshaped. I will maintain that this was a both a local and a global process. On the one hand the women operated in a local context; on the other, the hunger and malnutrition which the *olla* sought to address were explicable only with reference to global factors. I will argue that through these processes, complex and varying moral identities emerged.

2 Background to the interviews

Six taped in-depth interviews were conducted with the women who worked in the *olla*, almost all of the permanent workforce: Juanita Sanchez Villegas, Wilma Sándoval Turcois, Carmen Porto Carrero Narvaez, Nohemí Montoya, Glenda Beteto Perez and Erika de Los Angeles Lopez. Juanita, Wilma and Carmen were participants in the broader activities of the San Pablo CEB and spoke both about their experiences here and in the *olla* more specifically (see Chapter 4). Juanita, the co-ordinator of the *olla*, was keen that her name be used in the research. This was the result not of vanity but of a strongly stated contention that she had 'nothing to hide'. In this sense, she was testifying and did not want her words to be attributed to 'Señora X'. As the co-ordinator of the *olla*, Juanita felt that the research should be undertaken openly. In her view, the work of the *olla* and the attitudes and opinions of the women who worked there need not be hidden behind a cloak of anonymity. After much agonising, I acceded to this view. In using the names of the women who participated in the project, I was indeed compromising their privacy. At the same time, more 'controversial' statements from these and other women were made anonymous. In this way, I struck a compromise which allowed the women to be formally recognised as contributors to this research project and at the same time did not allow for any of the women to be too 'exposed' within the context of a published work.

Another difficulty which I encountered sprang from the power relationship that is almost inevitably part of the interview process. Until I began to conduct my interviews, I had never been in a position of overt 'authority' with the women. I had always been positioned as a novice and I had generally sought the advice of the women with regard to the correct manner of performing different jobs. Now as an interviewer, I was in control of the environment and they were now in the position to wonder, ' Am I doing this the right way?' I was using a tape recorder and notebook, tools with which I was much more familiar than a broom and cooking pot. Thus no matter how unassuming and sensitive I was, there was a shift in the balance of power.

The open character of the research did mean that Juanita in particular was concerned about how the *olla* would be represented to the world. Here different visions of the research were at odds. As a researcher, I wanted to present a multi-layered examination of the way in which the *olla* functioned, the attitudes of the women who worked in it and the difficulties that arose. As the co-ordinator of the *olla*, Juanita wanted to use my research as an opportunity to present an unambiguously perfect picture of the *olla*. As my research demonstrates, painting an accurate portrait of the *olla* was not incompatible with presenting a sympathetic and supportive one. However, while I was interested in publicising the good works of the *olla* and the courage and endurance of the women who ran it, I was also anxious to explore how and why the women came to be committed to the project.

In this effort, I wanted to interview all of the women who formed the core group of *olla* workers. Juanita resisted this idea because the women in this group had differing levels of commitment to the CEB, different political perspectives and even different religious affiliations. She was keen for the *olla* to be represented as a CEB project and for the religious and political views of the interviewees to reflect a 'renovated' Catholicism. For me, understanding why, for example, a young relatively apolitical evangelical woman would participate in a CEB project was just as important as understanding why a highly articulate and committed long-standing CEB member like Juanita was involved. Eventually, I was able to persuade Juanita that interviewing all of the women would demonstrate the ability of the *olla* project to generate true neighbourhood participation and she agreed to me interviewing any member who consented.

The diversity of the *olla* workforce was reflected in the interviews. Although I developed a trusting relationship with many of the women, this trust was based on work in the *olla*. The issue of work was where I began the interviews, asking questions about the *olla* and then moving to questions about politics and gender. In this way, I, as the interviewer, was located if not exactly as a colleague, as someone who shared an interest in and a concern for the *olla*. In some of the interviews the women were not very interested in or reflective about religious and political issues. In others these issues came across as central to their lives. The idea of the *olla* as a specifically religious or political project was not really put forward by any of the women. This was arguably an indication that the change in government, the worsening of the economic situation and the lack of a consensus on the way out of the prevailing crisis had weakened the connection between moral identities constructed around revolutionary politics or praxis-oriented religion and concrete action. Thus, the *olla* was generally seen by interview subjects as a practical response to malnutrition rather than an explicitly religious or political project.

Because of their lack of involvement with the CEB, or their relative youth, Nohemí, Glenda and Erika spoke mainly about their involvement with the *olla*. They did not have a long history of political and religious activities that complemented their participation in the *olla* and thus their responses, while generally thoughtful, did not reflect deeply held religious or political convictions. The interviews of the other three women were of a different character entirely. Here the women's responses to questions were richly textured and reflected many years of struggle and contemplation around religious and political issues. These were more akin to *testimonios* than to interviews.

I attempted to make the interviews as open-ended as possible in order to allow the women the opportunity to speak for themselves. Within this context, some interviews emerged as interviews while others emerged as *testimonios*. From my own experience, it was clear that the personal / collective dichotomy which characterises the *testimonio* was not universally meaningful to the women in the *olla*. Or at least it was not the way that all of the women in the *olla* chose to represent their experiences. I would speculate that the age difference between the two groups of women was significant in this respect. The older group of women had lived through and participated in the insurrection and had supported the subsequent revolutionary government while the younger women had been too young to participate.

The women in the *olla* were separated by a number of different factors including age, religion, educational levels, status within the *olla*, and domestic situations. There were also 'ideological' differences that were reflected in incongruous 'class ideologies' rather than in distinct economic position. Although, middle-class women (in this *barrio*, the shop owners and small business proprietors) did occasionally help with the cooking or cleaning in the *olla*, their contributions were more often in the form of donations, for example ice or small items from owners of small shops or grain milling from the local *polvorista* or grain miller. The middle-class women seemed to see the *olla* as a charity rather than a neighbourhood self-help project. This 'volunteerism' or middle-class ideology was common to some of the 'core' *olla* workforce even through they did not share this class position.

Despite the hardship and unemployment created by the neo-liberal policies of the Chamorro government, this was a 'stable' neighbourhood. In contrast to some of the shanty settlements on the shores of Lake Managua, Barrio Venezuela had the permanency and infrastructure of a neighbourhood rather than a settlement. Families had lived there over a number of years and there were well established friendship and kinship networks. Further, although unemployment was a problem, the neighbourhood sustained a number of tradespeople and several shops and small businesses. These characteristics set it apart from the more marginal *barrios*, which were often on the periphery of other more

144

prosperous communities and populated by very recent migrants from outside Managua. While there was surely a measure of cohesion and unity within marginal *barrios*, it was in more stable *barrios* like Barrio Venezuela that CEB activities were strongest. Ironically, the need for projects like the *olla* was greater in the marginal *barrios*.

3   Everyday life in the olla

In this section of the chapter I will detail the everyday functioning of the *olla*. To this end I will provide a description and analysis of a typical day in the *olla*, exploring the type of work performed and the way in which it was allocated. Throughout I will highlight the *olla*'s relationship to 'external' organisations such as Soy Nica, INSSBI (the government social security agency) and Casa CEB (the Managua office coordinating CEB activities). I will delineate issues of status and power and some of the problems that arose when the *olla*'s structure was implicitly challenged. Finally, I will briefly consider the implications of documenting the *olla*'s problems.

Lancaster argues that 'if Marxism is to be reinvented in its own critical and interrogative spirit, it must begin again - and always - with the conditions of everyday life and with an examination of power in its most mundane forms' (Lancaster, 1992, p.xvii). Hence, everyday life must be explored so that the seemingly 'prosaic' becomes the 'profound'. This is a particularly important consideration when looking at women because they are often locked out of the power structures that would render their activities profound. The public man/private woman dichotomy has been expressed throughout history in a series of binary oppositions that assign women to the domestic/reproductive/nature sphere and men to the public/productive/culture sphere (Bethke Elshtain, 1981). Women's lives have been marginalised, so a move to make the prosaic the profound is an essential strategy when looking at the *olla*. This micro-analysis of power cuts a swathe through the more macro class analysis which forms the basis of many Marxist critiques. However, far from positing the *olla* and the women who staff it as disconnected from the profound changes in Nicaraguan society, I will, through a detailed description, highlight the *olla*'s connection to the larger community in the economic and political context of the post-1990 period.

Barrio Venezuela, the location of the *olla* at San Rafael church, was a 'working-class' neighbourhood in eastern Managua. San Rafael was one of the churches that formed part of the larger parish structure of San Pablo the Apostle. While the *olla* had a great deal of autonomy, it was

145

clearly integrated into the Managua CEB structure. The kitchen's staples, the bags of soya, corn and rice, were provided by Casa CEB which served to co-ordinate CEB activities across Managua. Further, even the items which were donated as international food aid and distributed through INSSBI were collected by *olla* co-ordinators in a truck provided and driven by Casa CEB. However, perhaps the most obvious example of the *olla*'s status as a CEB project and indeed its identity as a Catholic undertaking was its location in the hall adjoining the San Rafael church. The women who initiated the *olla* tapped into the resources that were at the disposal of the CEBs in order to realise a project that they deemed necessary in their neighbourhood.

The San Rafael *olla* was also affiliated with the organisation Soy Nica which worked with both CEB-run and independent *ollas* Soy Nica provided financial, administrative and educational support to *ollas* throughout Nicaragua. In Managua, there was a close working relationship between the Casa CEB and Soy Nica, with an overlapping of both responsibilities and personnel. One of the key strategies of Soy Nica was to encourage the consumption of soya, an inexpensive and practical form of protein. Soy Nica trained the women to prepare soya beans and to add them in place of meat in traditional Nicaraguan dishes. In addition the organisation arranged workshops in soya preparation and nutritional education. Despite the support of Casa CEB and Soy Nica, the *olla* project in Barrio Venezuela was founded and run not by these organisations but by some of the more senior women in the San Rafael parish of the San Pablo CEB.

The *olla* was open to all nursing mothers, pregnant women, children under the age of six, any child who was underweight for her/his age and people with disabilities. There were no religious qualifications and anyone who fitted into these categories was welcome. Those who used the *olla* were required to register and attendance was recorded. In addition the children were weighed and measured on a monthly basis to check for signs of malnutrition and stunted growth. Approximately ninety people were registered, but on an average day between sixty and seventy of them were served.

Occasionally, after mealtime there was a talk presented by Soy Nica or some outside organisation and some of the mothers and *olla* workers stayed behind to listen. Health, nutrition and sexual education were some of the topics covered. These issues were also taken up in the Wednesday evening classes organised by the CEB. One of the most well attended talks was by a doctor who came to promote child vaccinations and made himself available to answer questions relating to child health. He passed out a health quiz that the women were asked to fill out in small groups; the ensuing discussion demonstrated the high degree of education among the women in health and sanitation issues, if not in the art of multiple-choice quizzes.

The above examination of the *olla* marks it out as an essential service to the immediate community. At the same time, there was a high degree of social integration between the *olla* and the surrounding *barrios*. The *olla* was clearly a site for social interaction and, as I will explore later in the chapter, many women moved easily between the status of *olla* client and *olla* worker. Many of the women from the surrounding community saw the *olla* as their own project, regardless of how large or small their contributions were. The presence of a number of some of Barrio Venezuela's oldest and most respected residents in the *olla* workforce enhanced the integration of the *olla* into the social fabric of the *barrio*. Most of these women were long-standing members of the CEB, and the *olla* was not the first time they had approached the larger community in a service capacity. Finally, because the project was focused on children and women in the roles of mother and future mother, it fitted well with the established 'common sense' of the *barrio*.

In order to illustrate the *olla*'s relationship with the larger community, it is useful to explore the events around its first anniversary celebration. Most of the guests were women and their children although there were a few fathers in attendance. Many of the children who usually came to the *olla* alone or accompanied by an older sister, came to this event with their mothers. There were also a number of children that I had never seen in the *olla* before. In total, about two hundred people attended this first anniversary party, including a number of progressive priests and sisters and representatives from Casa CEB, INSSBI and Soy Nica. Also in attendance were a few of the workers from the neighbouring Ducualí *olla*.

On the day before the fiesta, the *olla* was fastidiously cleaned. In the morning the *olla* was much more crowded than usual with all of the regular faces plus a few new ones. Amalia and Esmeralda had the responsibility for preparing the food and there was a lot more cutting and chopping than usual to be done. The food for the day was a sweet and sour rice dish with chicken and hot-dog meat. A woman from INSSBI brought an orange tiger *piñata* and a large number of shirts for the children. Gift bags were prepared for the children who regularly came to the *olla*: these contained one of these shirts plus an assortment of sweets. Balloons were blown up and hung around the *olla*, which had already been festooned with green and pink decorative plastic cut into thin strips. A large banner which covered the width of the *olla* was hung outside welcoming the guests to Olla San Rafael. Inside new posters and collages with nutritional information and encouragement to breast-feed were added to those already placed around the walls.

147

In a short speech, Father Arnaldo, the ubiquitous CEB priest, extolled the accomplishments of the *olla*. He then led everyone in a kind of nutritional call and response. 'What is the best nutrition for young children?' he asked with his fist raised in the air. He then supplied the answer, 'Mother's milk', so that when he repeated the question the crowd gave the desired response. He followed this format with a few other nutritional facts. This form of communication bore a striking resemblance to the call and response of political slogans or *consignas*. In line with the homily-dialogue that is common to popular church masses, this call and response format represented an incorporation of a political grammar into the language of the popular church in both its religious and educational activities.

Following Padre Arnaldo's speech, Juanita and the older women were publicly thanked and given gifts. At this point, the gift packs were distributed to all of the children registered with the *olla*. This gift distribution, along with the *piñata*, was the highlight of the afternoon for the children. Although the *olla* was extremely untidy after the guests left, the regular *olla* workers were not responsible for cleaning it. This was done the following day by a group of women from the CEB who had volunteered especially for this task.

Through my experience at the *olla*, it became evident to me that despite the relaxed ambience, there was a particular form of social organisation at work. It was a pecking order of sorts in which roles - sometimes formalised, other times not - were relatively fixed. Juanita and a group of older women held the most senior positions and were deferred to by both the younger 'core' workers and the casual volunteers. Within the group of older women, Juanita, as co-ordinator and storeroom keeper or *bodeguera* was the ultimate authority, although both her temperament and the character of her responsibilities meant that she did not exercise this authority as overtly as some of the older women. The cooks most frequently issued directives to the younger women in the form of demands while to the older women these instructions were always in the form of a request. In this way, there was a willingness to take orders as long as they were given with respect to the positions of both the order giver and the order taker.

The importance of this tacit power structure was reflected in the difficulties that emerged when, after a prolonged absence, one older member of the 'core' group returned and attempted to initiate a number of changes. She maintained that because the women and children were coming in 'when they felt like it' rather than at the appointed time (10 a.m.), the *olla* was having to stay open longer than necessary. This was interpreted not only as an explicit criticism of the women and children who arrived late but also as an implicit censure of the *olla* workers who tolerated this tardiness. Further, and more divisive, was the unsolicited advice that she gave to some of the other women; here she called into question established roles and generally accepted practices. She objected to one woman's failure to dry the dishes that she washed prior to serving the food in them. To another, she objected to the way that the area around the cooking fire was being kept. She murmured darkly about poor hygiene and cholera.

As a result of these interventions and the ensuing conflicts around them, three of the 'core' women left the *olla*. It was not clear when or even if they would return. In the course of these difficulties, two opposing conceptualisations of the *olla* emerged: 'self-help' and 'charity'. Was the *olla* a self-help project and a service to the community or was it closer to a charity? The discussion that emerged highlighted the different ways that participants viewed the *olla*. The women were positioned differently in terms of what they contributed to the *olla*, what they received from it, and how they conceptualised their relationship to it. Those who held the 'self-help' view were more relaxed about the *olla*'s time-keeping and were happy with the situation as it was, preferring a more 'laid back' atmosphere. Indeed, when more rigorous time-keeping was instituted at the *olla*, some of the sociability and informality of the 'old order' disappeared. The second view was similarly motivated by a desire to serve the community but suggested that the recipients of this service should not 'take advantage'. The dispute, too, was not entirely about different versions of the *olla*. There was also a degree of interpersonal conflict.

Alluding to the conflict in the *olla* Juanita stated: 'It is difficult. It is hard because there are different characters and they need to be understood.' This was as far as Juanita would be drawn on the issue. In my interview with her, I asked in a number of different ways if there were any problems that the *olla* itself had in terms of its structure or functioning, and if she saw any way that the *olla* could be improved. Juanita responded in a general way, citing the external factors (i.e. US intervention, the economy) which could be ameliorated. I felt that if I pressed any harder on this question it would imply that I thought that there was something wrong with the *olla*.

In fact, I was trying to open a space for critical reflection. With hindsight, however, I realise now that, given my stance as an 'outsider' gathering research information, albeit one who had by this time worked in the community for over two months, it was perhaps unrealistic to expect a frank delineation of any difficulties the *olla* might have. I was going to be providing a picture of the *olla* to the world outside Nicaragua and Juanita understandably wanted it to be an unblemished one. To this end, Juanita, aware that her comments might be aired in

Europe and the United States, tailored them to suit this particular audience. She asserted:

> I wish that there were more job opportunities, that the United States would not deny the loans [that it had promised], because there would be more sources of work. Because of this, there are vagrant men, women selling their bodies... Here in Nicaragua, there are many obstacles.

Clearly the *olla*, despite its difficulties, was a key site of resistance to these very conditions that Juanita described. Through their work, this group of women responded to the critical needs of their community and through this everyday practice they empowered not only themselves but also the women and children who used the *olla*.

4   The motivations for participation in the olla: religion, politics and pragmatism

The question of motivations is a complex one. Participation in CEBs has been attributed to various factors, amongst them religious commitment, political commitment and gender. More generally, establishing why people participate in political struggles or even what constitutes political struggle is a far from straightforward task. Simply asking people why they do what they do and how they would categorise the project that they are taking part in is an essential part of any attempt to ascertain motivations and perceptions. However, as I discovered in my interviews and informal conversations, different people are apt to express things differently or, conversely, in similar words which may or may not express the same meaning. Both present challenges to the theorist.

In Nicaragua the link between religious faith and political praxis was encapsulated in the notion of the Christian/Marxist alliance. Yet such an alliance, which had been so productive in the period of the insurrection and the revolutionary government, was, in the post-1990 period, no longer as practically or theoretically useful as it had been. It was not that the alliance had collapsed or been repudiated; indeed the popular church and the various institutions which sustained it continued to play a visible and vocal role in Nicaraguan society. Rather, the optimism and imagination contained in the meshing of particular versions of Christianity and Marxism had ceased to be recognised by many Nicaraguans. In effect, *Sandinismo* no longer 'hailed' Nicaraguans

150

as it once had. It had ceased to make 'common sense' and if it did, this alliance no longer seemed to indicate the way forward.

Sandinismo, fuelled by the merged goals of 'creating the kingdom of God on earth' and building a socialist Nicaragua, failed to maintain its hegemony in Nicaraguan society. Thus although a large minority of the population classified themselves as FSLN supporters, it was evident that the hegemonic consensus which sustained over a decade of revolutionary government had been broken. Further, it was unclear how in the current crisis, and with the present leadership structure, the FSLN would be able to reconstitute this consensus.

The collapse of the Sandinista consensus did not occur with the 1990 electoral defeat. Rather the election results were a reflection of a 'loss of faith' precipitated not only by 'sacrifice fatigue' but also by uncertainty about the ends and possible duration of such sacrifices. The FSLN election posters showed a virile and smiling Daniel Ortega pronouncing 'All will be better'. The majority of the population clearly did not believe this to be true. Yet despite the war, the economic embargo, quadruple-digit inflation, and the impending cessation of economic and military aid from the Soviet Union and the Eastern bloc countries, the Sandinistas still received over 40 per cent of the vote.

Thus, while the hegemonic consensus of *Sandinismo* was ruptured, a significant proportion of the population remained, in spite of great hardship, committed to the Sandinistas. Yet if the Chamorro government had been able to achieve the stability and prosperity that it had promised, even the loyal supporters of the FSLN might have appreciated the 'quiet life' after so many years of war and sacrifice. However Nicaragua was, at the time of this writing, one of the poorest countries in the western hemisphere, teetering on the precipice of economic ruin. Just as worrying as the dire economic statistics was the apparent political vacuum whereby the vast majority of Nicaraguans were alienated from the existing political system.

It is against this backdrop that I came to the *olla* at the San Rafael church. In fact, the *olla* owed its existence to the current economic crisis and the collapse of Sandinista policies and accompanying structures (e.g. the CDSs) which addressed food distribution, nutrition and health. At the same time, the local context of the *olla* generated its own set of issues and power relations. The Christian Marxist dynamic or the more neutrally phrased religion/politics construction was a chief concern of mine and I was keen to gauge its applicability in the context of the *olla*. The picture which emerged referenced this configuration but was far too textured and multi-layered to be contained strictly within this paradigm. The women who worked in the *olla* had individual and shared histories (and indeed herstories) which shaped and influenced their motivations

151

for participating and their experiences of this involvement. Further, although there were obvious convergences, the attitudes and opinions of the women were in no way uniform.

These differences were at least partially a feature of the relative heterogeneity of the group. It is clear from the biographical information given in the previous section that the women who formed the core of the *olla* workforce varied considerably in terms of age, work history, marital status, religion and involvement with and commitment to the revolution. Further, and often belatedly, there was a distinction between those who were long-standing members of the CEB and those who participated only in the work of the *olla*. Of the women I interviewed, Juanita, Wilma and Carmen were members of the CEB while, Nohemí, Erika and Glenda were participants only in the work of the *olla*. In looking at the relationship between participation in the CEB and involvement in the *olla*, it was striking that almost all of the 'older women' (over 40) were members of the CEB. In contrast, none of the younger women were members.

Membership of the CEB was based on a commitment to a praxis-oriented, renovated Catholicism. The *olla*, however, was open to anyone able and willing to contribute without expectation that religious transformation would occur. In daily practice, the *olla*, while receiving financial and administrative support from the CEB structure, functioned as a secular, apolitical organisation. Yet participants in the *olla* who were not members of the CEB were, in effect, CEB collaborators in addition to being full members of the *olla* workforce.

The women in the *olla* were similar in many respects, most notably in terms of class background and years of residence in the *barrio*. Most women had lived in this working-class *barrio* for at least the past twenty years or, in the case of the younger women, 'all of my life'. The class and other social factors which may have been contributory factors in the women's decision to participate in the work of the *olla* help to construct and highlight the manner in which activism, in whatever form, is not just the result of remarkable individuals but also of the social and political contexts which delivered them to the point of initial involvement. But - as I explored earlier in the chapter with reference to the differing version of how the *olla* should be run - similar class positions amongst the women did not translate into a unified adherence to a particular 'class ideology'. Manifestly, class position did not determine class ideology, as some of the women seemed to see the project within the terms most closely associated with middle-class notions of charity and volunteerism.

The observations of the women varied because they had individual histories which formed part of the prism through which they saw their actions and the actions of others. These prisms were also constructed by elements of their shared experience of gender, class and nationality. Finally, the usefulness of placing their understanding of themselves, the project, and their reasons for participating in it in the context of terms such as 'religion', 'politics' or 'gender specific-interests' in many ways cuts across the pragmatic grain which forms the basis of much community-based activity. According to the women that I spoke with, the reason for the *olla* was obvious: 'to help the children'. While this rationale can be usefully unpacked with reference to politics, religion and gender, amongst other factors, it is important not to imply that the commentator has any greater understanding of the speaker's motivations than the speaker herself does.

One of the primary purposes of the interviews was to give women the chance to speak for themselves above and beyond the informal conversations and my observations. When I first became involved with the *olla*, I assumed that, because it was a project of one of the first and most politically active CEBs in Nicaragua, the women who participated in it would have explicit religious and political rationales for their involvement. Some of the women did have strong religious and political beliefs but they did not necessarily relate these to their work in the *olla*.

In addition, just as there was great diversity amongst the women in both political and religious convictions, there was similar variance amongst those who were willing to discuss these issues within the context of the interview format. One of the most overtly political participants in the work of the *olla* did not want to be formally interviewed while another woman consented but gave very matter-of-fact answers when our interchange moved beyond a strict discussion of the pragmatic functions of the *olla*. For the latter, any discussion of politics and religion within the context of the *olla* was clearly an absurdity.

The most oft-cited reason or motivation for participation was the welfare of under- and malnourished children. In explaining how the *olla* came into existence, Juanita cited the visible signs of malnutrition as the motivating factor. 'Seeing so many skinny children', as Juanita simply stated, is what prompted her and other members of the community to initiate the project. *Ollas* had already existed in some of the other communities and because of the critical need in her community, she thought that the parish of San Rafael should have its own *olla*. Juanita, together with Isabel, Amalia, Carmen and Wilma, set up and organised the *olla*. Other members of the CEB, the parish of San Rafael and residents of Barrio Venezuela and neighbouring *barrios* soon became involved.

153

The motivations of this latter group were equally pragmatic and service oriented. Nohemí chose to work in the *olla* in order 'to help with the development of the child'. Yet her decision to participate was not unconnected to her experience as a mother nursing a young child. For Glenda too, participation was related not only to a desire to help children but also to her personal experience. Glenda first came into contact with the *olla* because her little sister was underweight and supplemental nutrition was a necessity. She began to bring her little sister to the *olla* and soon after began to volunteer on a daily basis. She was motivated, she contends, simply by a desire to 'help the project'. Similarly, Erika's participation in the *olla* arose from the needs of a sibling. She remembered:

> My little brother was fatigued and he went to the hospital gravely [ill]. It was not so serious but he remained undernourished. Doña Isabel told my mom that he should come here. When I brought him here [to the *olla*], I realised that I wanted to learn how to cook the soya. I wanted to help. I liked cooking the soya and little by little I learned.

Yet the women had more to say about themselves and the *olla* than the pragmatic character of the work and their participation. The women, especially the three older ones, had much to say about both politics and religion. Juanita in particular was keen that the achievements of the CEB and the religious and political context in which they were made should be conveyed to the 'people of the United States'. She and Isabel were also curious about churches in the United States and wanted to know if organisations similar to the CEB existed there.

Age seemed to be a determining factor in the degree to which religious and political beliefs were expressed. One of the results of Nicaragua's very young population is that the roots of the present political situation are inexplicable in terms of the personal experiences of a large segment of the population. The older women who participated in the *olla* had lived under Somoza and through the insurrection and the subsequent period of revolutionary government. They were members of the San Pablo CEB so had political and religious experiences which set them apart from the younger women.

Here it is significant that the scope and content of political and religious beliefs emerged in the course of more general discussions around the CEB rather than from any consideration of the *olla*. While Wilma, Juanita and Carmen all cited pragmatic reasons for their participation in the *olla*, they drew upon explicitly religious rationales to explain their affiliation with the CEB. For example, Wilma maintained

154

that she was motivated to join the CEB by 'the Bible, the word of God'. Like Juanita, Wilma associated her commitment to work in the community with a 'gaining of consciousness'.

Juanita defined Christianity in large part as a sensitivity to human suffering. For her, 'The Christian is [s/]he that sees the pain of others.' This recognition should, according to Juanita, generate a praxis which attempts to address not only suffering but also its underlying causes. Juanita contrasts this version of Christianity with the Catholicism that she was initially introduced to. She observed: 'I was born in this religion and it grieves me because when I came to know the Gospel, I realised that Catholicism can be a soporific religion. Now I am a Catholic but a renovated one.'

Carmen, too, expressed a strong religious commitment. However, unlike Juanita and Wilma, she did not describe any renovation of her Catholicism through the CEB. Her original involvement in the CEB was at the behest of a much respected woman religious working in the area. The significance that Carmen placed on this and other personal contacts indicated that her attachment to the community, like her initial involvement, was more rooted in immediate personal relationships than in any expressed need to pursue a praxis-oriented vision of Christianity.

Carmen asserted that her understanding of Christianity was deepened and enriched by a study of the Bible within the CEB. For her the measure of Christianity was one's behaviour in the context of interpersonal relationships. According to her stringent definition, neither she nor many other members of the CEB could accurately describe themselves as Christians. For Carmen then, Christianity was posited more as a ideal towards which one strives than a lived experience. She explained:

> Here in the community, we have a way of saying "we are Christians". Right? But I say that to know the Christian is a very good thing, very good. But hypocrisy is not acceptable for me, because I know Christians. I am not a Christian because it is a little bit of a lie to say that we are practising Christianity. If we are living in disagreement looking to cause harm... In the church there are members of the community that I would not call Christian because if we come to the church, it is to come together, to be better, to recognise our faults, not to become worse, not to throw dirt at one another. I recognise my faults and for this reason I say: I am not a Christian. I am not doing my duty directly as one could to be a Christian because if I have two garments and I see my brother without but and I do not give him even one, is this Christian? If I see another that is hungry and I do not share with him, is that Christian? (Interview, 1992).

Here Carmen put forward a version of Christianity that is inseparable from one's relationship with others; religious faith is not enough to designate one as a Christian. In one sense this was extremely exclusive in that very few people were entitled to call themselves Christians because of the difficulty of living up to this ideal. However, in another sense, her version of Christianity was inclusive because the appellation 'Christian', with little reference to professed religious beliefs, was open to anyone who was selfless and sacrificing in their dealing with others. In this latter sense, Carmen was akin to Juanita who emphasised the importance of praxis.

Juanita viewed her 'renovated' Catholicism and her involvement with the CEB as inextricably linked. She maintained: 'We in the CEB complement our work with our faith because, if I do many things but do not have faith, nothing has value for me.' However, she held that although religious faith was a defining feature of her own involvement, for her it was not an absolute prerequisite for participation in the activities of the CEB. As she asserted: 'I believe that it is not necessary [to have religious faith]. I understand that [for] the obliging person, born with a heart for service it is not important. What one has to do is to struggle against injustice.' Wilma was more light-hearted in her consideration of religious faith in the CEB. When asked if it was necessary to have a religion to work harmoniously with the CEB, she replied: 'No, but it helps a lot!' She then went on to say that all the activities of the CEB were open to anyone, regardless of religion.

Certainly involvement in the *olla*, the largest project of the CEB, was perceived as particularly open to people with a range of different religious and political beliefs. Of the women I interviewed, Nohemí was the only non-Catholic. An evangelical 'because my father was', Nohemí did not believe that one needed to be motivated by religious faith to work in the *olla*. She said: 'It is as it is. It is the same... Christian or Catholic, it is the same.' It is interesting to note that most of the interviewees referred to religious preference rather than absolute lack of religious belief. The possibility that some people might have no religious beliefs at all seemed unlikely to the women that I interviewed and spoke informally with. This was in line with Lancaster's assessment that atheism is a vary rare phenomenon in Nicaragua (Lancaster, 1988).

In common with Nohemí, Erika and Glenda were not involved in other projects of the CEB. Both young women said that they attended mass, and to this extent they were, unlike Nohemí, involved in the religious life of the community. However, neither Glenda nor Erika believed that it was necessary to have a religion to work in the *olla*. Erika categorised Glenda as a religious person, in contrast to herself. For Erika, one did not 'have to use religious words' in order to help with the work of the *olla*. But, while Glenda did claim that her religious faith was important to her, she did not necessarily link it to her involvement with the community. For these young women, their work in the *olla* was seen as a pragmatic response to the problem of hunger and under-nourishment rather than a political or religious act. While this was more or less true for most of the women who worked in the *olla*, Glenda and Erika did not have the lived experience or history of involvement with the CEB to identify junctures when religious faith and/or political conviction carried projects such as the *olla* beyond the pragmatic.

Just as the *olla* was marked out as more 'open' to participants of all religious persuasions than some of the other projects of the CEB, it was also seen as less political. But while the *olla* was not classified as political work, connections between political faith and religious beliefs were made. When I asked Juanita if all the women in the *olla* shared the same political beliefs she responded: 'No, no, no, not all. Here there are some that do and others that do not. Some are Protestants, others Jehovah's Witnesses, others Catholics, and others [that have no formal religion].' Here Juanita implied that one's political beliefs are tied to one's religious affiliation.

Wilma made this connection explicit:

> I have my political beliefs but I have my faith and I ask the Lord to help us proceed well in our work because there are governments that are not interested in the situation of the poor. Then, in this same manner, I believe that they want to take away our rights. How does that slogan go: They took away from us the fruit, the branches, the stem. But the root, that is the hope.

The women I interviewed did not explicitly cite religious or political reasons for their involvement in the *olla*. However, it became evident that many of the women held religious, and to a lesser degree political, convictions which dictated praxis in the light of social need. Clearly the *olla*, as a response to increased hunger, fell within these parameters and for many women, religious and political convictions were implicit motivating factors. Yet, given the backgrounds and beliefs of many of the women in the *olla*, it is initially difficult to understand why they themselves did not make explicit connections between deeply held religious and political beliefs and their work in the *olla*. I would posit that the ethics of the *olla* was inculcated with a set of political and religious values which were continuous with those found in the CEB during the insurrection and the subsequent revolution. However, the absence of a revolutionary government to highlight and reinforce these linkages, coupled with the lack of a cogently articulated alternative programme to neo-liberalism, contributed to a pragmatic rather than a strategic understanding of the *olla*'s work.

In this section, I have drawn together a number of disparate elements relating to the motivations of the women who participated in the *olla*. The relationship between Marxism and Christianity or politics and religion has been a central concern of this research and here I attempted to locate this dynamic within the context of a popular women's project in Chamorro's Nicaragua. The women themselves confirmed the exhaustion although not the extinction of this dynamic. Crucially, though, it was evident that participation in the *olla*, at this particular juncture, did not serve as a stage in politicisation for the younger women as the CEB experiences of the insurrection period had for the older women.

In the next section I will explore the issue of gender and its connection with 'pragmatism', the stated rationale for most women's participation in the *olla*. I will examine the possibility of the polarisation of practical gender interests in the *olla*, a key step in organising around strategic gender interests.

5   The olla and gender-specific interests

Many of the things that we need can wait
[But] the child, no!
They are creating themselves at this very moment
their bones, producing their blood and testing their senses.
To [s/]he we cannot respond 'Tomorrow'.

[S/]he calls upon you NOW. (Mistral, 1992, p.48)

This sentiment was echoed by a leaflet put out by Casa CEB, which asked 'Why a communal kitchen in our *barrio*?' The leaflet, through written text and illustration, explained how *ollas* could be set up and admonished the reader that 'the children are waiting for us "now". Not tomorrow....' The sense of urgency conveyed here was borne out by the dire infant mortality statistics (83 per 1,000 live births: *Barricada Internacional*, November/December 1993). According to Alvaro Ramírez, national epidemiology director of the Ministry of Health, malnutrition and poor sanitation resulted in the death of approximately 4,000 infants in 1992 (*Envio*, August 1993, p.25).

'Nicaragua,' according to Marta Peralta, 'is a country of women and children.' This statement is attested to by the country's demographic breakdown: 50.4 per cent of the population is female (Peralta, 1993) and 47.9 per cent are under the age of 15 (*Barricada Internacional*, August 1993, p.22). Given the fact that most women will at some point in their lives be single parents (*Envio*, June 1991), the absence of men becomes key to understanding how women perceive their interests and their identities. In fact, because Nicaragua has the highest rate of population growth in the hemisphere and the second highest in the world (*Barricada Internacional*, August 1993, p.22), the prominence of this mother/child dyad is expected to increase in significance.

In this section I will look specifically at gender issues within the context of the *olla*. First, I will examine the *olla* with respect to Molyneux's distinction between practical and strategic gender interests. I will secondly explore how the women conceptualise the lack of male participation in the *olla*. Thirdly and finally, I will analyse how Linda Mayoux's classification of the three different levels of benefits (economic, social and strategic gender) traditionally ascribed to women's co-operatives can be applied to the context of the *olla*.

The concept of 'women's interests' is hardly a straightforward one. Yet because women's interests are mediated by a range of factors, in particular class, it is well nigh impossible to present an agenda which is equally relevant or even acceptable to all women. For example, the issue of inclusive non-sexist language was raised at a women's conference held in Managua in 1992. For some delegates the issue was a pivotal one; for others it was 'excessive' and a diversion from other more 'fundamental' issues. The idea of 'women's interests' as a monolithic construct was further challenged by the failure of many women to countenance the legalisation of abortion or lesbian rights, often considered key women's issues in the 'West' (Cuadra et al., 1992).

I return now to Molyneux's distinction between strategic and practical gender interests. Strategic gender interests are often centred around the removal of legislative and other institutional forms of discrimination, access to abortion and child care, and a challenge to the present division of labour, amongst other demands. As my experience in the *olla* demonstrated, strategic interests are often not what women prioritise in their own lives. On the contrary, the issues of more concern to women were clearly tied to practical gender interests. This category includes interests that do not necessarily represent an attempt to redress or challenge the gender imbalance. Instead they are concerned with concrete responses to problems that women experience in their lives, even if these responses reinforce traditional gender roles or fail to address gender inequality.

The women in the *olla* were clearly operating according to their practical gender interests rather than their strategic gender interests. In

Nicaragua, as in most other countries, the responsibility of child-rearing falls on the female side of the sexual division of labour. This factor, coupled with the material deprivation experienced by the vast majority of Nicaraguans, makes providing for children a central preoccupation in the lives of Nicaraguan women. Projects like the *olla* are designed to address these practical gender interests. However, it could be asked, do they in the process serve to entrench the underlying assumption that children, and the domestic tasks which caring for them entails, are the sole responsibility of women?

This gendered division of labour is confirmed through practice as making 'common sense'. Clearly young women were being socialised into traditionally 'female' roles. A large number of children were accompanied to the *olla* and attended to, not by their mothers, but by older sisters. Maria Elena was one such young woman I became friendly with. She was a 12-year-old who came in daily with her younger brother Elvis and was often accompanied by her 10 year-old cousin who also came with an infant sibling in tow. Maria Elena was very serious about her responsibility for her brother and diligently fed and cared for him. Very young girls (from about the ages of five to nine) did not have responsibilities for younger siblings but would often imitate other traditional women's roles by, for example, pretending to sweep or mop the floor. Sometimes they were called upon by one of the women to help with simple tasks such as 'picking out the garbage' from the soya and other grains.

Many of the older women who participated in the *olla* no longer had young children and for them the work in the *olla* was part and parcel of their commitment to the larger base community. While the older women that I interviewed did not articulate a programme of gender-specific interests, it was clear that throughout their years of involvement with the community, they had challenged gender stereotypes through their participation in non-traditional jobs and their assumption of leadership roles. While the older women who did not have young children, or childless young women like Glenda and Erika, expressed their motivations in term of helping children, they were also assisting the mothers of these children to meet their practical gender interests. So while the language used was focused on the needs of children, these needs were almost by definition the needs of the women who were responsible for them. Thus, concern for children implied solidarity with their mothers.

That children and women in the role of mothers were the focus of CEB activity was explicable not only in terms of the church's emphasis on traditional women's roles but also as a feature of the larger Nicaraguan women's movement. As I discussed in Chapter 3, one of the perceived weaknesses of AMNLAE, the official women's organisation of the FSLN, was that it did not comprehensively address women's strategic gender interests, focusing instead on the critical priority of mobilising women in support of the war effort. In this effort, women were organised primarily as mothers, a tactic that tapped into matrifocal aspects of Nicaraguan culture and 'common sense' Catholic discourse. AMNLAE prioritised mobilisation at the expense of the slower and riskier strategy of organising around strategic gender interests. The irony is that women quite reasonably associated their short-term practical gender interests (and their responsibility to their children) with a change in government if this would mean an end to the war and economic embargo and the restoration of US aid.

The *olla* attracted participants because its efforts were focused on children and mothers and thus geared towards the very critical practical gender interests of women. Given the women's resistance to seeing the project as anything other than a practical response to the problem of under- and malnutrition, it is doubtful that the *olla* would have garnered the same degree of support and participation had its stated intentions extended beyond the pragmatic and into the strategic. At the same time, women were being empowered as they engaged in collective practice to address practical gender interests even as the gendered division of labour was being reinforced though the assumption of these responsibilities. In the area of women's health, the CEB was allowing some space for the articulation of strategic gender interests. In providing a space for Ixchén to hold low-cost gynaecological consultations, the San Rafael church was potentially providing women with access to artificial contraception, although this was not acknowledged as it would have been a direct challenge to the edicts of the church.

In my observations, the work of the *olla* was done by women. On the very rare occasions that men did contribute it was in a sporadic and highly gendered fashion. In one instance knives needed to be sharpened and a local man was asked to do this. In addition the periodic deliveries to the different *ollas* were made by a man. However, these were the only instances in which I observed male participation. Juanita's explanation for this was that perhaps they were embarrassed to do what was considered women's work. Nohemí maintained that her husband did not work in the *olla* because 'he does not have time'.

Glenda speculated that men did not participate because: 'Perhaps they are working. The may not have any free time.' This view was echoed by 11-year- old Marta Perez, an occasional volunteer who speculated that, 'Perhaps they do not know [about the *olla*] or they do not have time.' Men did, on rare occasions, come to the *olla*. However, according to Glenda, they came only 'to give food to their children' and not to help with the work. For Erika, this lack of male participation was not very significant. 'Only mothers come' because, unlike fathers, they have 'a reason to come'.

It was obvious that for these young women, the absence of male participants in the *olla* was not really an issue and it was difficult for them to fathom why I was raising it as such. While Nohemí had been somewhat dismissive when asked about men's role in the *olla*, Glenda and Erika were genuinely perplexed by my interest in the matter.

In the other activities of the CEB, Juanita maintained that although men participated, women generally worked harder than men. She observed that men did jobs like announcing a meeting while women generally did the less glamorous jobs like mopping floors. The CEB did have a male co-ordinator of the community. Other men 'come to sing at the mass, play the guitar, and do construction work' and various other tasks. However, Juanita estimated that in the San Rafael section of San Pablo, there were only about four men who worked in a consistent and organised way. Wilma also highlighted the female character of CEBs, stating that: 'Women are always more committed.' Male participation, Wilma posited, may be constrained by the breadwinning role that men play in the family and the time and energy that this requires. This was the case with her own husband who had been an active participant in the CEB during the insurrection period, 'but when the revolution came, he decided to work and now when he returns from work he says that he is tired'. Juanita's husband also used to participate in the community but his involvement became restricted due to illness.

Carmen also stated that women were a numerical majority within the CEB. She said: 'There are more women than men. There are very few men [who participate].' However, a number of young men did help out with various projects on an *ad hoc* basis. In several different ways, I asked Carmen why more women than men participated in the activities of the community. She resisted offering any specific reasons or even thoughts on the matter.

Thus far I have considered why men do not participate and have documented the reasons given by some of the women who worked in the *olla*. One reason that I have not yet considered is that perhaps men did not participate because the *olla* was a female domain in which women held the power and controlled the knowledge. Perhaps large-scale male participation would threaten the erosion of a traditional space of women's authority. I would posit that the female dominance of the *olla* was related as much to this sense of women carving out a space of power and authority independently of men as it was to do with male indifference.

162

In addition to a sense of authority, women accrued a number of benefits from their participation in the *olla*. In her analysis of Nicaraguan women working in tailoring co-operatives Linda Mayoux considers three different levels of benefits that have traditionally been ascribed to women's co-operatives: economic, social, and the potential that they provide for women to organise 'to improve their position as women' (1992, p.98). In economic terms, although women did not receive an income from their work in the *olla*, there was a clear economic benefit to those women who would not otherwise have been able to provide adequate nourishment for their children. In this sense all women who sent their children to the *olla*, regardless of their level of participation, gained. However, access to the *olla* for young children and pregnant and nursing mothers was not conditional upon their contribution to the *olla*. While there was some expectation that women would make an occasional contribution, many women did not and it was in no way mandatory that they do so. Further, as I have already stated, a number of the *olla*'s most active workers were not amongst the recipients targeted by the *olla*.

However, there were a few small perquisites for the women participants themselves. Women who worked in the *olla* would generally have a portion of what they had helped to prepare that day. Any perishable leftovers would be taken home by the women. In addition, the women who formed the core group of workers, those who came daily or almost daily received, according to Juanita, 'a small stimulus of rice, beans and soap' on a monthly basis. This package consisted of one pound each of beans and rice and two bars of soap. Yet for the women these rewards on their own were not sufficient incentive for participation. It is clear that for the women who worked in the *olla*, economic concerns, were not paramount. As Juanita stated emphatically in her interview: 'We are volunteers. We do not receive pay.'

This solidarity was inextricably bound up with the social benefits that women derived from their involvement with the *olla*. The burdens of domestic labour and child-rearing combined with a resistance to their entering the labour force can mean that women are isolated and may 'not be allowed to have a life outside of the home' (*Envio*, June 1991, p.32). For women who are in this position, work in a community project like the *olla* might be viewed as relatively non-threatening by themselves or by male husbands or partners.

The social benefits for women that are attributed to collective work were similarly evident in the *olla*. Lucy Morren, a Belgian religious, maintained that at times children are not brought into the *olla* because their mothers are 'many times ashamed ... even though [the children] may be dying of hunger' (Gabriel, 1992, p.38). While it is not possible for me to address the veracity of this statement for *ollas* in general, it was clear that in Barrio Venezuela there were more needy children than the sixty to eighty that regularly attended the *olla*. However, once mothers came into the *olla*, the 'sociability' of the setting helped to militate against a sense of shame.

In regard to the last benefit of women's collective that Mayoux outlined - the potential to organise around gender issues - it was evident that this potential was still inchoate. Within the terms of Molyneux's analysis the politicisation of 'practical gender interests' had not taken place (Molyneux, 1984). However, although this had not occurred, the setting of the female-dominated *olla* and the crucial role that it played in the surrounding *barrios* nurtured the potential of this consciousness. Further, as I explored in Chapter 3, this process was taking place within the context of the movement around women's health centres. As one of these organisations ran a weekly gynaecological clinic at San Rafael, the potential for these praxis-generated consciousness to directly cross-fertilise the *olla* was in place.

6 Conclusion

My findings suggest that the *olla*, as a site of organisation around 'practical gender interests', offered the possibility for the emergence of an agenda around 'strategic gender interests'. However, as with the politicisation of practical interests in general, this was not realised. In the case of both gender and politics, it was the older women who came closest to making these linkages between the practical and the strategic. Given the relative youth of the Nicaraguan population, this is a trend that should be well noted in any struggle to reconstruct an alternative political project.

In Chile *ollas comunes*, given that their rapid growth in 1982 and 1983 coincided with the imposition of neo-liberal economic policies, were visible manifestations of the suffering wrought by the Pinochet regime. Moreover, they were perceived as forms of collective action and, as such, a threat to the regime:

> their presence denounced a situation of misery and a keen pre-
> occupation with human rights abuses. The *ollas* were examples of the
> hunger that reigned in the authoritarian regime. The mobilisation of
> families to gather food and supplies for the *ollas* was viewed as
> subversive by the regime (Astelli and Henríquez, 1992, p.40).

The development of the *ollas* in Chile suggests interesting parallels for their Nicaraguan counterparts. In Nicaragua, many *ollas* were tied to Catholic parishes. In Managua, supplies to these parish-based *ollas* were co-ordinated by the Casa CEB, which served as a resource centre for the Managua CEBs. In Chile, the precursors of the *ollas*, the *comedores infantiles*, were initiated by Catholic parishes in 1975 (Astelli and Henríquez, 1992, p.40). These *comedores infantiles* were set up to provide breakfast and lunch for children suffering the effects of the poverty and widespread unemployment that were the lot of their parents. While the church was involved with the 'popular sectors' on a number of different fronts, notably in the organisation of brigades of unemployed workers called *bolsas de cesantes*, it was the *comedores infantiles* which gave birth to a large, and eventually autonomous, popular organisation.

The transformation of the *comedores infantiles* into the network of *ollas* known as the Asamblea Metropolitana de Ollas Comunes was shaped by two important factors: an increasing autonomy from the church beginning in the 1978-79 period and a broadening of its function from providing children with food to providing a collective framework for community food provision. The *ollas* were supported in different ways, from subscriptions paid by participating families to fund-raising activities and donations. What is significant here is that a once church-based form of nutritional provision broadened in scope and became independently run. Does this development in Chile have any implications for the Nicaraguan *ollas*?

Given the continuing deterioration of the Nicaraguan economy and the failure of the government or the FSLN to put forward a plan to address the poverty and hunger that is the lot of most Nicaraguans, it is clear that the need for organisations like the *olla* will continue to grow. Yet the likelihood of these organisations transforming themselves into a political movement comparable to that which developed in Chile is uncertain. The emergence of *ollas* is a relatively recent phenomenon in Nicaragua. In the San Rafael *olla*, even amongst politically active participants, the focus did not extend beyond child nutrition, although many women clearly linked under- and malnutrition to the current political situation.

6 Popular religion and culture in Nicaragua

1 Introduction

Popular religion is not just religion that has many adherents; rather its denotation as 'popular' reflects its lack of integration with or accountability to 'official' religion. At the same time, the practices and beliefs of popular religion, while in conflict with authorised forms of religious expression, are often held by their adherents to be consistent with and at times more 'genuine' than 'official' customs. Writing about popular religion in the United States, Peter Williams notes that all movements which fall within the parameters of popular religion 'exist apart from or in tension with established religious groups with regular patterns of organisation and leadership'. The distinction between popular and official religion does not necessarily imply a discordance between the two; as Williams notes popular religion may be 'tacitly welcomed' as a means of relatively contained expression of unacceptable but prevalent beliefs and practices (Williams, 1989, p.17).

The separation between popular religion and established religion, however, is not strictly demarcated and there is clearly an interaction and slippage between the two. Syncretism or the fusion of religious forms is often a feature of both popular and establish religion. Yet syncretism has been more recognised as a feature of popular religion because the origins of beliefs and practices that have been adapted and reshaped are hidden within the official discourse and codifications of established religion.

In Nicaragua, as well as other Latin American countries, pre-conquest religious practices and beliefs have been encased in Catholicism, both in its established and popular forms. But Catholicism itself has a syncretic character. In fact, Roman Catholicism itself represents the syncretic process by which the practices and thinking of the Roman empire came to influence the religion it initially persecuted and eventually accepted.[36] The issue of syncretism is germane not only to Catholicism in its movement from persecuted faith to imperial religion but also to its adaptation to differing cultural contexts. In turn, cultures that have come into contact with Catholicism have often been recast by this interaction. In Latin America, the conquest initiated a process of syncretism between Catholicism and indigenous or pre-conquest religion that can be witnessed most clearly in the practices and beliefs of popular religion.

My aim in this chapter is twofold. Firstly, I am concerned to explore some general issues around popular religion and its relationship to popular culture. Secondly, I wish to explore the indigenous roots of popular religion and thus examine the syncretic character of Nicaraguan popular religion. To this end, I will begin my analysis of popular religion in Nicaragua with an exploration of some of the general themes which dominate considerations of popular culture and popular religion. I will next examine how the issue of popular Catholicism has been taken up both by the 'official' church, particularly in the wake of Vatican II, and by liberation theologians. This discussion will lead to a more specific focus on popular religion in Latin America. I will then briefly analyse the proliferation of evangelical Protestant groups in Latin America, specifically addressing Bastian's argument that these groups are in fact re-articulation elements of popular and folk Catholicism that have been abandoned by the official Catholic church (Bastian, 1993). Finally, I will move to an analysis of the indigenous roots of Nicaraguan popular religion and the implications of this for both the 'traditional' and the 'popular' church in Nicaragua.

2 General considerations of popular culture and popular religion

Terms such as popular religion and popular culture are heavily dependent upon context. Religion is an important aspect of culture and thus popular religion is an aspect of popular culture. However, the relationship between popular religion and traditional or orthodox religion is not the equivalent of the relationship between popular culture and 'high' culture. Neither popular culture nor popular religion are hermetically sealed systems; there is an interaction between the two and also between themselves and their respective 'opposites'. This interchange blurs the distinctions between these various categories so that no category can be said to be designated 'pure'. While the obvious distinction between the 'orthodox' and the 'popular' is that the latter is an adaptation or a 'corruption' of the former, in fact all orthodoxies are themselves adaptations.

Popular religion often stresses allegiance to past religious practices. In this way, popular religious activities are often centred on previously prescribed religious practices which have lost their importance within 'official' discourses. Here '"little tradition" [e.g. popular religion] is often merely "great tradition" that has taken root in a particular place and lasted longer than its time' (Christian Jr.,1981, p.178). Williams has linked this tenacious adherence to 'outdated' religious practices as a resistance to the modernising impulses which have characterised 'official' religious discourses. In contrast to a rational system of beliefs, popular religion 'generally looks for signs of divine intervention or manifestation in the realm of everyday experience' (Williams, 1989, p.18).

Thus, popular religion is not a systematised set of beliefs and customs. Rather, popular religious practices reference orthodox religion and exist both within and in tension with this reference point. Popular religion is open to manipulation by the orthodox religion, particularly by clergy and religious, but it is never under their control. Often forms of popular Catholicism accord clergy and religious magical powers. Literature on popular religion often cites the belief that priests are invested with supernatural powers that they use to hold sway over their parishioners (Taylor, 1990; Badone, 1990). This attribution of magical powers to priests and religious has been used both to exert control and to correct perceived wrongs.

An example of the latter usage was given by Raquel Fernandez in her analysis of the Jesuit-run public service organisation Fe y Alegría, which operates throughout Latin America. She describes the case in which a woman religious saves a child born with a harelip from death at the hands of a fearful community who believed the deformity to be a diabolical manifestation. The sister took the child claiming, 'I have a more powerful magic'. She then took the child to have the harelip surgically corrected. When she returned some weeks later with the child who was now free of the deformity, her magical powers were confirmed and the community celebrated this triumph over the devil (Fernandez, 1993, p.38).

Was this action manipulative? Should the sister have respected the cultural practices which mandated that the child be killed lest the entire community be damned? In this construction, official religious discourse seeks to create a relatively rational and coherent belief system, an idea which might be said to correspond to Gramsci's understanding of 'philosophy'. Conversely, popular religious beliefs and practices might be said to spring from 'common sense'. In this way popular religion is not essentially a reactionary or progressive force. Gramsci contended:

> Popular religion is crassly materialistic, and yet the official religion of the intellectuals attempts to impede the formation of two distinct religions, two separate strata, so as not to become officially, as well as in reality, an ideology of restricted groups (Gramsci, 1971, pp.396-397).

Recent manifestations of popular Catholicism have often been concerned with preserving pre-Vatican II ritual and custom that have since been discarded. Vatican II was the Catholic Church's attempt to 'rationalise' the church by opening it up to 'modern' influences. In this way, many seemingly arcane practices were disregarded. According to Peter Hebblethwaite, with Vatican II, ritual 'condemned to become more meaningful.' (Hebblethwaite, 1978, p.33) For instance, the pre-Vatican II mass said in Latin with the priest facing the altar was abandoned in favour of mass in the vernacular with the priest facing the congregation. The council's goal was to strip away rituals and practices that had assumed the place of an authentic spirituality.

In addition to the rationalisation and updating that Vatican II initiated, it also generated an attempt within the church to critically engage with 'modern' systems of thought, particularly Marxism. Vatican II (1962-1965) and the Medellín CELAM conference (1968), wholeheartedly endorsed the Church which sought to open itself up to 'local' influences and were the forums that most resolutely signalled the Church's 'preferential option for the poor'. This option was linked to the church's more 'modern' stance and much of the intellectual backlash focused both on the shedding of 'out of date' rituals and customs as well as the church's openness to Marxist influenced notions of social change.[37] Thus, proponents of 'popular Catholicism' in the post-Vatican II period were often seen as both theologically and politically reactionary.

Vatican II, in line with a dominant strand in Marxist thinking, associated 'modernisation' with the struggle for social justice. This thinking also ran through the work of many liberation theologians who viewed the church's move away from ritual and ceremony and its openness to new forms of religious expression as a necessary stripping away of calcified and outdated traditions. This modernising impulse had at its heart the intention of (up to a point) sweeping away old ideas and old systems. In describing the impact of Vatican II on Latin America, Lernoux stated:

In less than a decade the church shifted its institutional allegiance from rich to poor, gave birth to liberation theology, and undertook the organisation of thousands of grassroots Christian base communities that would give the poor greater participation in their church and society and lead to the emergence of a new more militant faith (Lernoux,1989, p.91).

Popular religion in Latin America was varyingly affected by the dramatic changes which Lernoux outlined above. For all its commitment to open itself to 'local' influence, the impulse to 'modernise' meant that it was difficult for the church to incorporate the often patently 'anti-modern' and ritualistic elements of popular religion. The 'Pan-American Mass' featuring mariachi bands and South American folk music and 'put together by a Mexican bishop and designed to be a tourist attraction' was one example of the church's efforts to incorporate 'local' elements in to its newly honed ritual and practices (Rowe and Schelling, 1991, p.71). The universalising character of this attempt demonstrates the difficulty the church faced in meeting two often conflicting goals: accommodating both the modern and the local.

The modernising impulse was the stronger of the two and in the aftermath of Vatican II popular religion in Latin America received special attention. However, this was not only a move sought by the Vatican. It was a concern of proponents of liberation theology who often equated the rituals of popular religion with passivity and obscurantism and many times shared the suppositions of modernity which had driven Vatican II. In CEBs and other popular church organisations in Nicaragua and Latin American, the importance of understanding and action were stressed over ritual.

Gramsci contended that initially the masses would be unable to rationally understand or espouse Marxism because this would require study and time. In the meantime the masses could take Marxism on faith. Does popular religion and liberation theology function in the same way? If popular religion validates a praxis oriented Christianity, is it possible for people to hold a liberation theology tinged popular religion until they fully understand what is behind it? Successful socialism is ultimately and not just initially comprised of a good deal of faith and common sense as well as philosophical understanding.

Philip Berryman argues that popular religion can be seen as 'expressing a suppressed aspiration to peoplehood' (Berryman, 1987, p.70). At the same time, in Nicaragua the participants in popular religious practices far outnumber those active in liberation theology organisations. Here, the FSLN and the popular church were able to tap into popular religious understandings but they were unable to control them.

Many manifestations of popular religion in Latin America had never been sanctioned or controlled by the church and hence were not directly affected by the changes in ceremony and ritual initiated by Vatican II. However, because of Vatican II's emphasis on making ritual meaningful, the issue of popular religion received special attention in the CELAM Episcopal conferences at Medellín, Puebla and Santo Domingo. Popular religion, a true expression of the 'local' which Vatican II prioritised, was said to be in need of 'purification' and 'systemisation'. The 1968 CELAM conference at Medellín was the apex of official church tolerance of liberation theology. The 1979 Puebla conference saw a new and more authoritarian pope and conservative Latin American bishops attempt to regain ground 'lost' to the progressives. The Santo Domingo Conference in 1992 saw 'a powerful and sustained onslaught by the conservatives' that was resisted with relative success by proponents of the preferential option for the poor (Linden, 1993, p.5).

The battle between the 'progressives' and the 'conservatives' centred on the issue of the preferential option for the poor. Within this context positions on the issue of popular religion were not so clear cut. Some progressives conceived of popular religion as a sort of 'false consciousness' which impeded *conscientización* and induced passivity. Writing about Brazil, Thomas Bruneau concluded: 'Those in the popular Catholicism pattern are less likely to be aware of the possibilities of change by means of control, making demands and acting' (Bruneau, 1986, pp.116-117). Thomas Kselman identifies two positions espoused by proponents of liberation theology with regard to popular religion. He maintained that a 'traditionalist' perspective holds that popular religion serves to 'express and reinforce a hierarchical and authoritarian view of the church' (Kselman,1986, p.34). In contrast, a 'progressive' view contends that because popular religion is under the control of the laity and side-steps the rituals and sacraments controlled by the clergy, it 'undermines the ecclesial hierarchy' (Kselman,1986, p.35).

Here concerns centre around the effect that popular religion has on the process of *conscientización* and the transformation of the church. Conservatives have often supported popular religion because it reinforces a traditional view of the church rather than a modern one. At the same time this support has been selective and conditional. The view often expressed by the hierarchy was that popular religious festivals are legitimate expressions of devotion which are nevertheless in need of 'purification'. In other words, the aspects of popular religious festivals that most closely paralleled approved discourse and practice were lauded while other, more 'profane', aspects were questioned. For example, in describing the Nicaraguan church's attitude towards 'popular piety', Mons. Mondragón asserted:

in Popular Piety there is a mix of the divine and the human; there are lights and shades; the sacred and the profane are seen. We recognise this matter as a valid method of evangelisation, but there must be a purification of the cultural expressions of the people (Ubeda Bravo, 1992).

Yet, because of the contradictory and often independent character of popular religion, hierarchical responses to popular religious practices have varied greatly. Certainly where popular religion has been perceived as an apolitical alternative to liberation theology, it has been treated more kindly by the conservatives. Yet because popular religion is a shifting and unsystematised grouping of beliefs and practices it eludes the control and categorisation of the hierarchy. This unpredictable and insubordinate character makes it difficult for conservatives within the Latin American church to 'count on' popular religion. Furthermore, although popular religion does not 'parallel' the official church in the same way that the 'popular church' is said to, it does pose a threat to the authority of the hierarchy.

Popular religion in Latin America is a local phenomena. The unique pre-conquest cultures and conquest and colonial experiences of different regions plus varying experiences of urbanisation and modernity influence the character and prevalence of popular religion in a particular area. There is no single Latin American popular religion in the same way that there is no uniform Latin American culture. There are only popular religions and popular cultures. This cultural diversity and its expression in local forms of Catholicism was recognised in the preparatory document for the Santo Domingo conference produced by CEHILA (Commission of Historical Studies of the Church in Latin America) which maintained:

> the oppressed, never conquered were able to discover the presence of the Gospel in spite of the violence from states and churches. They recognise God as the one who hears the cries of the oppressed. The indigenous peoples and mestizos, the African and Caribbean groups, are reconstructing their popular religious world ... (Sandoval, 1991, p.62).

In line with this statement, the progressives reject the universalist discourse of the conservatives and seek to create an 'inculturated' church whereby Catholicism would become 'localised' taking a particular form based on the cultural and spiritual traditions of different regions. In this way, progressives argued for a 'local' rather than a 'universal' church.

Yet, at the same time, the progressives advance overarching principles of social change which seek to unite culturally diverse groups in the struggle for liberation. Here, elements of popular culture and religion which seem to impede this project are problematised. Further, while the doctrinal unity that the Vatican seeks to impose may be an anathema to the progressives, there is a basic Christology to which they subscribe and difficulties arise when popular religious beliefs and practices contradict this. After all, it was the progressives who advocated a return to the Bible in an attempt to strip away the layers of antiquated and authoritarian dogma that had masked Christianity's truly liberating message. Thus, liberation theology posits a universal message of liberation through Christian faith and praxis that prioritises the shared experience of oppression rather than cultural differences.

At the Santo Domingo conference, the notion of a 'Christian culture' as a force to combat secularism was advanced by Conservatives as a major focus of the conference. This focus on culture was an attempt to shift the priorities of the Latin American church away from the preferential option for the poor and towards a struggle against secularism. Because the urban middle classes were identified as most vulnerable to the nascent influences of modernism, they, rather than the 'poor' , were seen as most in need of the church's protection. In this construction, the poor are seen as pre-modern and therefore irrelevant in the struggle against secularism.

The notion of an inculturated church, which progressives and conservatives alike accept in principle, is often, in practice, beset by a pervasive Eurocentrism that 'sets the limits of acceptable diversity in the Church so narrowly as to deny the principle' (Linden, 1993, p.3). Further, the idea of a Christian culture not only essentialises the experience of Christianity in Latin America, it also flattens cultural differences. This restrictive notion of culture was expressed by Rafael Carías in a commentary on the CELAM preparatory document on culture for the Santo Domingo conference. He maintained:

> There exists, as a result of those long centuries of mutual influence, what is called the 'Latin American person', more noteworthy for what is held in common than for the regional diversities that, aside from isolated ethnic groups, could be termed subcultures (Carías, 1991, p.22).

Despite its often essentialist character, the debate around Latin American cultural identity conducted in conjunction with the Santo Domingo conference in many ways seemed to echo 'post-modern' debates around identity. The church is uniquely placed for these debates because it is an institution which is at once ephemeral and concrete, temporal and spiritual, national and global, personal and public. In line with some post-modern constructions of identity, the conservatives isolated notions of culture from an analysis of the socio-economic conditions that would allow for a concept of oppression to emerge. In the preliminary document to the Santo Domingo conference, the notion of an 'organic society' is proffered. Here a neo-pluralist society in which competition rather than conflict characterises the interaction amongst groups. In this way critical social analysis is reduced 'to a diagnosis of its pathologies and symptoms, ignoring the analysis of its causes and of the guilty parties' (Suarez, 1991, p.19).

Clearly with regard to culture there is considerable disagreement in the Latin American church. However, it is difficult to reduce these differences to a progressive/conservative polarisation because cultures do not necessarily bend to a particular political or religious agenda. For example progressives objected to the notion of a Christian culture because it proffered a uniform and essential Christian culture, thus undermining and denying the plethora of Latin American cultural diversity. At the same time, if cultural diversity is approached in a completely neutral fashion, as with the 'organic society' advanced by some conservatives, the culture of the urban bourgeois would be the 'moral' equivalent of, for example, an indigenous culture under threat. The progressives do not wish to create a unitary Christian culture. However, they do seek to prioritise some cultural expressions over others, particularly those that dovetail with liberating Christian praxis.

Thus both progressives and conservatives highlight elements of Latin American culture that support a particular type of church. Popular religion, an important feature of many Latin American cultures, is received with similar selectivity. While the progressives may be more respectful of cultural diversity than the conservatives, a fully syncretistic Catholicism is desired by neither.

Elements of Latin American 'high' culture are more easily incorporated into an inculturated Catholicism because of the European bias of many of these forms. In Latin America, popular culture is a mixture of the vestiges of indigenous culture that survived the conquest, cultural practices and beliefs that preceded urbanisation and the ensuing preponderance of mass cultural forms and the mass culture condemned by Adorno and Horkheimer. Yet the boundaries between 'high' and 'popular' culture are no longer as distinct as they once were. In an analysis of these increasingly blurred distinctions, García Canclini contended: 'High, popular, and mass are no longer to be found in their familiar places...' (García Canclini, 1992, p.30).

However, while the boundaries between high and popular culture in Latin America may be becoming more fluid, those between popular Catholicism and the official Catholic discourse have not. The distinctions between the two have remained relatively fixed, despite significant interaction and overlap in the discourses and practices of both. Yet popular Catholicism often operates in a dialectic rather than an oppositional relationship with 'official' Catholicism; they do not operate as discrete impenetrable entities. In Nicaragua, both the popular church/Left/FSLN bloc and the hierarchical church/Right bloc have used the symbolic grammar of popular religion to legitimise their positions. Although both groups are unable to control and unwilling to fully accommodate all aspects of popular religion, they ignore it at their peril.

The discourse of the 'popular' is infused with the language and logic of popular religion and it is on this ability to articulate and embody the popular that the legitimacy of FSLN and the popular church rest. In this effort to represent the popular, the popular church/FSLN bloc were in competition with not only the hierarchical church/Right bloc but also with the growing number of evangelical Protestant groups who, in the past decade, have grown rapidly in Nicaragua and throughout Latin America.

3   Protestantism, liberation theology and popular religion

Thus far I have considered the issue of popular religion with regard to the Catholic church. However, any analysis of popular religion in Latin America would be incomplete without a mention of the numerous and growing evangelical Protestant groups. The growth of Protestantism in Latin America was an issue of much concern for the Santo Domingo conference which sought to devise strategies for stemming the tide of evangelical Protestant conversions (Linden, 1993, p.4). The growth of these groups has often been attributed to the well-financed and highly organised missionary programmes of US evangelical groups who often engage in aggressive radio and television conversion campaigns (Bamat, 1992, p.14). The right-wing character of many of these missionary groups and the stated intention of the Santa Fe document (the governing policy document of the Reagan administration on Latin America) to promote evangelical Christianity as an alternative to liberation theology in Latin America have given credence to the view that the growth of evangelical Protestantism is the result of a concerted strategy to subvert social change.[38]

Indeed, the Pentecostal Protestant groups, in the main, serve to 'reinforce the order which accounts for their exponential growth and success' (Bastian, 1993, p.39). Yet it is important to distinguish between the generally conservative fundamentalist sects and mainline and progressive Protestant groups (e.g. Baptists, Lutherans, Methodists, Presbyterians). In Nicaragua, CEPAD, the Evangelical Committee for Aid to Development was a grouping of 49 member Protestant denominations that supported and worked closely with the revolutionary government (Norsworthy, 1990; Dodson and Nuzzi O'Shaughnessy, 1990). In this way, CEPAD, in line with the popular church, linked Christian faith to progressive political praxis.

As opposed to other expressions of Protestantism, the refusal of Pentecostal Protestantism to challenge the status quo 'helps to limit popular movements seeking social change. The poverty and political violence in Central America which fostered the growth of the popular church were also behind the rapid multiplication of evangelical Protestant groups. In difficult and dangerous times, the fundamentalists offer simple solutions, support networks and the motivation for personal transformation. Pentecostalism's emphasis on 'right conduct' translated into a decrease in alcoholism, gambling and participation in costly fiestas. In this way, members of Pentecostal groups often experienced an improvement in their standard of living. However, perhaps the most significant benefit that members derived from their participation was an increased sense of self-esteem. Through their involvement, they '...become human beings, they walk tall, they speak, they pray, they grow. They leave the world of apathy for the world of activity' (Bamat, 1992, p.15).

A number of commentators maintain that the attraction of Pentecostalism stems from its ability to rearticuate popular Catholicism in a way that meaningfully addresses the physical and psychological needs of its adherents (Bastian, 1993; Samandu,1988; Stoll, 1990). As with Latin America as a whole, Nicaragua has experienced an expansion in the number of adherents to Pentecostal religious groups. In explaining the success of these groups, Luis Samandu maintained:

> Pentecostal beliefs make possible free expression of the popular religious world [that is] inhabited by demons, spirits, revelations, and divine cures... in such a way that the believers recognise in Pentecostalism "their" religion with profound roots in popular culture, long discredited as superstition by the cultivated and educated classes (Samandu, 1988, p.8).

It is interesting to note that the growth of Pentecostalism has not been a boon to mainline Protestant churches in Latin America. The modernising thrust of many mainline Protestant religions initially garnered members from the educated urban middle classes beginning in the nineteenth century (Bastian, 1993, p.36). It was Weber who first theorised the relationship between Protestantism and development of Capitalism (Runciman, 1978) and it is this rationalising trait that has set mainline Protestantism against popular religion and hence undercut its ability to reach the popular sectors. The Pentecostal groups, in contrast, emerged from 'within the Catholic and shamanistic popular religious culture' and thus did not pose a 'modern' alternative to Catholic corporatism (Bastian, 1993, p.39). In response to the growth of Pentecostalism, many mainstream Protestant churches have successfully sought to 'Pentecostalise' themselves by incorporating charismatic elements into their religious practices (Bastian, 1993, p.49).

While liberation theology Catholicism has an agenda of transformation, Pentecostalism advances a program of adaptation and personal resistance. During the time that the FSLN held state power, US Pentecostals, particularly televangelists, targeted Nicaragua as a site for intensive conversion activity. The tenor of these efforts, including television, radio and print campaigns as well as more interpersonal approaches, was overwhelmingly anti-Sandinista (Norsworthy, 1990; 127). Further, US Pentecostals, particularly televangelists, generated considerable financial and political support for the *contras*. In contrast, their 'mainline' counterparts were often engaged in 'solidarity' work in support of the revolution.

Ironically, however, the Chamorro government has not rewarded the Pentecostals for their contribution to the anti-Sandinista crusade. All religious programmes must now be submitted to Cardinal Obando for 'review' prior to broadcast and the rates proposed for transmission have hardly been concessionary. The new government has also expressed its hostility to Pentecostals and mainline Protestants through the imposition of a sales tax on the low cost health care services they provided. Catholic organisations providing similar services were not subject to the tax.

The Nicaraguan hierarchy's hostility to the Pentecostals rests on the challenge that these groups pose to 'official' church's authority to define the parameters of religious expression. The hierarchy similarly objects to the 'popular church' because it challenges their version of what it means to be 'in church'. The hierarchy and many members of the Chamorro government seek to inculcate a more integral Catholicism and both the popular church and the Pentecostal groups threaten this notion of Nicaraguan society. While the Pentecostals' ability to articulate popular religion has fuelled their growth, they, like the hierarchical church and the popular church, do not control it. All of these religious configurations find themselves dipping into a pool of common sense practices and beliefs in order to make their particular version of Christianity more 'popular'. In the following section, I will explore the indigenous roots of popular religion and culture, laying the groundwork for an examination of how indigenous culture has been addressed in the construction of hegemony.

4   The indigenous roots of Nicaraguan popular religion and culture

The pre-conquest ancestry of present day Nicaraguans is rooted in the intermingling and changing ascendancies between the Mayas, Mixtecas, Zapotecas, Toltecas, Huastecas, Totonacas, Olmecas, Tabascos, and Xochicalocos, all early inhabitants of what is now Mexico. Around the year 800, a group of migrants from Mexico called the Nicaraos settled in the isthmus of Rivas in southern Nicaragua displacing the Chortegas. The Nicaraos had left the exalted city Teotihuacán while it was in its slow decline. The reasons for its decline and subsequent fall remain shrouded in mystery but what is certain is that the city of Tula carried on many of the old traditions and beliefs, albeit in a less grandiose fashion than its predecessor. In the twelfth century, a group of Toltecas left Tula and emigrated to Nicaragua settling in the area between Xolotán[39] (Lake Managua) and Cocibolca (*Barricada,(Gente)*   25 September 1992, p.7). At the time of the conquest of Nicaragua, 'four or five distinct languages' were in use. The main language was called 'Nicaraguan' and was the same as the primary language spoken in Mexico at the time, that is Náuatl. Other significant languages were Chortega and Chontal (Fernández de Oviedo y Valdés, 1992, p.7).

Present day Nicaraguans are said to speak 'nahuañol' because of the preponderance of Náuatl words that are still in common usage. It is in language that Nicaraguans experience and recognise their indigenous roots. In group discussions at the CEB 500 Years conference and in numerous informal conversations, most Nicaraguans I spoke with were able to list, with relative ease, scores of words which had indigenous origins. The continuity between past and present that language in Nicaragua provides is characterised by author Carlos Mántica, who contended: 'Our history is spoken, speech is our history' (*Barricada, (Gente)*, 25 September 1992, p.11).

Another area where indigenous culture is easily identifiable is the area of traditional medicine. However, the persistence and resurgence of 'traditional' medicine says as much about the persistence of indigenous

178

healing practices and the religious systems to which they were tied as it does about 'underdevelopment' and lack of access to 'modern' medicine. Thus, with this caution in mind, a consideration of Nicaraguan 'traditional' medicine yields a wealth of information about indigenous religion and provides some signposts to its incorporation into popular Catholicism. Alejandro Dávila Bolaños, an anthropologist and medical doctor killed by the National Guard in 1978, contended that religion played a vital role in pre-Columbian understanding of health and disease. Many indigenous gods were accorded a particular medical function. With the conquest and forced Christianisation, these saints took the place of indigenous gods and often there was a direct correspondence between a particular god and a particular saint. For example, San Jerónimo replaced Quetzalcoalt, the curer of all illnesses, San Lazarus and San Lucía took the place of Xipe Totec, the healer of skin and vision problems, and San Isidoro Labrador was a substitute for Tlaloc, the god of the harvest (*Barricada Internacional*, November/December 1992b, p.25).

Here there is clearly a syncretism of indigenous gods and Catholic saints. Yet in Nicaragua, the connections between indigenous religion and contemporary religious practices and beliefs are not widely recognised. For example, while religious festivals were characterised by many people with whom I spoke as uniquely Nicaraguan or specific to a particular region, this singularity was not generally attributed to the persistence of indigenous religious traditions. Indeed, Nicaraguan popular religion could not be characterised as an exclusive syncretism of indigenous religion and Catholicism because it referenced a whole range of past and present cultural forms. As I will discuss in the following chapter, the popular religious festivals of La Purísima and Santo Domingo manifest a melange of divergent influences, many of them rooted in indigenous religion.

5 The struggle to redefine Nicaraguan identity through debates on the conquest and indigenous identity

In the context of the conquest, Catholicism was a crucial instrument of subjugation and the means of both literal and cultural genocide. 'With the cross and the sword' was the phrase used by many commentators to denote the central role played by the Church in the conquest of the Americas. This phrase was freely employed by priests and religious associated with the popular church whose involvement with the 500' Years of Resistance Campaign 1992 Conference was extensive. There was a recognition of the role played by the church in the conquest and a genuine attempt to grapple with the implications of this complicity.

In addition, great strides were made to 'popularise' indigenous culture through the construction of a post-conquest 'indigenous' identity. In The Labyrinth of Solitude, Octavio Paz located the origins of Mexican 'isolation and solitude' in the rejection of the Indian 'Mother' whereby 'we condemn our origins and deny our hybridism' (Paz, 1961, pp.86-87). The Nicaraguan post-conquest identity seemed more rooted in a 'mestizoism' which acknowledged the indigenous influence on Nicaraguan culture but placed this within the context of a relatively neutral 'coming together of two worlds', in effect a celebration of hybridism. Following from this paradigm was a lack of identification with the 'Indian', a phenomena which was neatly encapsulated in a single frame cartoon that appeared in Barricada in October 1992. Pictured were two characters with identical features facing each other. One of the men, dressed in 'western attire' said to the other, clothed in an animal skin, 'You poor Indians, I really feel sorry for you.'

1992, the quincentenary year of Columbus' arrival in the Americas, was the catalyst for a number of important debates throughout the Americas. Often these debates were prefaced on whether 1992 was conceived of as the five-hundredth anniversary of the 'discovery' or the 'invasion' of the Americas. The former view was a positive or neutral conception of the process seen as a 'coming together' of two worlds. The latter view was a negative version of the process, characterised as a 'conquest'. The continental 'campaign of resistance' took the latter view and further made explicit links between the negative consequences of the conquest and contemporary 'indigenous, black and popular' struggles. One of the most popular slogans heard at the 1992 campaign of resistance conference was 'Five hundred years on, we're still here!'. This slogan encompassed the notion that the 'discovery' of America initiated a period of struggle that was on going thus forging an explicit link between past and present forms of oppression and resistance. Thus, the issue was politicised to the extent that a positive or neutral view of Columbus' 'arrival' implied support of, or indifference to, current forms of oppression in the Americas.

In addition, both negative and positive views had implications for understandings of contemporary culture and religion. Because Columbus' arrival in the 'new word' initiated the process of Christianisation, the Vatican initially saw the 1992 Santo Domingo CELAM conference as an opportunity to celebrate '500 years of evangelisation'. In fact, the timing of the conference, beginning 12 October 1992, and its location in Santo Domingo were chosen with the Quincentenary in mind.[40] Not surprisingly positive and negative views of the conquest were associated with conservatives and progressives respectively (McDonagh, 1993, pp.9). As I explored in the previous section in my discussion of inculturation, amongst conservatives there was a valorisation of European high culture and a resistance to 'localising' the Church.   In envisaging the elements that comprise 'Christian culture', aspects of indigenous religion received short shrift. Yet, in this respect, the conservatives were only adhering to official church dogma which held that 'syncretism' was not a feature of Catholicism because it was the received word of God and thus not influenced by other religious systems.

However, the indigenous roots of many forms of Latin American popular religion have long been recognised (Paz, 1961; Léon-Portilla, 1980; Boff, 1985, 1986; Carraso,1990). In the following chapter I will explore in more detail examples of the indigenous elements in the Nicaraguan religious festivals of La Purísima and Santo Domingo. However, here I will consider the way in which indigenous religion has been conceived of by the FSLN and the Nicaraguan popular church. I will begin with a brief delineation of the pre-conquest Nicaraguan population configuration.   I will then move to an analysis of the relationship between the FSLN and indigenous culture and religion with particular reference to the controversy over the 'Day of the Race'. Finally I will consider the relationship of the popular church and indigenous religion in Nicaragua.

The popular church and the FSLN, during and after its tenure in government, have focused not only on education about the damage to indigenous life wrought by the Spanish, but also around a widening of the concept of 'conquest' to incorporate a group of oppressors and forms of resistance much more complicated than a simple 'Spanish vs. Indians' opposition would suggest.   '500 Years of Resistance' suggests half a millennium of struggle, initiated by the 'invasion' of the Americas but continuing in the myriad of struggles which centre around race, ethnicity, gender, class, nationhood (i.e., the resistance to imperialism). Here the concept of '500 Years of Resistance' invites a two-fold identification: firstly, a 'reclaiming' of indigenous identity and secondly the forging of a continent-wide unity based on a shared experience of oppression and opposition which transcends differences in race and gender and to some extent class.

The Nicaraguan popular church was actively involved in educational work around the '500 years'.   In the run-up to October 12th, popular church personnel described 'the cross and the sword' as the conquistadors' two most powerful weapons.   Here the popular church explicitly acknowledged the role that the church played in the conquest. In fact, a poster featuring a conquistador figure holding a sword in one hand and a cross and the phrase 'with the cross and the sword' graced the wall of many popular church establishments and was for sale in the Centro Ecumenico Antonio Valdivieso book shop. Thus, the Nicaraguan popular church directly acknowledged and sought to educate laity and CEB members about a shameful chapter in church history. While the hierarchical spoke in positive or neutral terms about the 'discovery' of the Americas, the popular church stressed the notion of 500 years resistance against the conquest. Further, it sought to re-educate people about Nicaragua's pre-conquest history and to instil a sense of pride and identification with indigenous history. This was seen as a way of educating people and giving Christians a point of identification with their ancestors in an effort to mediate against the negative images of indigenous culture.

However, the popular church was in somewhat of a quandary here. For if the introduction of Christianity was so brutal and so integral to the conquest's project, how could a reinvigorated sense of pride in indigenous ancestry be compatible with a continued adherence to Christianity? This very question was raised by the participants in the CEB 500 Years conference that I discussed in chapter four. Most of the people in attendance there were committed CEB activists who saw themselves as adherents to a renovated Catholicism, one which had broken with the traditions of the conquest. In this respect, the popular church's willingness to engage with indigenous religion and to discuss the church's dubious history was unlikely to produce a mass 're-conversion' to indigenous religion. The popular church tried to equalise the 'essential' elements of Christianity and indigenous religion. For example, at the CEB conference indigenous poems and prayers which seemed to express a monotheistic concept of god were compared with Christian thinking. The difficulty was that the emphasis on indigenous culture was selective in that it tended to stress the monotheistic elements of indigenous religion or areas where there was correspondence or convergence between the two; in this sense, the popular church was true to the ecumenical spirit of Vatican II.

In this way, the popular church in its participation in the 500 years of resistance campaign stands in contrast to the more neutral and positive attitude taken by the Right and the Nicaraguan hierarchy. Hence, on the one hand, the Nicaraguan hierarchy tended to follow the Vatican line that 1992 should mark if not a celebration then a recognition of 500 years of Christian evangelisation in the Americas. On the other hand, the popular church was actively involved in organising conferences (such as the CEB conference described in chapter five), discussion groups, masses and commemorative events and in the continent-wide

'Campaign of Resistance' which held its 1992 conference marking the Quincentenary in Managua.

During the time it held state power, the FSLN challenged the underlying assumption of the 'Dia de la raza' or the 'Race day', celebrated every 12 October. They problematised the notion of a benign 'mixing of the races', highlighting the brutality of the conquest. In fact, the revolution was located in a continuum of struggle against oppression incited by the conquest. The FSLN rejected the notion of a neutral 'mixture of races' and with it the 'Creole' spirit of 'Race day' which had been a celebration of 'the white Nicaraguan, the "chele"'. In this way, it reflected a 'deference towards Spanish culture that deep down symbolizes deference towards the US' (Kattenberg, 1991, p.4). To this end, the FSLN discontinued official celebrations marking the day and encouraged an awareness of Nicaragua's indigenous roots (Argüello, 1992). In fact, on the Pacific coast, they received significant support from indigenous communities during the insurrection and the subsequent years of revolutionary government.[41]

Yet one of the bitterest aspects of the contra-revolutionary war was the conflict between the Miskitos, one of the indigenous groups on the Atlantic coast, and the FSLN which resulted initially from mutual misunderstanding and was greatly exacerbated by the bellicose activities of the CIA.[42] The FSLN's attempts to integrate the Atlantic coast into the structures of the revolution reflected a desire to spread the benefits of the educational, health and development projects that were being undertaken. Yet to many Miskitos, these efforts were interpreted as a form of colonialism by the 'Spanish'. The Somoza regime had largely ignored the region, with the exception of its mineral resources, and this 'benign' neglect was seen by many Miskitos as preferable to the Sandinistas' sometimes heavy handed attempts to share the gains of the revolution. Yet, through negotiations between the various ethnic groups on the Atlantic coast and the revolutionary government, the Autonomy Project emerged. This agreement achieved something of a rapprochement between the Miskitos and the revolutionary government. Further, it accorded the people of the Atlantic coast an autonomy, unprecedented elsewhere in the world, which covered not only political affairs but also, significantly, the natural resources of the region.

The widespread support for the Autonomy Project on the Atlantic coast did not translate into electoral success for the FSLN in this region. In both the February 1990 and 1994 elections on the Atlantic coast, the Sandinistas failed to garner a majority of the votes. While the results of the 1990 elections could be put in the context of a general war weariness and lingering distrust of the FSLN, the February 1994 regional elections provided the opportunity to reaffirm an embattled Autonomy Project.

Yet Arnoldo Alemán's neo-Somocista Constitutional Liberal Party (PLC) won a majority of seats at least partially on the strength of vague promises to bring investment into a region which suffers from unemployment rates as high as 90 per cent. The electoral fortunes of the PLC were also boosted by the armed groups that prevented the FSLN from campaigning in rural areas. Despite the loss, the FSLN took some comfort in their second place standing amongst a number of different parties. As the FSLN's political secretary in the South Caribbean region, William Schwartz, maintained: 'This confirms that *Sandinismo* is a true political alternative in the region' (Cuadra, 1994a, p.15).

Thus, given their difficulties on the Atlantic coast, many in the FSLN viewed the election results as a confirmation of the party's successful struggle to develop a meaningful discourse with the people on the Atlantic Coast. Through the Autonomy Project, the FSLN demonstrated a true respect for an acknowledgement of indigenous cultures. Since losing state power in 1990, the FSLN has continued to defend the autonomy project. The FSLN, in common with the popular church, also participated in the Continental Campaign of Resistance Conference. In fact, the organiser of the October 1992 Continental Encounter held in Managua was Myrna Cunningham, a FSLN member of the National Assembly as well as a *costeña* (woman from the Atlantic Coast). In addition, Daniel Ortega, Tomás Borge and Henry Ruiz, all members of the National Directorate, addressed the conference. The participation of prominent members of the FSLN was matched by the involvement of many pro-FSLN grass roots organisations.

In this way, it was evident that the FSLN and the popular church sought to build a link between indigenous identity and a commitment to a socialist project. Thus, elements of indigenous religion and culture were highlighted by both in an effort to foster this identification. The hierarchical church and the Right were content to use a non-identificatory discourse in relation to the 500 years and to rely on the traditional lack of explicit identification with indigenous culture. In making the 500 years an explicit point of discussion and debate, the popular church and the FSLN used indigenous practices and beliefs (selectively) as a tool of organisation and politicisation. Despite these efforts, FSLN/popular church did not generate 'mass' adherence to an indigenous national popular identity. Yet, indigenous practices and beliefs, as they are inscribed in popular religion and culture, served to create a sense of national identity even if these influences were obscured and unacknowledged.

The CEBs have been at the forefront of a synthetic process whereby popular religion and culture, indigenous practices and tradition and revolutionary commitment were synthesised. An example of this process was provided by the July 1994 national CEB mass 'revolutionary mass' to commemorate the fifteenth anniversary of the Sandinista Revolution held in Monimbó, the city of Masaya's indigenous district and an FSLN stronghold. Padre Arnaldo Zenteno, who worked with Managuan CEBs, helped to celebrate a mass where photographs of the 'heroes and martyrs' of the revolution from Masaya were enshrined in special altars or *enramadas* decorated with palm. Similar to the 'All Souls' mass (also co-celebrated by Padre Arnaldo) which I discussed in chapter 4, this fifteenth anniversary mass included the homily-dialogue in which people variously condemned structural adjustment, privatisation, environmental degradation, etc. There was also a 'call and response' in which Padre Arnaldo asked, as he had done at the first anniversary celebration of the San Rafael *olla*, a series of questions to which the congregation answered in unison. Following the mass, traditional instruments of the Monimbeños were played as fifteen *quinceañeras* or girls celebrating their fifteenth birthdays cut a cake into fifteen pieces. Each girl wore a wide sash with a slogan for each of the years of the revolution, for example one young woman wore a sash that read: '1981, year of defence and production'.

Was this a Catholic mass, *quinceañara* fiesta, indigenous encounter, revolutionary rally or resolutely all of these? This was a mixture of politicised traditional and popular religion fully cognisant of its indigenous roots. There the traditional Catholic mass was recast through the popular church and popular culture and religon. The creativity and adaptability of this hybrid form demonstrates that popular religion is not just confined to long-standing practices and traditions, such as those associated with the festival. Further, as I shall explore in the following chapter, these long-standing forms are themselves changing hybrids.

6 Conclusion

In this chapter, I have explored the willingness of the popular church and the FSLN to engage politically and intellectually with indigenous culture and religion. The example of the CEB's fifteenth anniversary celebration of the revolution was a reflection of this willingness but also of the autonomous and adaptive character of popular religion, as expressed in the practice of CEB members. In Nicaragua, popular religion operated outside the control of both the hierarchical and popular churches. However, each sought to exercise influence over popular religion. The hierarchical Catholic church sought to exercise greater control over popular religion in order to 'purify' and 'rationalise' it. The popular church has, at times, seen popular religion as retrograde in its seemingly apolitical expression and has, in many instances, attempted to politicise it.

Within the Catholic church as a whole, the struggle over inculturation produced a bifurcation between 'conservatives' who sought a universal church and 'progressives' who supported a 'local' or 'inculturated' church. Yet a problem for the 'progressives' is that inculturating the church with local traditions and practices may mean introducing discourses and customs that run counter to some of the universalist positions that the progressives may hold, for example, the principle of diversity which underlies inculturation. Thus, it seems that inculturation, even for its most ardent supporters, cannot be absolute. Yet, given the Eurocentric, centralised and hierarchical character of the church, the inculturation debate will remain significant. In Nicaragua, the popular church has engaged in an inculturation process with respect to popular religion. In the context of the 500 years of resistance campaign, the popular church engaged in education about pre-conquest religion and culture and attempted to revalue and incorporate elements of these traditions into a progressive Catholicism.

To the extent that indigenous practices and beliefs form a part of contemporary Nicaraguan popular religion, they serve a function different from the organisational efforts of the FSLN and the popular church. In other words, popular religion is not a wholly 'rational' or systematised system. In Gramscian terms, organised religion is philosophy while popular religion is common sense. As I will explore in my examination of two popular religious festivals in the following chapter, popular religion in Nicaragua has played a part in developing 'moral indentites' in support of the revolution by fostering a 'common sense' understanding and acceptance of socialism. The common sense understanding of the revolution fostered through popular religion enhanced the expressly political linkages between religion and politics made by the popular church and the FSLN. Yet does popular religion, in and of itself, form the basis of revolutionary transformation?

The notion of non-rationalised religion acting as a barrier to capitalist development was at the heart of Weber's *The Protestant Ethic and the Spirit of Capitalism* and has been advanced by other scholars of popular religion (Schneider, 1990). Michael Taussig offers an analysis of pre-capitalist culture that highlights the popular religious dimensions of class struggle in Latin America (Taussig, 1980). He argues that 'irrational' and fetishistic pre-capitalist forms of practice and belief often serve as a form of resistance to capitalist development. While capitalism may seem to be a rational discourse, it has its own fetishistic practices and beliefs particularly around the commodity. Taussig argues that the 'pre-existing cosmology' of peasants and the newly proletarianised allows for a subversion of capitalist development (Taussig, 1980, p.94). But for Taussig, whilst pre-capitalist forms of practice and belief, inculcated in popular religion, offer the opportunity to mediate and disrupt capitalism, they cannot transcend it.

Lancaster provides a critique of Taussig that accepts the negative impact of capitalist encroachment. However, he views Taussig's characterisation of popular religious practices as too hopeless and futile. In particular, Lancaster references examples of popular religious practice which provide the basis for the transcendence of capitalism. Further, he locates the impetus for a popular adherence to socialism in the very popular religious practices that Taussig classifies as merely disruptive. In my view, Taussig's argument is based on the false assumption that popular religion in Latin America cannot fulfil the liberative function that Lancaster ascribes to it. Yet in Nicaragua, where Right and Left struggled on the terrains of both organised and popular religion, the most significant issue was not whether popular religion was 'liberating' or merely 'disruptive' but rather how effectively it was reinterpreted and built upon by blocs competing for hegemony. In the following chapter, I am concerned to look not only at how popular religion is expressed but also how popular religion has been used and engaged with by blocs competing for hegemony. To this end, I will explore the festivals of La Purísima and Santo Domingo, as popular religious manifestations which incorporate not only elements of indigenous religion but also popular cultural practices and aspects of both subversive and 'approved' religious discourses.

Notes

1   The price of this acceptance was the incorporation of authoritarian and hierarchical power structures which fundamentally changed the egalitarian and communal character of early Christianity.

2   Perhaps the strongest exponent of this reactionary weltanschauung was French bishop Marcel Lefebvre who risked open schism with the Vatican over his refusal to "follow the Rome of neo-modernist and neo-Protestant leanings" (quoted in Nowell, Robert, The Guardian, 26 March 1991). In addition to his veneration of the Latin mass, he expressed support for military dictatorships in Chile and Argentina.

3   For a more detailed analysis of the Santa Fe document and the links between evangelical protestant groups, US televangelists and

support for right-wing governments and counter-insurgencies see Lernoux, 1989: 90-91 and 153-164.

4   Although opinion polls always demonstrated that the majority of the American public oposed aid to the Nicaragan contras.

5   Xolotlán means "place of Xolotl". The indigenious god Xolotl was the twin brother of Quetzalcóatl.

6   The Pope said a mass to inaugurate the controversial "Columbus Lighthouse" that had been erected to commemorate the "discovery" of the Americas and to house the alleged skeletal remains of Christopher Columbus. Numerous objections had been raised to the project including the eviction of almost 1000 families from the site and its excessive cost (McDonagh, 1993:11).

7   Masaya, a town of largely indigenous farmers, was an FSLN stronghold during the insurrection. Support was particularly fervent in Monimbó, a Masayan barrio where indigenious cultural traditions were especially strong. Pragmatically and in reference to their indigenous status, the people of Monimbó used bows and arrows to repel the National Guard (Lancaster, 1988:51).

8   The CIA capitalised on Miskito discontent by funding and providing logistical support to armed groups on the Atlantic Coast (Lernoux, 1989:397).

7 Popular religious festivals and popular power: Constructing the 'popular' in Nicaragua

1 Introduction

In this chapter, I will focus on the way in which the religious, mythical, spiritual and common sense dimensions of the popular have been taken up, both consciously and unconsciously, within the context of popular religious festivals and political and religious discourses. I will begin with an exploration of the popular religious festivals of La Purísima and Santo Domingo. In addition to unpicking the remnants of indigenous religion in contemporary popular religious festivals, I also wish to examine how these festivals related to both the 'popular church' and the 'traditional church' and their respective political allies.

I have selected these two festivals because La Purísima is the most widely observed national religious festival and Santo Domingo is the most widely celebrated festival in Managua where I carried out my fieldwork. In addition, I wanted to expand upon Roger Lancaster's exploration of these two festivals in his seminal text, *Thanks to God and the Revolution*. Here he examined La Purísima in light of the revolution and, correspondingly, the revolution in light of popular religious manifestations. However, and central to the project of this book, he did not explore questions of gender in relation to the popular church and popular religion. Furthermore, his analysis did not consider in any detail the indigenous character of these festivals and this is another gap that I will attempt to rectify. Finally, Lancaster's analysis was written before the 1990 change in government. For this reason, I wanted to access any changes that might have occurred in popular religious festivals since this time.

After a consideration of La Purísima and Santo Domingo, I will move to a more general analysis of how political and religious discourses intersect and overlap in attempts to construct hegemonic blocs. I will investigate the 'construction' of the 'popular' in Nicaragua. To this end, I will consider the way that the 'people' and hence the 'popular' are an essential element in the discourses of all the forces competing for hegemony in Nicaragua. In politics and religion, the spectre of the 'popular' looms large and various groupings claim not just to represent the people but also to be the 'people'. These points of unity are posited around sites of identification such as 'faith', 'class', and 'nationality'. I will specifically examine the use of religious imagery in the construction of the popular exploring in detail the FSLN's use not only of existing religious imagery but also the continuities between revolutionary and religious festivals and marches. I will argue that the FSLN, during its it years in insurrection and government, was able to successfully provide not only a rational imperative for socialism but also a truly 'popular' ethical and spiritual framework. In this way, they provide an example to other movements seeking to gain popular support and significantly the means to regain national power.

Throughout this book, I have sought to highlight the interplay between religion and politics. This chapter represents a continuation of this line of analysis but seeks to explore in more detail how, in Nicaragua, competing discourses invoked 'the popular'. Yet the reality was more complex than a simple 'competition' between different forces and their respective attempts to embody the popular. Clearly, for example, economic factors influence the extent to which the popular 'myth' retains its power. For example, the Sandinista popular discourse was exhausted when the unrelenting US aggression eroded the standard of living to a point where a change in government seemed to offer the only way of reversing the downward economic spiral.

Thus, while it is clear that a grasp of the popular is key to achieving hegemony, it is not enough to retain power in the face of a deteriorating economy and a tantalising alternative. Yet the 1990 elections were not lost on economic factors alone. There was a strong appeal to popular religious sensibilities made by the UNO coalition and if the FSLN are to regain power, they will not only need to demonstrate their ability to restore some measure of economic stability to the impoverished populous but also to reconstitute their hold on the popular.

2 La Purísima: Marian devotion and 'shouting'

La Purísima is a popular religious festival unique to Nicaragua. It is initiated with a novena (a nine day period of devotion) to the Virgin Mary that culminates in a celebration on December 7, the eve of the Catholic feast day of the Immaculate Conception. Altars in devotion to the Virgin Mary, many of which have been in families for generations, are set up in homes throughout Nicaragua. These altars are visited throughout the evening by groups of people who 'shout' for their 'gorra', the gifts given out by those who sponsor the altars. The traditional gifts include sugar cane, toasted maize, chicha (a fermented maize drink) and pumpkin with honey (Nuevo Diario, 7 December 1992). Writing in La Prensa, Eloisa Ibarra A. noted that due to the difficult economic situation, rice, beans and soap were replacing or supplementing these traditional gifts. There is an expectation that the maintenance of these altars and the distribution of these gifts will be undertaken by members of the community who are able to afford it. Throughout the evening revellers shout the question, 'Who causes such happiness?' (¿Quien causa tanta alegría?), and the response, The Conception of Mary! (!La Concepción de María!).

For the faithful, La Purísima 'is one of the clearest expressions of popular religiosity and is, in its original sense, a revelation to a poor, humble, suffering and believing people' (Aragón Cárdenas, 1992). Aragón Cárdenas alludes to the common confusion between the Immaculate conception of Mary and the Virginal birth of Jesus. Indeed, many of the people that I spoke with assumed that La Purísima was a celebration of the 'immaculate', i.e. non-sexual conception of Jesus. In fact, the Immaculate Conception was a reference to Mary's lack of original sin and thus her suitability to be Jesus' mother. Mary's 'sinless' state from conception became official church dogma in 1854 by Pope Pius IX's papal bull Ineffabilis Deus. According to Aragón Cárdenas, the notion of Mary's Immaculate Conception was a source of great division between two theological schools, the 'immaculistas' and 'maculistas'. The former supported the concept of the immaculate conception while the latter maintained that Mary was born with original sin.

It is significant that the debate between the immaculistas and the maculistas did not affect the preponderance of Marian devotion in Catholic popular religion. In fact, the papal bull decreeing the Immaculate Conception was not the initiation of Marian piety but an expression of an existing devotion that was reflected in, but not contained by, the discourse of the immaculistas. An 8 December feast of the Immaculate Conception was celebrated as early as the seventh century (Warner, 1985, p.239). In Nicaragua, the earliest written reference to the celebration of La Purísima came in a document dated 7 December 1742, almost one hundred years prior to Pius XI's 1854 bull. Here the Mayor of León, Alfonso Navas, declared that on this day residents of the municipality should clean their patios and put out lights or face a five peso fine. The traditions surrounding La Purísima had their origin in this northern city and it is here that the oldest altars are found (Armando Quintero M.,1992). The festival was initially promoted by members of the Franciscan order (El Tayacán,1987, p.24) in keeping with the keen Marian devotion that has long characterised the order (Warner, 1985, pp.181-184).

Although La Purísima is a singularly Nicaraguan festival, Marian devotion is prevalent throughout Latin America (Rowe and Schelling, 1991). Marian devotion represents a syncretism of aspects of indigenous religions and Catholicism. In this way, reverence to indigenous female divinities was incorporated into a devotion to the Virgin Mary. In Catholicism, the Virgin Mary is the exemplar of both virginity and motherhood. According to Marina Warner, conceptions of the Virgin Mary posit a unique transgression of the opposition between the categories of mother and virgin (Warner,1985). Mary's virginity is remarkable because of her motherhood and in particular her role as the mother of Jesus Christ. As 17th century Mexican mystic and philosopher Sor Juana Inés de la Cruz contended: 'His August Majesty could not fit in the greatness of the Heavens, yet he fitted into the generous cloister of the virginal womb' (Franco, 1989, p.52). In Latin America, the conquest gave the figure of Mary a particular significance. There was a syncretism of Mary and existing indigenous goddesses. Mary was defined in terms of two highly gendered roles, the virgin and the mother, and was singular in that she was simultaneously the standard bearer of both. Officially her sanctity rested on her exemption from original sin, articulated in the doctrine of the Immaculate Conception. Yet clearly her privileged position within popular Catholic discourse was not based solely on this theological distinction.

Mary's virginity referenced not only the presence of a state of 'purity' but also the absence of a state of violation. The indigenous people were the 'victims' of the conquest, yet with victimhood came the self-loathing and the stigma of collaboration. This was particularly strong for women as the mixing of the races was almost always a result of the union of a European man and an indigenous women. In this way, women were responsible for the 'betrayal' of their own race. At the same time, rape and coercion were often the defining features of these unions and thus the violation of indigenous women became a living metaphor of the violation of all indigenous people and their surroundings. Thus there

192

was a conflation of impurity and violation. La Malinche, the much mythologised indigenous woman, who was 'given' to Cortés gaining infamy as his mistress and interpreter (Franco,1989, p.xix). She became the archetypal representative of all that the Virgin Mary was not: a violated, impure woman.

In considering a number of issues surrounding 'the cult of the Immaculate Conception' Sofía Montenegro is concerned to reconcile the veneration of the Virgin Mary with the shabby and often violent treatment that Nicaraguan women receive (Montenegro, 1992). For Montenegro, this 'Virginity in the sky... violation on the earth', is borne out not only by the statistics (estimates place the number of women suffering from physical and verbal abuse as high as seventy per cent) but also in the details of the case of María de Los Angeles. An accompanying article by Mildred Largaespada details the case of this fifteen year old girl who was battered and raped six times by four different men, three of whom were professional baseball players and one of whom was a good friend of the victim. Because the girl had been drinking and socialising with the men prior to the attack, she was accused by many commentators as 'looking for it'.

In Nicaragua, this veneration/violation binary, according to Montenegro, is rooted in the experience of the conquest. My aim is not to establish the veracity of the version of the indigenous people as victims/resisters of the conquest. It has been noted that some indigenous people fought alongside the Spanish against other indigenous people, in this way undermining the concept of a generalised conquest of Latin America. However, my intent is to reflect on how indigenous identity was used as a tool of political motivation and identity formation. To this end, I have sought to examine the discourse around popular religion that took place in Nicaragua during the time of my field work which coincided with the 500th anniversary of Columbus' arrival in the Americas. In this way, Nicaraguan analyses of La Purísima often drew upon the notion the conquest to explain the significance of Marian devotion in Nicaragua.

In Nicaragua, the 'mixing' of indigenous and European peoples began at least partly through the violation of indigenous women by the Spanish conquistadors. Montenegro argues that because of this experience Nicaraguans, 'like the rest of Latin Americas are marked by this original violence and therefore obsessed with a feeling of impurity and stigma by virtue of their birth' (Montenegro,1992). The violated land and culture have been personified as a violated woman 'Mother earth'. Montenegro maintains that the representation of Mary as a European virgin rather than as an indigenous mother has an impact on the way that women are perceived within Nicaragua society. As she holds:

> It is from this perspective that one can better understand the neurotic and ambivalent attitude of the Nicaraguan man before the figure of the mother and therefore before women in general. The maternal cults of today are an expression of the identity of the victim that we all share and therefore they reflect a deep pain: the self-negation that obligated the mestizo population to be ashamed of their colour, their ancestry, and of the culture of their maternal ethnicity (Montenegro, 1992).

In this way, the emphasis on Mary's virginity and the ascription of European characteristics to her created a sense of distance between her and her devotees. Yet as well as the white virgin who bore the son of God, Mary was also the mother who raised Jesus and stood by him through the passion. In this sense the Virgin Mary came to represent the ideal nurturer and comforter. Further, the suffering that she experienced through the loss of her son and the brutality of his execution established her as a supremely empathetic figure. In this way, the Virgin Mary became the comforter of the suffering and the oppressed. In the context of the conquest, solace from a comforting and maternal presence took on heightened significance. Thus, although there was a syncretism between the Virgin Mary and indigenous goddesses, the role of the female divinity in the indigenous cosmology under assault shifted from provider of fertility and fecundity to the giver of consolation and succour. As Octavio Paz maintains:

> The Indian goddesses were goddesses of fecundity, linked to the cosmic rhythms, the vegetative processes and agrarian rites. The Catholic Virgin is also the Mother..., but her principle attribute is not to watch over the fertility of the earth but to provide refuge for the unfortunate. The situation has changed: the worshipers do not try to make sure of their harvests but to find a mother's lap. The Virgin is the consolation of the poor, the shield of the weak, the help of the oppressed (Paz, 1961, p.85).

Sofía Montenegro also notes the difference between the role of indigenous earth goddesses and the figure of the Virgin Mary. (The number of households headed by single or abandoned mothers is over thirty-eight per cent.) For Montenegro, Mary's virginal status signalled the 'amputation' of 'pre-Christian sexuality' from the female divinity (Montenegro, 1992). Lillian Leví, however, is concerned to express the genuine devotion to Mary and like Paz uses the metaphor of the maternal lap. According to Leví, '... all Indian America likes to fill the sky with firecrackers and gunshots in that unique collective ritual,... in order to send pleas to "María Purísima", whose maternal lap protects all our orphaned' (Leví, 1992). In Nicaragua, La Purísima is also referred to as La Gritería or the 'shouting' and Leví highlights the relationship between the different forms of shouting that are central to Nicaraguans. Throughout 7th December vigil, the revellers shout their praises to the Virgin Mary, shout about the happiness that they feel about the 'conception of pure Mary', and through these cries also shout for their gorra or gifts. In addition, Leví contends, Nicaraguans have a history of shouting about injustice and oppression.

Leví's reflections on Nicaraguans and 'shouting' was just one of the ways in which a Nicaraguan national identity was constructed or 'conceived' of through the Virgin Mary. The figure of the Virgin Mary served two seemingly contradictory roles: the intercessor and comforter of the oppressed and the representative of National unity. Newspaper coverage of La Purísima in all three Nicaraguan dailies tended to reinforce the perception of the festival as a point of national unity. The overriding thrust of La Prensa's coverage seemed to be that La Purísima was a tradition that united all Nicaraguans in spite of social class and that the festival would endure in the face of all difficulties. As Armando Quintero wrote: 'Neither war nor earthquakes, nor volcanic eruptions, nor acts of terrorism, nor economic difficulties has been able to dampen the fervour of the Nicaraguan people...' in their celebration of La Purísima (Armando Quintero M.,1992). Here La Purísima is presented as a tradition that has retained its centrality in Nicaraguan life despite all 'natural' and 'man-made' disasters. La Purísima is said to fulfil 'our religious race' (La Prensa, 7 December 1992). Clearly La Prensa is drawing on a notion of national unity as constructed through Marian devotion.[1] In this view, class and racial distinction are unimportant because all Nicaraguans are one in their dedication to the Virgin Mary.

Through feature articles, such as those by Montenegro and Leví, a number of race and gender themes around La Purísima were explored in Barricada. Yet Barricada's coverage did not deviate greatly from the notion of La Purísima as a conduit for national unity. Yet references to 'we Nicaraguans' in Barricada had a more 'popular' intonation. For example, Barricada's list of 'precautions and advice' for a 'safe and enjoyable La Purísima' (Barricada, 7 December 1992) were directed primarily towards those who would be travelling from house to house to collect their 'gorra' rather than towards those who had the means to sponsor a purísima. Evidently Barricada was working with a different version of national unity than La Prensa but one that nevertheless tapped into the pervasive Marian devotion that characterised Nicaraguan popular religion. Nuevo Diario also highlighted the theme of national unity when they stated: 'Nuevo Diario wishes all Nicaraguans a happy day'. In all the three national newspapers there was very little secular or distanced coverage of the festival.

In the informal interviews that I conducted, respondents gave very similar responses when asked what significance the festival of La Purísima had for them. Typical responses were: 'Its a tradition of the Nicaraguan people'; 'It is very traditional for our country'; 'It is part of our religious beliefs'. All the people that I interviewed maintained that La Purísima was the most important Nicaraguan patronal festival. One woman that I interviewed contended: 'La Purísima is the maximo (maximum). It is the most dear of all patronal celebrations. She is the queen of all of Nicaragua.' One reason that La Purísima was accorded such prestige by the respondents was undoubtedly its national standing; unlike other Nicaraguan patronal festivals, La Purísima was celebrated in every region of the country. My status as a foreigner also shaped the answers given by respondents as they were proud to explain the uniquely Nicaraguan character of La Purísima and the way in which it manifested the depth of Nicaraguan Marian devotion.

In fact, everyone seemed to be happy with and involved in La Purísima. Much of the popular discourse around La Purísima was descriptive and 'common sense' rather than analytical and 'philosophical'. In the days leading up to the 7th December vigil, many different organisations and institutions of all political stripes gave purísimas, or parties in which small gifts were given out. This 'pre-vigil' phase had the atmosphere of the lead up to Christmas in the US or England, not least because of the commercial aspects of the festival. Television and newspapers were filled with advertisements for the items necessary to 'give a purísima'. Further, because people from all social classes gave 'purísimas', supermarkets, luxury outlets, small shops, and market stalls alike all did a brisk trade in the weeks preceding the La Purísima vigil. Unlike its more riotous Managuan cousin, the Santo Domingo festival, the La Purísima vigil seemed to arouse no controversy whatsoever.

The tension between 'popular' and 'official' religious discourse was not a contentious issue in the 1992 La Purísima celebrations. The content of popular Marian piety and the manner in which it was expressed in La Purísima were, by and large, sanctioned and in many cases directed by the 'official' church. In contrast to the more freeform Santo Domingo revelry, the La Purísima festival did not threaten the church's authority to control and define the proceedings. Whereas traditional forms of religious devotion seemed to parallel many of the Santo Domingo

196

events, church-based activities and approved forms of religious expression such the 'novena' were integral to the La Purísima celebrations. People fulfilling 'promises' made to Mary for favours received (pagadores de promesas) honoured their obligations through prayer, giving purísima gifts, maintaining the traditional altars and other forms of sanctioned religious expression. The more 'carnal' character of Santo Domingo, as exemplified in the all night drinking and dancing often undertaken by 'pagadores', was not a feature of La Purísima.

During the years of revolutionary government, however, La Purísima was the subject of antagonism between the hierarchical church and the FSLN. When the FSLN held state power, they sponsored La Purísimia events and gave out toys and candy to children. In this way the FSLN used the resources of the state to give the biggest purísima of all. The government sponsored a competition for the best public purísima altar and businesses, organisations and various government ministries participated. This state involvement in the festival of La Purísima was irksome to the hierarchy because it was perceived as a threat to their authority and in particular their influence over popular Marian devotion.[2] The hierarchy protested strongly about what it experienced as FSLN interference in 'Church affairs' (Crahan, 1989, p.87; Dodson and Nuzzi O'Shaughnessy, 1990, p.152). In this way, the controversy around La Purísima was part of a larger conflict between the FSLN/popular church and the Right/hierarchical church blocs over the control of religious imagery. In the next section of this chapter, I will come back to a discussion of the battle over religious and political symbolism. Yet, in looking specifically at La Purísima, it is clear that since the 1990 change in government, there seems to have been less struggle around this festival. This marked decrease in tension or political neutralisation of the festival events seemed to be due primarily to the fact that the FSLN no longer had the resources of the state to give a purísima although Sandinista individuals and organisations continued to host purísimas. For example, Tomás Borge's child development foundation, La Verde Sonrisa, distributed traditional gifts to the children who participated in its projects (Barricada, 6 December 1992).

While the FSLN held state power, the events around La Purísima were often a barometer for tensions between 'church' and 'state'. Yet the festival itself was never remotely subsumed by the these tensions. In assessing the prominence of La Purísima in Nicaraguan society, Stener Ekern calls it the 'only event that unites everybody, everywhere in a single activity' (Ekern, 1987, p.98). However, for Ekern, La Purísma is more of a social than a religious manifestation and he maintains that the organised church is seen mainly as a 'service institution' (Ekern, 1987, p.105). He seems to conflate religious expression and faith with formal religious practice and affiliation. In this way, Ekern equates a lack of formal religious participation with a dearth of religiosity - an equation which leads him to question the authenticity of the religious content of popular religious festivals. Throughout this book, I have striven to demonstrate the diversity of Nicaraguan religious expression, much of which takes place outside of the formal, 'approved' contexts. Further, I would disagree with Ekern's contention that La Purísima was more of a 'social' than a 'religious' manifestation because the distinction is in many ways a false one - in popular religion as in liberation theology, the religious and the social are inextricably bound. In this work, I have focused on the centrality of religious discourses in shaping the 'moral identities' that underpin social action. Despite my objections to some of the assumptions behind Ekern's observations on Nicaraguan popular religion, he does effectively highlight La Purísima's 'everyday' importance on the neighbourhood level. From these observations, however, he incorrectly concludes, in my view, that: 'religion' is a family rather than community activity and thus that religious festivals are more social than religious in character (Ekern, 1987, p.106). He seems to erroneously assume that the social precludes or undermines the spiritual.

I would speculate that the integral role La Purísima played in many Nicaraguan neighbourhoods was the factor which accorded it a relative autonomy from religious and political discourses which attempted to subsume it. Roger Lancaster, in an insightful analysis of Nicaraguan popular religion, argues that La Purísima serves to reinforce a set of values antithetical to capitalist accumulation (Lancaster, 1988). In Nicaraguan neighbourhoods, those with the financial means were expected to 'throw' a Purísima for their neighbours, while those without the necessary resources were free from this social pressure. In this way, Lancaster argues, La Purísima played a 'levelling' role in many neighbourhoods because it served to eliminate or greatly diminish material differences between neighbours. As he explains:

> throwing a Purísima has the effect on those who have been more prosperous during the preceding year of effectively wiping out their savings and eliminating any material advantage that they might have accumulated over their neighbours. The annual celebration of the Virgin Mary's purity, then, is not coincidentally also the approach of a great levelling device that vigorously levels the economic distinctions that have accumulated in a community over the year (Lancaster, 1988, p.53).

Thus, Lancaster argues: '...it is difficult for one to get ahead of one's neighbours in an economic sense if affluence imposes an incumbent obligation to sponsor the community's lavish religious displays' (Lancaster, 1988, p.51). Through this levelling mechanism, La Purísima built neighbourhood cohesion and served to release interclass tension. In this way, La Purísima was redistributive within classes rather than between them.

Since the 1990 change in government and the subsequent increase in poverty and unemployment, the practices around La Purísima have taken on new meaning. As noted earlier, the traditional *gorra* was now being supplemented with or replaced by more critical items such as rice and beans. Thus, it is highly likely that the levelling function of La Purísima will be undercut as throwing a 'purísima' becomes less affordable to those in the 'popular classes'. It this way, it may become a form of charity from the rich to the poor rather than an interclass redistribution of surplus. The situation is further complicated by the return of so many relatively well off exiles since 1990. I would predict that La Purísima, barring an end to the present government's neo-liberal economic policies, will increasingly become more a site for class tension than national unity. Ironically, for all the hierarchy's complaints about FSLN interference in La Purísima, the socio-economic conditions fostered by the revolutionary government, despite the very real constraints of a war economy, actually provided the conditions for a less 'political' celebration of this festival.

3 Santo Domingo: relajo, religion and the observer

A few days prior to the commencement of the festival the route that the procession will take is prepared. This is referred to as the *roza* or clearing. More than an actual clearing, this event seems to be a pre-festival celebration with dancing and general merriment. The festival itself begins on the evening of the 31st of July when crowds gather at Las Sierritas church in the foothills of Managua. After a night of revelry including copious drinking and dancing both inside and outside the church, the statue of Santo Domingo is carried down through the city to the Santo Domingo church where it remains for the next nine days. The statue is transported in a festooned vessel known as the boat (*el barco*). Those that carry the statue are known as carriers (cargadores) and the crowd that surrounds the statue in the procession is referred to as the vigil (la vela).

The festivities continue once Santo Domingo reaches his temporary home. For the nine days that Santo Domingo is in residence, there is a fairground atmosphere both inside and outside the church. There are a number of masses and special religious services that are performed in the Santo Domingo church during this time frame. On the 10th of August, the statue is returned to the Sierritas church where it rests until the next year. The procession that accompanies the statue on its journey between the two churches, called 'la traída' or 'the bringing', is a loud, boisterous and colourful celebration on the move. In 1992, more than fifty thousand people accompanied the statue on its nine kilometre journey between the two churches (Trejos Ubau, 1992). The revelry and boisterousness of the celebrants on their journey to Managua was not matched in the calmer return procession to the Sierritas church (Talavera,1992). The people that I spoke with maintained that the return journey was usually more contained than the commencing excursion.

Unlike La Purísima, Santo Domingo was much less under the control of the church. This was manifest, not only in the event itself, but also in the history of the statue. The origins of the small Santo Domingo statue are obscure. In one version, the statue was found in 1811 by a local woodcutter. In another rendition, the statue was found in a puddle of muddy water. According to La Prensa the present day festivities date from 1926 when they were initiated by Santos Ocampo. The festival continued until 1961, when church officials, decrying their lack of control over the proceedings, decided to end Santo Domingo's yearly pilgrimage and decreed that it was to remain in the Las Sierritas church. Lisímaco Chávez6 stole the statue from the Las Sierretas church and brought it to Managua despite the prohibition. For his pains he was excommunicated. Notwithstanding his status in the Catholic church, Chávez continued in his role as unofficial 'jefe' or boss of the proceedings ever since.

While La Purísima was focused on innumerable shrines, Santo Domingo was centred around a small statue and its journey from one end of Managua to the other. In the former, there were a plethora of images of the Virgin Mary, albeit almost all depicting her as a light skinned European woman; no particular image had been invested as the sole representative of Mary as was the case with the tiny statue of Santo Domingo. This sacred identification is often a feature of the 'cult of saints' whereby saints take on a sanctity above and beyond their designated role as intercessors between God and the faithful. Writing about Latin American popular religion, Cristián Parker asserts that the icon itself serves as a 'concrete symbol of a transcendent reality' and serves as a 'catalyst of emotions and desires in a precise time-space [the patronal festival]' (Parker, 1993, p.196).

Yet in my observations, the Santo Domingo statue seemed to be invested with sacredness that went beyond the notion of a 'concrete symbol'. In effect, the statue not only represented Santo Domingo but also in a very real sense embodied him, in both a 'sacred' and a 'profane' sense. In terms of its status as a sacred incarnation, it was clear that the statue itself was considered sacrosanct as many participants were keen to be as close as possible to it during the procession. For the days when the statue was temporarily at rest in the Santo Domingo church, religious services held in the patron's honour were largely ignored. The centre of attraction was the statue which sat in the corner of the church. Here, there were long queues of parents and children waiting to touch the glass casing around the statue. This popular emphasis on the statue itself reflected not only its accorded sanctity, but also the fact that actual control over the statue and its movement was ambiguous and contested. Meanwhile, the official church services were squarely under the control of the church who sought to curb the festival's excesses.

Thus, the devotion to the statue reflected not only a genuine sanctification of the statue itself but also demonstrated both an intentional, as well as an unconscious, repudiation of the official church's attempts to exercise greater control over the festival, in particular the drinking, dancing and general 'party' atmosphere. It is this notion of the 'sacred in aid of the profane' that characterised the Santo Domingo festivities. In terms of the statue's profane embodiment, there was an intimacy and familiarity between the statue and the faithful that manifested itself in the popular perception of Santo Domingo as 'one of us'. In conversation and newspaper stories alike, the statue was referred to by the diminutive nickname 'Minguito'. During the festival Barricada nominated him one of the 'people of the week' (Barricada, 1 August 1992).[3]

This investiture of sacredness in an icon is a feature of popular religion that is not restricted to Nicaragua or to Latin America. Throughout the world, popular Catholic festivals and rituals have often centred around a particular image of a saint that has taken on a sacred character for its devotees (Behar, 1990; Badone, 1990; Taylor, 1990; Schneider,1990; Parker, 1993). In analysing contemporary popular religious practices and beliefs in rural Spain, Ruth Behar notes the resistance of villagers to post-Vatican II attempts to 'desancitify' images and icons and to 'supplant the pantheon of saints'. Despite its rational and modernising thrust, the church's attempts to demystify concrete representations of saints and to downplay patronal devotion is continuous with a centuries long battle waged by the church against 'idolatry' (Behar, 1990, pp.79-81). However, while the struggle over the meaning of icons is not unique to the Santo Domingo festival, Nicaragua's particular history of colonisation is significant in the sanctity accorded to 'Minguito'. In the next chapter, I will examine the issue of syncretism in more detail.

However, it is important to indicate here the particular significance of the syncretism between indigenous religion and Catholicism for the Santo Domingo icon and the festival that surrounds it. With particular reference to saints within Nicaraguan popular religion, it is significant that early evangelisers in Meso-America encouraged the process of syncretism through their use of the Nahuatl word ixitla to mean 'saint'. However, in Nahuatl ixitla indicates 'effective presence and immanence' (Rowe and Schelling, 1991, p.69) rather than merely intercessor or mediator as Catholic dogma stipulates.

The Santo Domingo festival itself is a syncretism of elements of indigenous culture, traditional Catholicism and mass cultural images. Most of the participants in the procession wore some type of costume; the most prevalent costumes were devils/'Hollywood Indians', women in embroidered dresses and flowers in their hair and cows. There was also a woman giant (La Gigantona) usually portrayed by a man on stilts. In this way, the popular religious festival is 'faithful only to itself' (Lancaster, 1988, p.203).

The devil/Indian is one of the symbolically richest characters in the cast of Santo Domingo characters. This figure simultaneously portrays the devil and an indigenous person prior to the conquest. The costume usually consists of a feathered head-dress, a stick/spear and a complete body coating of thick black motor oil. The origins and meanings of this costume are somewhat obscure. The equation of the indigenous person and the devil is a complicated one. Although the conflation initially seems retrograde the character is usually presented as more mischievous than evil. At times it seemed that the devil/Indian was not a confirmation of Spanish prejudices but rather the embodiment of their worst nightmare: a proud and emboldened opponent with access to magical powers. In the Santo Domingo procession, the devil/Indian, not the Spanish conquistador, has the power. Further, one Managuan told me that the greasing was also meant to symbolise the African slaves who were brought to Nicaragua. From this costume emerged the practice of 'greasing', i.e. smearing motor oil on bystanders or other participants. 'Greasing' someone in the 'audience', particularly someone perceived as 'privileged', was a way of taking them down a few pegs. 'Tarring' them, as it were, with the brush of slavery. The tradition of 'greasing' grew out of the copious quantities of oil that were used in creating the devil/Indian costume.

Standing at the sidelines of the traída procession, I experienced this 'greasing' first hand. A group of four or five youths, a couple of which were completely covered with grease saw a companion and myself and cried ¡cheles! (in this instance white foreigners). They laughed and smeared our heads, face, and clothing with 'grease' which was in fact thick black motor oil. This was done in 'fun' and one of the young men urged us to dance with him. However there was an air of intimidation to the whole process. Other people in the crowd and on the side lines repeatedly assured us that there was no need to worry because the grease would wash out. Walking away from the procession many people laughed, pointed and smiled; my 'painting', neither the total body look nor the smudges that were more the norm, was quite noticeable.

Although all of my informal interview subjects maintained that La Purísima inspires more genuine devotion and less drunken merriment than Santo Domingo, it was also clear that acts of extreme religious fervour were often more commonly witnessed in conjunction with the latter. The more extreme character of this devotion can be attributed at least partially to the incarnate character of the Santo Domingo icon. In keeping with the sacred/profane dichotomy of perceptions of the icon and of the festival that surrounds it, the promises or promesas made to Santo Domingo were often paid through either extreme piety or extreme indulgence. Thus, on the one hand, some of these 'promise fulfilers' (*pagadores de promesas*) walked a part of Santo Domingo's journey on their knees. In 1992, for example, Josefa Delgado accompanied the procession returning Santo Domingo to the Sierritas for five blocks on her knees. She was 'paying her promise' to Santo Domingo in order to 'give him thanks' for curing an infection in her knees (Talavera,1992). On the other hand, some promise fulfilers kept their promise to dance through the night.

In 1992, the Santo Domingo festivities marched 'to the style of the present mayor Arnoldo Alemán'. Under Alemán's instructions, the route of the procession was altered for the first time so that it bypassed the San Judas barrio. This was an affront, not only to the residents of San Judas, but was also meant as a challenge to the authority of Sandinista supporter Chávez. According to Chávez, 'the traditions of the popular festival of Santo Domingo are beginning to disappear because they are being used for political ends'. Because of this conflict with Alemán, Chávez remarked that he was considering giving up his participation (*colgar los guantes*) although in the end he did retain his central role in the proceedings (Nuevo Diario, 31 July 1992).

The Jesuit priest Jesús Hergueta who had occupied the position of steward (mayordomo) of the festivities resigned just prior to the commencement of the festival in 1992. He blamed the change of route as the primary reason for his decision. The residents of San Judas had already purchased fireworks and made preparations for the procession. It was unfair, Hergueta argued, that the route should be changed. Hergueta and Chávez had worked closely together in the past and one festival organiser speculated that this relationship was at the root of the discord between Alemán and Hergueta (Barricada, 27 July 1992). Whatever the full dimensions of the internal wrangling may have been, it was clear that the conflict over the route of the procession and Alemán's eventual triumph in the matter were a reflection of the changed political situation in Managua. Alemán used his control of the city's budget in order to condition funding of the fiesta on the fulfilment of his conditions. Erken contends that the patron/client relationship is a central part of Nicaraguan social and political life. In the case of the dispute between Alemán and those that objected to the changing of the route, some of the festival organisers supported or did not challenge Alemán because he 'would have withdrawn the economic support of the fiesta (Barricada, 27 July 1992). Here the power of the office and the risk to those who challenged it was clearly recognised.

As with La Purísima, the commerce element of the festival was of primary importance. On 1st August 1992, Barricada led with the story 'War of the Beers'. Contrary to his stated commitment to the free market, Managua's mayor Arnoldo Alemán gave Toña, the beer manufacturer owned by the family of Violeta Chamorro, the exclusive right to set up stands and sell beer outside of the Sierritas church and the Santo Domingo church. At the same time La Victoria, the state owned beer company claimed to have paid for the same exclusivity. Eventually an agreement was reached whereby both beers were freely available during the festival and the significance of the contradictions and attempted fraud of the mayor and his functionaries faded. However, the competition between the two beer companies, equalled only by the Coke/Pepsi rivalry, was evident throughout the festival in the form of banners and copious loudspeaker announcements extolling the virtues of one beverage or the other.

Small groups danced around cars with loud speakers blaring out music interspersed with advertisements for a particular product. The 'cows' which danced in the parade often had advertisements across the contraptions which supported their horns. There were a number of vendors selling fireworks, straw hats, t-shirts with likenesses of Santo Domingo on them, crucifixes, and other religious mementoes. In addition, a variety of food and drink was on offer - from a humble plastic bag full of water to an elaborate meal wrapped in banana leaves. I observed a remarkably gendered division of labour which was most extreme in the case of a family of vendors. A woman was packing up a cart with a few small children and the items that she had been selling. The cart was the type that is usually hitched to a horse, however, in this instance it was the woman who pulled the cart. Her male companion made no effort to help with either the packing or pulling of the heavy

204

cart. In general there seemed to be a disproportionate share of female vendors, particularly with respect to food items.

In my observations of the Santo Domingo festival, it was through their economic activities that women were most efficacious. Although women were responsible for 'dressing' the saint and 'perfuming' his special pedestal (*peaña*), they were largely excluded from positions of power in the organisation and administration of the festival. The office of 'pretty Indian' (*la bonita india*), in effect a beauty queen, was the most senior position held by a woman. In contrast, in the La Purísima festival, the numerous home based shrines, the purísima parties and the distribution of gorra are usually organised by women. Given the 'free for all' that the festival usually becomes, this lack of integration into the festival's organisational structure, would not necessarily indicate or limit female participation. However, women clearly did not participate to the same degree as men in some of the defining (profane) activities of the festival.

There are a number of factors that underlie this difference. Firstly, given the highly gendered division of labour, women are significantly less 'free' to engage in all night drinking and dancing. Secondly, traditional constructions of femininity limit both women's ability to participate or engage in behaviour which contravenes these conventions (i.e. physical aggression, public drunkenness, etc.). Thirdly, and related to the above two factors, many women simply do not want to fully participate in the Santo Domingo festivities. Most of the women that I spoke with expressed reservations about the festival - generally that it was 'out of control', potentially dangerous and not indicative of genuine religious devotion. As one woman that I spoke with maintained: 'It is better to celebrate it inside the church rather than outside. In the streets there is too much violence. There is more devotion (inside the church). It is more Christian inside the church.'

Thus, in broad strokes it would seem that La Purísima is a 'female' festival while Santo Domingo is a 'masculine' celebration. This distinction would also follow Ekern's development of the male-street/female-home dichotomy whereby the 'street' was the male sphere of authority while the home was the female domain (Ekern, 1987, p.98). Yet, this distinction is somewhat simplistic because it was evident from my observations and informal interviews that the 'male' elements of the Santo Domingo festivities alienated not only women but also men who voiced many of same objections as the women. A number of the men with whom I spoke dismissed the activities around the processions and simply chose to stay away. The male/female distinction is further complicated by the fact that a number of women did participate actively in the festival, albeit usually in a more relaxed fashion. A good example of this distinction was the difference between the cows portrayed by men and by women. The costume consisted of a circular rigging held up by a strap around the neck. Attached to the apparatus were two bull horns which rested at the level of the genitals. The cow role was played by both men and women who danced on their own and with other revellers. One male cow that I observed 'charged' those around him, encouraging them to play the role of the matador. He even playfully pinned a police officer to the side of his vehicle. The female cow did not engage in this mock fighting, preferring to dance on her own or with willing partners.

From my observations, it was clear that most people, both male and female, were primarily observers rather than participants in the Santo Domingo festivities. Much of the literature detailing popular religious festivals tends to concentrate on the attitudes and experiences of active participants (Badone, 1990; Lancaster, 1988, 1992; Parker, 1993). However, the riotous, 'male' character of Santo Domingo meant that the majority of the people seemed to be observers rather than full participants in the festivities. Clearly, observing can be a form of participation and the lines between the two, particularly in the popular celebrations, were often blurred. Often those on the side lines were smeared with grease and thus were drawn into more active participation. Sometimes those on the periphery had brought small children in costume but held them back so that they would not be jostled or lost in the crowd. I spoke with a former soldier who said that he did not attend the popular celebration at all for fear of violent reprisals from emboldened right-wingers. Indeed, the large jostling crowd that comprised the vela had a markedly different feel than that of other crowded public events that I attended - there was more threat of violence and more actual violence. During the ten days of the festival, it was forbidden to carry arms. This was a measure designed to limit intentional injury as well as accidental injury that might accompany the firing of live ammunition into the air that had become something of a Santo Domingo tradition. The tradition of setting alight fireworks that sounded ominously like gun shots continued unabated.

Roger Lancaster describes Santo Domingo as a 'turning upside down' of normal social relations. This view of popular religious festivals is echoed by Parker who maintains that they constitute 'the introduction of an extraordinary time-space' that introduces 'a means of expressing freely the contradiction of discontinuity, the grotesque and the spontaneous' (Parker, 1993, p.190). The term that Nicaraguans use to describe this is un relajo [4] It is utilised loosely but conveys the sense of breaking free from every day or commonsense moral and, at times, political, conventions. It also implies a group context - a lone individual engages in a transgression; a group has un relajo. In speaking revolution, many Nicaraguans say that the Sandinistas had a 'big rela Sometimes the speaker uses the term critically, other times approvingly The Santo Domingo festival was considered a relajo because of its transgression of accepted notions of propriety; here anything could happen. People ate, drank and danced continuously throughout the all night vigils and processions which marked the beginning and the end of the festival.

For Lancaster, participation was turning the world upside down. In my observations, there were many more people on the side lines and partial participants than those who had surrendered themselves completely to the relajo. In a sense this partial participation could be described as 'audience participation'. Those on the sidelines generally entered the fray with a sense of guardedness. One person lowered a hose down to the participants so that they could drink and cool themselves down. Many people danced and clapped on the sidelines. Sometimes the parade moved between participation and spectacle.

While the Santo Domingo festival was 'opened' and 'closed' by large and boisterous processions through Managua, it was also framed by more middle and upper-class equestrian parades. The parades them-selves, besides a show of horses and equestrian skill, featured a number of large lorries sponsored by various companies in which bands played and people danced. There were also a number of pick-up trucks with groups in the back waving to the crowd. Most of the people on these lorries and pick-up trucks looked relatively young (late teens to early twenties) and seemed to have better quality clothes and lighter skin than the participants in the processions. There were none of the extremes of the procession: no costumes, no exceptional acts of religious devotion, and certainly no grease. Instead of the relajo that characterised the processions, the parades were relatively tranquil; the participants observed traffic signals and there was a negligible police presence - a total contrast to the popular processions.

This was in marked contrast to the equestrian parade where there was a marked distinction between the performers (those with access to horses, pick-up trucks and connections to the companies sponsoring the floats) and those who watched in a very passive way. In the equestrian parades, the middle and upper middle classes rode horses and danced on the truck floats in contrast to their conspicuous absence from the popular celebrations either as participants or observers. Here, the upper and middle classes were the participants because they had the horses, the pick-up trucks and the corporate connections - everyone else watched.   There was little of the fluidity between participant and observer that characterised the processions. Fittingly, given the social

207

articipants the most common costume in the equestrian
e 'cowboy' rather than the 'Indian'.

on sense' of Nicaraguan popular religion: class, gender
m

er persuasively locates popular religion as the normative
basis for socialist transformation. An issue which he does not consider,
however, is how values which deviate from these 'norms' can be
incorporated into a socialist programme. I would concur that popular
religious 'common sense' can be a conduit for social transformation and
I will explore this notion in greater detail in the following section.
However, here, it is of primary importance to examine the lack of a
feminist sensibility in the 'common sense' which underlies popular
adherence to socialism and to examine the possibility of such an
incorporation. It is a difficult issue because many of the factors which
build cohesion within a community can also serve to undermine
diversity and suppress demands for change that do not reference the
'timeless time'. Three key factors, integral to the 'common sense' of
Nicaraguan popular religion, militate against just such a unity: the 'class'
character of the solidarity constructed through popular religion;
traditional notions of 'womanhood' and women's roles contained within
popular religious practices and beliefs; and the 'nationalistic' character
of many Nicaraguan popular religious practices.

Firstly, the linkage between the levelling acted out in popular religious
practices and the levelling project of socialism focuses the locus of
popular identification and praxis on 'class'. This 'class' component, on
the one hand, is the key to popular religion's power to 'lay the ground
work' (Lancaster, 1988, p.54) for the acceptance of socialism. At the
same time, political projects constructed around class have often been
notoriously remiss in their ability or willingness to concretely prioritise
issues of gender, race and sexuality. Often the resolution of 'non-class'
issues is linked to an a priori socialist transformation of society; in this
way, it is posited that all 'non-class' issues will be resolved after, if not
through, the introduction of socialism. Here issues of gender, race and
sexuality become subordinated to the issue of class. Throughout this
book I have attempted to develop an analysis of *Sandinismo* that
highlights its complexity, creativity, and flexibility. However, it is clear
that there was a strand of *Sandinismo* that reinforced this 'class bias' and
rendered women's strategic gender interests 'petty bourgeois'.[5]

Secondly, and particularly in relation to La Purísima, Nicaraguan
popular religion is infused with a particular model of 'womanhood'. As

noted earlier, Sofía Montenegro has highlighted the contradictions of this model both in its inculcation in popular religious beliefs and practices and in the resulting 'veneration/violation' dichotomy that she describes (Montenegro,1992). Thus, there are particular attitudes and beliefs proffered within popular religion that undermine the status of women. The church's sexism has been challenged by some liberation theologians (mostly women and Leonardo Boff, more or less alone amongst prominent male liberation theologians) often through biblical references that demonstrate strength and courage manifested by women in defence of their families and communities. Yet this discourse takes place outside of the realm of popular religion; it is conducted in the domain of 'philosophy' rather than 'common sense'. Furthermore, as I argued in chapter 2, many strategic gender interests are never addressed within the church because to do so would contradict official church teachings on issues such as abortion and contraception.

Thirdly, Nicaraguan popular religion is uniquely 'Nicaraguan' and in this way it serves to reinforce and transmit patriotic and nationalistic impulses. This nationalism, as expressed in the revolutionary slogan *'patria libre o morir'* (free country or death), was a key component of *Sandinismo* . Given the level of US aggression against Nicaragua, anti-imperialism was the inevitable corollary of nationalism. 'Feminism', or the articulation of 'strategic gender interests', was erroneously considered as a 'foreign' or 'imported' discourse. In this way, women who sought to address strategic gender interests were often greeted with a resistance based on a defence of Nicaraguan 'traditions' and a rejection of a 'foreign' discourses. As Maxine Molyneux contends: 'there is a tendency for nationalist movements to reject it [feminism] in the name of their own national authenticity' (Molyneux, 1981, p.4). Clearly, Nicaraguan nationalism is not reproduced solely through popular religious practices and beliefs. However, they are one of the underlying supports for Nicaraguan nationalism because they shape and reinforce a particular version of 'Nicaraguaness'.

These three elements contained within Nicaraguan popular religion - a 'class' orientation; traditional notions of 'womanhood' and women's roles; and a nationalist bent - have served both to underlie a 'revolutionary class identity' as well as to limit the ability of women to identify and peruse strategic gender interests. Although normative constructions of womanhood (particularly notions of passivity and self-sacrifice) almost invariably constrain the formulation and expression of strategic gender interests, issues of class and national identity offer more scope for adaptation and recasting in the light of a feminist agenda. Gramsci contended that the 'philosophy of praxis', or Marxism, must build upon 'common sense' thus 'renovating and making "critical" an already existing activity' (Gramsci, 1971, p.331). Yet in teasing out these underlying elements of Nicaraguan popular religion, it is important to stress that the idea of renovating common sense discourses, particularly those around popular religion, is not straightforward. As Lancaster maintains: 'To underscore the political content of popular religion is to negate the form of that practice and to transform it into something else, whereby it loses its appeal as popular religion' (Lancaster, 1988, p.48).

Lancaster presents popular religion as the base on which both the FSLN and the popular church built the often intersecting and over-lapping discourses of *Sandinismo* and liberation theology. In this way, the values and identities generated through popular religious practices and beliefs have, in 'political' terms, their greatest significance outside the discourse of popular religion. Yet the values and beliefs inculcated through popular religion were often under-recognised by the FSLN and the popular church who sought to make it more 'critical' and 'politically' focused. Yet in attempting to recast popular religion itself, they failed to see the politics of popular religion, 'a politics that operates on a subtle unselfconscious and metaphoric level' (Lancaster, 1988, p.48). However, Lancaster does not consider how to build upon popular religion, and in particular the awareness around class and national identity that it constructs, whilst at the same time challenging some of the retrograde applications of these values. Clearly, from a feminist perspective, attempts to build on popular religion must be accompanied by a corollary vision that seeks to challenge some of the common sense beliefs and practices that limit strategic gender interests. However, challenging some of the norms of popular religion's 'timeless time', in particular those around the reproductive sphere, is most effectively done outside of the sphere of popular religion itself. In this way changes in the larger society can and will give rise to changes in popular religious practices and beliefs.

Further, although strategic gender interests are not generally supported by popular religious practices and beliefs, practical gender interests often are. Women exercise a high level of control over popular religious festivals. In La Purísima, women are generally responsible for maintaining the shrines of the Virgin Mary and organising the customary gift giving and parties. Images of female passivity and self-sacrifice are often accompanied by images of female agency and strength. These contradictions are found within the popular religious discourse around the Virgin Mary. While Mary represents idealised notions of purity and passivity, she is also seen as a very powerful figure capable of dramatic and decisive interventions into the lives of the faithful.

In recent years, Marian devotion has been associated with a conservative anti-secular movement within the Catholic church which has placed itself in opposition to Liberation theology (Perry and Echeverría, 1988, p.274). In Nicaragua, both Right and Left have drawn upon religious and religiously imbued secular imagery in an attempt to create a compelling national popular myth. The convergence of Marian devotion and right-wing politics is a phenomenon not limited to Nicaragua. Pope John Paul II pursued a policy of Marian devotion which linked it to an anti-liberation theology stance. Despite this strategy and use of popular religious symbolism, by both the Right and the Left in Nicaragua, Marian imagery has not been definitively incorporated into any particular political programme.

5 Constructing the popular in Nicaragua

We struggle for bread but also for beauty (J. Mariátegui).

The importance of culture in the triumph and the subsequent shaping of the revolution in Nicaragua was seminal. The massive popular support that the FSLN were able to garner was not due simply to the desire to redress economic inequalities. The FSLN also managed to create a national 'myth' which enabled them to capture the public imaginations as well as their souls. The revolution, with its veneration of the guerrilla fighter, the chavalos, presented a vision of personal transformation. Here Ché Guevara's notion of the 'New Man'[6] figures prominently. This notion of personal transformation and sacrifice echoes the crucifixion and resurrection of Jesus Christ, a powerful image in an overwhelmingly Catholic country.

The revolution did not just use popular culture - it was popular culture. This sense of leading the people and being the people was a dialectic tension which fuelled the insurrection and the subsequent years of revolutionary government. Marx argued in the German Ideology that 'The class that has material power also has spiritual power' (Girardi, 1987, p.172). This competition for 'spiritual power' was an important part of the hegemonic and counter-hegemonic struggles that saw both the Left and the Right dipping into the pool of religious and religiously inspired secular imagery.

In this section, I will explore how the popular has been constructed in Nicaragua through the use of religious and 'secular-religious' imagery. I will firstly explore the FSLN's use of religious imagery in the construction of their successful hegemonic bloc. I will secondly examine the FSLN's creation of a 'secular-religious' imagery through the compelling symbolic representations of sacrifice, redemption and personal transformation. The FSLN/Popular Church bloc was not the only grouping to draw upon popular religious imagery. The Right/hierarchical church was also active on this terrain. I will thus thirdly consider the attempts of the hierarchy to create a counter-hegemonic project through the use of popular religious imagery. Since the 1990 change in government, the two blocs have been unable to retain the unity that they achieved during the period in which the FSLN held state power.

The confluence between the projects of the FSLN and the popular church have been considered in Chapters three and four. Here I will concentrate on the way in which there was an intermingling of Sandinista and Christian imagery which was fostered by both the FSLN and the popular church. In many ways, the popular church's attempts to make existing religious practices and beliefs more 'popular' was a political act in support of the revolution. The reference in the Nicaraguan Popular Mass to Jesus being 'born of our people' is a good example of how the issue of the 'popular' itself galvanised such controversy. Furthermore, in this and other services and publications of the popular church, Jesus Christ was addressed in the familiar Nicaraguan 'vos' rather than the more formal 'usted'. In placing Jesus literally in the realm of the popular by highlighting his humble and human origins and referring to him in a familiar rather than a formal sense, the popular church hit a nerve in the hierarchical church, as well as the Vatican, who objected to this emphasis on Jesus' popular roots. This construction of Jesus and the 'official' reaction to it reflected each side's vision of the church.

While Tomás Borge claimed that there was no contradiction between the revolution and Christianity, Ernesto Cardenal often seemed to imply that there was in fact no difference between the two. While this lack of differentiation did not represent the entire panoply of thinking within the popular church, there was a solid consensus around the centrality of the revolution to the project of the popular church. In this way, the popular church often mixed religious symbolism with Sandinista imagery. As part of a solemn oration in a mass of gratitude held a few days after the triumph of the revolution, the congregation gave thanks to God for the revolution. The oration stated: 'The red and black banners are undulating throughout our free territory. They are raised today to give thanks to You, Father and Liberator' (El Tayacán, 1987, p.56). Here, for the popular church, the red and black flag of the FSLN was being flown as a form of homage and worship.

Humberto Belli, fervent anti-Sandinista in exile and minister of Education in the Chamorro government, voiced the objections of the

212

Right and the hierarchy to this mixture of religious and political symbolism. In describing the actions of the popular church, he contended:

> the revolutionary Christians were putting into practice the FSLN's call to re-invest religious symbols and celebrations with new revolutionary meanings...In the liberation theology being preached in the country, the revolutionary Christians identified sin with capitalism; Satan with the bourgeoisie and US imperialism; salvation, or deliverance from sin with revolution; the Messiah - Jesus being a revolutionary zealot - with the vanguard or the revolutionary party; the kingdom of God with revolutionary socialism. All this was the Marxist-Leninist world view and eschatology;only the terms changed (Belli, 1985, p.160).

While many revolutionary Christians rejected the suggestion that they held a 'Marxist-Leninist' paradigm, they openly strove to make connections between their spirituality and their commitment to the revolution. In this way, rather than on the instructions of the FSLN, revolutionary Christians reinvested religious symbols with revolutionary meanings. For the popular church, this reinvestment of religious symbols was not incompatible with their 'essential' meanings. Indeed, liberation theology holds that the struggle against oppression has always been at the core of Christianity and that Christ's message was fundamentally a liberating one.

In this case, Belli's consternation was aimed at the revolutionary Christians whom he implied were being manipulated to do the FSLN's bidding. However, what angered the Right and the hierarchical church even more was the manner in which the FSLN itself drew upon popular religious imagery in building support for the revolution. In many ways the distinction between the FSLN's usage of religious symbolism and that undertaken by the popular church was a false one because the two often worked in tandem. Furthermore, there was a genuinely popular association between Christian and revolutionary symbolism that was not manufactured by either the FSLN or the popular church. In an extremely religious country, it was not surprising that many Nicaraguans saw revolutionary struggles through a filter of religious imagery.

The FSLN's use of religious imagery was both calculated and unconscious. In addressing a crowd with the words 'People of Sandino! People of Christ!' (Ormrod, 1988, p.7), Daniel Ortega could hardly fail to appreciate the emotive power of such a juxtaposition. In this construction, both Sandino and Christ are posited as figures who symbolise Nicaraguan identity. In this way there was an equivalence between the figures of Christ and Sandino. The Right and the hierarchy were also concerned by what they interpreted as a substitution of the figure of Sandino for that of Christ. For example, during the 2nd January procession of Christ the King, people chanted 'Christ today! Christ Yesterday! Christ forever!' The FSLN utilised this slogan replacing Christ with Sandino (Ekern, 1987, p. 175). The Right responded to this adaptation by adopting the original formulation as something of a rallying cry and a pointed snub to the notion of Christian/FSLN unity (Dodson and Nuzzi O'Shaughnessy, 1990, p.149). This slogan was used in both religious and political contexts highlighting the power of religious symbolism for both the Right and the Left.

The syncretism of Christianity and *Sandinismo* was particularly irksome to the hierarchy and the Right whose claims of religious persecution were seriously undercut not only by the significant participation of Christians in the revolution but also by the religious language employed by the supposedly godless FSLN. The genuine receptiveness of the FSLN to religious imagery demonstrates the degree of the FSLN's inculturation and this is where the power of *Sandinismo* resided. The Peruvian Marxist José Carlos Mariátegui contended that socialist revolution must emerge from the particularities of a national culture (Rowe and Schelling, 1991, pp.154-157; Burbach and Nuñéz, 1987, pp. 21-22). He argued that the impetus for change must arise from the 'force of myth' which includes elements of transcendence, a 'need for the infinite', and offers a deep sense of personhood or identity. While identifying the religious imperative of this myth, he argued that 'the religious motives have shifted from heaven to earth' (Rowe and Schelling, 1991, p.155). Writing in the 1920's, he anticipated the power of liberation theology's brew of utopian myth (creating the kingdom of God on earth) and praxis.

Gramsci also stressed the importance of a mythical language in creating the conditions for social transformation. While he condemned the Catholic church, he saw in the utopian impulses of primitive Christianity one of history's greatest 'moral and intellectual reforms' (Gramsci in Girardi, 1987, p.228). Yet the role that the Church played in the maintenance of bourgeois hegemony blinded Gramsci to the possibility that Catholicism could ever be involved in the creation of a utopian myth to challenge the status quo. For him, Catholicism 'insists on putting the cause of evil in the individual man himself, or in other words it conceives of man as a defined and limited individual' (Gramsci, 1971, p. 352).

At the same time, Gramsci's notions of common sense and faith recognised the impossibility of social change without reference to popular religious sensibilities. For Gramsci, it was only through faith that social transformation was possible. He maintained that 'in the masses, as such, philosophy can only be experienced as a faith' (Gramsci, 1971;339). In this way, it is not necessary for the 'masses' to have an intellectual grasp of all the finer points of Marxist theory. Gramsci does not disavow the possibility that the masses will gain a philosophical understanding of what they take on faith. However, this educative process demands considerable intellectual rigor as philosophy is the highest order of knowledge. Yet, he attributed the acceptance of a particular philosophy to a moment of 'conversion'. He explained:

> The fact of having once suddenly seen the light and been convinced is the permanent reason for his reasons [in support of a particular political position] persisting, even if the arguments in its favour cannot be readily produced (Gramsci, 1971;339).

Yet Gramsci acknowledged that the myth which generated this conversion cannot sustain it indefinitely (Gramsci, 1971, p.129). The promised social transformation must be concretely realised at some point and discrepancies between the myth and the reality can provoke a loss of faith. In his experiences with the Turin factory councils and in his subsequent writings, Gramsci developed the notion of prefigurative practice. He maintained: 'The socialist state already exists potentially in the institutions of social life characteristic of the exploited labouring class' (in Joll, 1977, p.38). For Gramsci, prefigurative practice involved attempts to develop co-operative and democratic practices which would not only portend a revolutionary society but would also presage the 'new man' necessary to affect and sustain this transformation.

In Nicaragua, the FSLN constructed a powerful and highly productive myth. Yet they did not maintain hegemony merely through a generative myth. Rather, the FSLN sought to create a civil society, a task that years of corrupt dictatorship had precluded. The grassroots democracy that the FSLN endeavoured to build through mass organisations and national campaigns such as the Literacy crusade was the concretisation of the national popular 'myth' that had brought them to power. Yet with the institutionalisation of the revolution came a lessening of revolutionary mysticism. As Tomás Borge mused:

> we should be in conditions to redeem something that has diminished, that is revolutionary mysticism, the mysticism that we had in the war,

215

the mysticism that we had in the mountains, the mysticism that we had in the struggle against Somoza (in Girardi, 1987, p.149).

In his testimony, *Fire from the Mountain*, Omar Cabezas recounted his experiences fighting in the insurrection. He described the transformation that he and his counterparts experienced as they moved from raw recruits to skilled and experienced combatants. When Cabezas joined the FSLN, he took a new name and this renaming signified the beginning of a personal transformation in the midst of a collective struggle for social transformation. This taking of a pseudonym or 'nom de guerre' was a customary part of the FSLN induction and signified dedication to a new vocation, similar to the way religious change their names when they begin training. Not only did Cabezas experience his own transformation and that of his compañeros, he also experienced a transformation in his own perception of the mountain. It moved from a hostile and frightening place to a protective and mysterious entity.

This sense of personal transformation through revolutionary struggle and valorisation of the 'mountains' was not unique to the Nicaraguan revolution. Indeed it was Ché who spoke of 'the new Man'. Further, the equation of 'sacrifice' in times of war with the death and passion of Christ has often been a recurring war-time motif throughout the world. In this construction, in times of war, 'the soldiers' role becomes analogous to the redemptive act of God in Christ' (Martin, 1985, p.6). However, because of the pervasive Christian component of the Nicaraguan revolution, notions of personal transformation and sacrifice were brought into even sharper relief. The 'heroes and martyrs' who died in the insurrection were paid homage to in song, poetry, prose, paintings murals, graffiti, monuments and small neighbourhood shrines. In fact, the political geography of the country was transformed with the names of neighbourhoods, streets, places and buildings being 're-christened' in order to honour those who had fallen.

For Roger Lancaster, sacrifice and charisma are key elements in both Christian and Latin American revolutionary imagery. He finds parallels between 'The Story of Christ', 'The Authority of the Priest', and 'The Charisma of the Guerrilla'. While the priest, in line with both Christ and the guerrilla, rejects material comforts and resists the temptations of the flesh, he plays a more intermediary and secondary role than the other two. Christ and the Guerrilla are set apart from the rest of society by the depth of their sacrifice - Christ is crucified and the guerrilla often gives his/her life in the struggle. As a result, 'Christ is resurrected, ensuring Christendom's victory, the 'new man,' and life after death.' Thus '"Man" ascends to heaven'. In the case of the guerrilla, s/he is 'symbolically resurrected in the revolution, ensuring victory of the poor, the socialist

216

new man, and transcendence over the present conditions'. Here, 'heaven descends to Christ' (Lancaster, 1988, p.134).

Representations of the heroes and martyrs utilised religious imagery which drew upon and re-deployed religious imagery in a secular fashion. Here there was not only a borrowing of emotive religious imagery to create a secular saint but also an open identification of the fallen person with Christ. For example, the paintings of Solentiname are replete with Christian/revolutionary imagery which explicitly portrayed Jesus as a guerrilla and the Roman soldiers as National Guard members. This linkage was not limited to those who had fallen, although it is here that the two 'myths' most closely converged. Rather, all participants in the struggle were compared, in varying degrees, to Christ. [7] In fact, because of the popular nature of the revolution there was an association between the suffering and sacrifice of Christ and the hardship experienced by the Nicaraguan people as a whole.

Further, in a country where Marian imagery was particularly resonant, women combatants were often venerated in both their roles as guerrilla fighters and as mothers. Stener Ekern maintains that Nicaragua is a matrifocal culture where 'anything associated with motherhood is sacred' (Ekern, 1987, p.104). In this way, the imagery surrounding not only Christ but also the Virgin Mary was rearticulated through representations of women guerrillas. In this maternal role, women guerrillas did not pose a threat to machismo, which Ekern contended placed great store on the reproductive capacity of women as the flip side of an emphasis on the procreative ability of men (Ekern, 1987, p.97). However, the symbolic power of the woman guerrilla, suffering and sacrificing in the mountains along side her male counterparts, was a particularly powerful challenge to machista conceptions of the acceptable female behaviour.

The imagery surrounding the suffering and sacrifice of the guerrilla was suffused with the sensibilities of Nicaraguan popular religion. Yet the process by which popular religious imagery was incorporated into revolutionary discourse was one of mediation and mélange rather than wholesale incorporation. Further, although *Sandinismo* was the 'ideology' of the FSLN, it was not a paradigm that was under the control of the party; it was more the discourse of an inculturated revolution than a party line. Liberation theology, the 'ideology' of the popular church, also utilised elements of popular religion. In this case, popular religion was rearticulated, emerging rationalised but more overtly religious than in its reincarnation through *Sandinismo*. At the same time the distinction between the way in which popular religion was articulated in *Sandinismo* and liberation theology was something of an artificial one as in Nicaragua there was often not a strict demarcation

217

between the two. In effect, liberation theology became incorporated into *Sandinismo* and for many in the popular church, *Sandinismo* was a Nicaraguan liberation theology. In his analysis of this relationship between popular religion and its embodiment in both *Sandinismo* and liberation theology, Lancaster maintained:

> Revolutionary class consciousness excavates and redeems the subterranean treasures of the traditional popular religion; it takes the form of a partial rationalisation of such impulses. The resultant 'ethical religion' is still popular to be sure, but it is a popular religion rationalised on a higher plane than the antecedent, traditional one. In Nicaragua, such ethical trends were originally distinguished into a secular version (*Sandinismo*) and a religious one (liberation theology). These distinctions are now being blurred in practice, although each has its theoretically separate role and place (Lancaster, 1988, p.212).

As Lancaster maintains, the distinctions between religious and secular expressions of revolutionary class consciousness began to break down in the context of revolutionary practice. I would argue that 'moral identities', the manner in which people publicly and personally recognise themselves and others vis-à-vis a commitment to a particular project, are in fact the individual and collective inoculation of this ethical religion. In this way, 'ethical religion' provided the basis for the moral identities that were created in the crucible of the insurrection and the revolution. Yet there was more of a dialectical than a causal relationship between the two; each informed and shaped the other. If a revolutionary ethical religion was the leading 'ideology' or 'myth' of Sandinista Nicaragua, then moral identities were the spaces in which myths became true or at least true enough to generate action and commitment in support of the revolution. Mariátegui's notion of the 'force of myth', with its power to fulfil a need for the infinite and to accord a deep sense of personhood, suggests a route between personal and collective experiences of revolutionary consciousness and the more formal codifications of these impulses in *Sandinismo* and liberation theology.

Thus far, I have considered the power of the national popular myth and in particular the generative power of *Sandinismo*. Yet some of the basic premises outlined with regard to the creation of national popular myths are neutral. Thus myth creation is available to socialist and fascist, Right and Left alike. Rowe and Schelling attempt to establish how the notion of the national popular myths found in the work of Mariátegui and Gramsci can be distinguished from the national popular myths of Fascism. When Gramsci writes of a political ideology that creates a 'concrete phantasy which acts on a dispersed and shattered people to arouse and organise its collective will' (Gramsci, 1971, p.126) he could, as Rowe and Schelling contend, be referring to the mobilising power of fascist ideologies (Rowe and Schelling, 1991, p.156). In this context, is essentialism unavoidable?

The notion of the national popular myth or governing ideology seen in both Gramscian and Mariáteguian terms is a neutral concept. Both were primarily concerned with how to construct a compelling socialist national popular ideology or myth. In this way, ideology provided the impetus for class consciousness and class-based liberative praxis. In contrast, Marx held a negative concept of ideology because he held that it was a manifestation of a distorted consciousness at the service of the ruling class. A neutral concept of ideology means that the critical distinction between ideology and truth is broken down because both ruled and rulers use ideology in the battle for hegemony. Obviously Mariátegui and Gramsci had a notion of truth and believed that Marxism was true. However, the concept of ideology could no longer illustrate this critical distinction when used in a neutral fashion. In Nicaragua the 'national popular' was appropriated by all sides. I have analysed the conditions in which was successfully adopted by the FSLN/popular church bloc.

6   The 1990 elections and counter-hegemonic strategies

The 1990 elections saw the emergence of a counter hegemonic myth which, although not entirely convincing, seemed to represent the possibility of a break with war and economic hardship. Chamorro presented herself as the 'Mother' of all Nicaraguans offering stability, reconciliation and prosperity vis-à-vis her favourable relationship with the US government. Ortega, in contrast, presented himself as a virile 'macho man' promising 'all will be better'. In a country where the Virgin Mary was a central focus of popular religion, the pull of Chamorro's Marian imagery was indeed powerful, especially to a population weary of conflagration and fearful of the further erosion of living standards. The Chamorro campaign was particularly effective amongst women who, as some studies suggest, were decisive in determining the outcome of the election (Envio, June 1991, p.39). Clearly, the election was not won merely on the strength of the Chamorro campaign, rather it was a campaign that capitalised effectively on a national mood of weariness and rather disingenuously since many of the participants in the UNO coalition had actively supported and encouraged the war and economic embargo.

219

Yet the Chamorro victory did not mean that a new national popular myth or governing ideology had emerged to replace *Sandinismo*. While UNO may have won the election, the battle for hegemony rages on. While in previous chapters, I have considered struggles in the political and economic arena, I will here consider the not unrelated battle over popular symbolism that has emerged since the 1990 UNO victory. One change has been that state support for maintaining the concrete symbols of the revolution has disappeared. For example, during the years in which the FSLN held state power, the tomb of Carlos Fonseca was one of the country's most revered monuments. An eternal flame burned brightly and visitors were advised to keep a respectful distance. After the change in government, the far Right placed a bomb on the statue which, while only doing minor damage, outraged FSLN supporters who protested loudly and violently. Since the explosion, the eternal flame has been replaced by an eternal light bulb encased in a flame shaped plastic cover and FSLN supporters have kept a watchful eye one the monument. In fact in 1992, José Jesus Zamora, a retired ESP soldier, lived in a tent pitched adjacent to the tomb in order to stand guard over it.

Many attempts to eradicate the presence of Sandinista symbols have taken place with the support of Managua's far Right mayor Arnoldo Alemán. He has been intent on removing the visible landmarks of *Sandinismo* that have continued to dominate the Managua cityscape. To this end, a number of revolutionary murals have been painted over by city workers on Alemán's instructions (Kattenberg, 1991, p.3).[8] Further, efforts to strip away the physical manifestations of *Sandinismo* extended to renaming barrios which formally bore the names of 'heroes and martyrs' of the revolution. For example, under instructions from the mayor's office, city workers removed the plaque designating Barrio Christián Pérez, a Sandinista fighter slain shortly before the triumph of the revolution, and put up another with the barrio's pre-revolutionary name 'Salvadorita', Anastasio Somoza's mother.[9] Daniel Ortega maintained, 'Just like Nero, who wanted to erase all that had to do with Christianity, he [Alemán] wants to erase all that has to do with the Sandinistas' (Barricada Internacional, March 1993;22).[10]

While in *Sandinismo* religious imagery has powerfully underscored a political message, the far Right has attempted to use religious symbolism to signify the restoration of the pre-revolutionary status quo. One example of this is the proposed construction of a giant statue of the Virgin Mary modelled on the Christ figure with outstretched arms that overlooks Rio de Janeiro. Because politically it would be extremely difficult to take down the silhouette statue of Sandino that dominates the Managua skyline, the statue of the Virgin Mary would be a rebuke to

220

this and other still standing Sandinista monuments. Not surprisingly, Alemán had been involved in the project which was set to cost five million dollars. Given the prevailing economic conditions, the project provoked outrage amongst many. The San Pablo community had been quite active in protests against the construction of this monument, arguing that the money would be better spent building houses for people who had been left homeless by torrential rains in the Spring of 1993.[11]

The battle over the Virgin Mary statue demonstrated the importance of religious symbolism to the Right in their efforts to build a national myth to challenge *Sandinismo*. Yet nowhere was the battle over symbolism more intense than over the construction of Managua's new cathedral which after months of delays was finally inaugurated in mid-1993. In chapter five, I discussed some of the objections raised by members of the San Pablo CEB to the construction of the cathedral. These rested primarily on the cost of the construction in the face of the critical economic situation. For these women, the church symbolised the intransigence of the hierarchy and its lack of demonstrable concern for the deprivation experienced by the majority of the Nicaraguan people. However, to the hierarchy, the cathedral was a powerful symbol of its reasserted authority within Nicaraguan society and a concrete (literally) representation of the type of church that it sought to promote.

The cathedral also symbolised for the hierarchy and the Right a new national mood. In the department of Chontales, a small plaster statue of the Virgin Mary, kept in a shrine that was thought to be the site of an apparition, was accidentally broken by the caretaker. With no evidence, the Right accused the Sandinistas of committing a 'sacrilegious assault' on the basis that: 'only they would attack a place which shelters the most basic and durable values held by Nicaraguans' (*Barricada Internacional*, November/December, 1993c, p.27). The speciousness of this claim aside, the furore created by the Right over the statue illustrates one of the key components of their myth-making strategy, e.g. to present themselves as a counter to the areligious tendencies of the Sandinistas. During the time that the FSLN held state power, this attempt was seriously impeded by the degree to which *Sandinismo* implicitly and explicitly incorporated popular religious imagery and sensibilities. As a response to this, the hierarchy and the Right often pointed to supposed apparitions and supernatural occurrences as extraterrestrial support for their anti-government stance.

The Right's discourse on the broken statue specifically referenced the 'brutal persecution of the church' during the FSLN's tenure in government (*Barricada Internacional*, November/December 1993c, p.27). In this way, the Right and the hierarchy made constant reference to the religious subjugation supposedly suffered under the FSLN and pointed to the continued threat to popular piety posed by the FSLN's enduring power and influence. Yet this attempt to besmirch *Sandinismo* was not a sufficient basis for a new national popular myth. Even if it were widely accepted that the preservation of Nicaraguan religious traditions depended upon the eradication of *Sandinismo*, this in and of itself would not constitute an ideology capable of achieving hegemony. The problem for the Chamorro government and the moderate Right is that, besides traditional religious values, they have allied themselves, through design and necessity, to a neo-liberal economic policy which has clearly been to the detriment of the population. To the extent that sections of the FSLN ally themselves to the Chamorro government they are similarly identified as part of the problem and the regeneration of *Sandinismo* is stunted.

The far Right on the other hand, with its standard bearer Arnoldo Alemán, is attempting to foster a nostalgic national popular myth which harks back to an imaginary period of benign *Somocismo*. Alemán, who has declared his intentions to run for president in 1996, is a charismatic figure who presents himself as a populist 'caudillo' with the ability to improve Nicaraguan fortunes through his extensive political and economic connections in the United States. Although Alemán has been tainted with well documented accusations of corruption, these have not greatly affected his credibility with the large number of Nicaraguans who resist political categorisation. Talk on the streets of Managua has often viewed possible mayoral corruption with selective resignation. 'The mayor steals, but he gets things done. The government steals too, but it doesn't do anything' (Envio, January1994, p.19). Alemán's paternalistic leadership style and his perceived ability to 'get things done' have enhanced his popularity with many Managuans. While it is difficult to see a unifying ideology emerging from the far Right, it is possible to envisage the improved electoral prospect for Alemán and his colleagues if *Sandinismo* fails to coherently reassert itself on the national scene.

In his study of 'street power' in Nicaragua during the 1980's, Sterner Ekern contended that the FSLN's emphasis on notions of the vanguard and the 'supreme command' prevented it from completely throwing off the 'patron-client' model of government which had characterised the Somoza regime. It is significant that, as the FSLN was striving for greater internal democracy, a 'party line' was no longer being proffered. The shifts and disagreements within the FSLN, while perhaps a healthy and necessary process for the party, seemed to create confusion for rank and file supporters and made it more difficult for a cohesive revolutionary myth to reassert itself. The FSLN had lost the 'street power' that Erken had said was central to its moral authority. In describing the effects of the divisions within the party over the issue of privatisation, Danilo Silva, President of the Association of Retired Combatants, held that the attitude of many of his members was: 'Oh screw them, they can go to hell and leave us alone, so that we can find a way out of this poverty and unemployment' (Silva, 1993, p.6).

Culture Minister Gladys Ramirez's assertion that the Sandinistas had been 'abolished and pulverised by history' (Kattenburg, 1991, p.2) was more a statement of a goal than an assessment of actual fact. The danger, however, is that while the Right and the hierarchy have failed to create a governing myth or ideology capable of achieving hegemony, the FSLN and the popular church have thus far been unable to reinvigorate the 'ethical religion' which guided the insurrection and the years of revolutionary government. That is not to say that a large percentage of the population does not remain true to the notion of a revolutionary Sandinista Nicaragua. However, a governing ideology does not just need to keep the faith of the militants but also and more importantly to create a sense of faith and hope which will carry the 'average' man and woman along. In this respect, *Sandinismo* has lost its unifying appeal.

7 Conclusion

Although festivals like Santo Domingo and La Purísima fell into the category of popular religion they were not recognised as such by the participants who generally saw them as 'popular' religious manifestations rather than manifestations of 'popular religion'. In other words, for the people who participate in popular religious celebrations there is a continuous relationship with 'traditional religion' rather than an opposing relationship as a popular vs. traditional conception of religion may suggest. The use of the word popular is also misleading in the context of the popular church. The traditional church was actually more 'popular' than the popular church. However, what makes both the popular church and popular religion popular is that they appeal to a constituency beyond the classically 'faithful'. Put another way, popular religious festivals drew on active church participants plus a group of people that did not ordinarily participate in the traditional religious activities. In the same way, the popular church reached a group of people or tapped into a vein of religious common sense that may not have resulted in actual participation in popular church activities but did award them respect and recognition.

It is clear from the analysis provided in this chapter that popular religion in Nicaragua helped to construct support for a revolutionary project. In the festivals of La Purísima and Santo Domingo, it is possible to locate some of the values and assumptions that predisposed Nicaraguans to the revolution. For Lancaster, Nicaraguan popular religious practices and beliefs are the basis of the 'norms' that underlie the 'self-consciousness of the poor', in other words revolutionary class consciousness. Yet in looking at the contradictory way in which women are positioned within Nicaraguan popular religion, it is clear that this normative function of popular religion can serve to reinforce traditional conceptions of gender in addition to fostering class consciousness.

Yet it is clear that popular religious common sense is not in and of itself able to generate revolutionary social change. In harnessing its project not only to the 'philosophical' discourse of the popular church but also the 'common sense' discourse of popular religion, the FSLN created a revolutionary hegemonic bloc. Yet the Right, too, sought to use religious discourses to undermine the FSLN's hegemony. Particularly pronounced was the Right's use of Marian imagery in an effort to create an anti-Sandinista national unity. That said, Nicaraguan popular religion did clearly help to instil the moral identities which underpinned a deep and personal identification with the revolution. If the FSLN is to regain hegemony in Nicaragua, it will need to find new ways of tapping into the well of popular religious common sense.

Notes

1   Marian imagery has been used elsewhere in Latin America in the construction of national unity. In Argentina, during the years of military dictatorship the Virgin Mary was used in an effort to legitimate the status quo (Rowe and Schelling, 1991). In Peru, President Alberto Fujimori identified himself with three statues of the Virgin Mary that were said to cry and cure disease. The emergence of the three crying Marys, in the midst of a crippling economic crisis, a cholera epidemic and a series of national strikes, seemed to be anything but a coincidence. Two of the statues were the property of ruling party activists. Further, a military document was said to describe the strategy of a campaign based upon Christian imagery in order to take advantage of what was considered the "excessive credulity of the Peruvian people" (*Barricada Internacional*, June 1991:34).

2   In fact, the hierarchical church had been heavily involved in the promotion of an alleged apparition of Mary to a *campesino* called Bernardo Martínez in the northern village of Chupa, Chontales.

The initial apparition was said to have happened in May 1981, followed seven years later with another one to the same fortuitous *campesino* in May 1987. In the 1987 apparition, Mary, appearing under the name of "Virgin of the Victories", asked that Nicaraguans pray the rosary, "return to the traditions of the Church and the holy water" and burn "bad" books. Arch-conservative bishop Bosco Vivas himself carried out "Mary's" wishes by organising a bonfire to burn Marxist or suspected Marxist publications. To some commentators this apparition became known as "St. Mary of the Contras" and "Our Lady of Oliver North" (Envio, December 1987:43; Perry and Echeverría, 1988:302-4)

3 That Santo Domingo was a herbal doctor who worked amongst the poor (Lancaster, 1998:39) only served to enhance his standing as a "man of the people".

3 Thanks to Carlos Arturo Jiménez Campos for his comprehensive and witty elaboration on the Nicaraguan usage of this term.

4 Thanks to Carlos Arturo Jiménez Campos for his comprehensive and witty elaboration on the Nicaraguan usage of this term.

5 This point is well illustrated by an anecdote related by Sofía Montenegro. At a 1987 women's "De Cara al Pueblo" (Face the People) public meeting in which FSLN leaders answered questions, Montenegro attempted to focus the meeting on "strategic gender interests" of sexual discrimination at work, sexual harassment, rape, abortion, etc., rather than "practical gender interests" centred around economic and community issues. The usually diplomatic Daniel Ortega publicly reproached her for being "petty bourgeois" (interview in Küppers, 1994:175-6).

6 Although, given Ché's "old-style" relationships with women, he was clearly not presaging the gender studies/popular discourse meaning of the term "new man".

7 Interestingly, a famous photograph of a Sandinista with a machine gun strapped to her back and a crucifix around her neck, featured on the cover of Margaret Randall's *Christians in the Nicaraguan Revolution*, was used in a Soviet poster extolling the virtues of international solidarity. However, the crucifix had been airbrushed out of the reproduction of the photo. This alteration says much about the wilfully atheistic character of the Soviet national popular myth.

8 During the late 1980's, fine art experts from Italy had helped with the restoration and preservation of many of these public murals. It

is ironic that after this effort to save the murals was undertaken, they were ultimately painted over.

52 Alemán justified his actions as a response to demands from residents for the name change. As proof he cited a survey of residents carried out under his auspices which was published in *La Prensa*. Closer scrutiny of the survey by *Barricada* revealed that the survey was invalid. It found that a number of the so-called respondents, were in actuality former residents, never participated or were dead (Barricada International, March 1993: 22).

10 The reference to ancient Rome was apt given the 1993 Managua "Ben Hur"-style chariot race with participants dressed in full Roman regalia and driving horse-drawn carts. The contest, with carts and drivers adorned with company logos, drew over 20,000 spectators (*Barricada Internacional*, September 1993:27).

11 There were plans to build this statue on "expropriated" land, the owners of which would be amply compensated for their loss. In fact, the compensation proposed was far in excess of the actual value of the land, demonstrating that for some in Nicaragua their piety and personal enrichment were not irreconcilable.

Conclusion

1 Introduction

This book has explored the institutional and extra-institutional processes by which political consciousness was shaped in Nicaragua both prior to and since the 1990 elections, highlighting the gender dimension of these processes. Processes of identification in Nicaragua in the period of revolutionary government were mediated through a dense web of religious and religiously shaped political discourses. However, in the post-1990 period, support for the revolutionary process was no longer seen as the basis of 'moral' or 'right' action. The breakdown of this linkage underlay the FSLN's electoral loss and has hampered their attempts to reconstitute their former hegemony. This has a gendered process insofar as women, due to the war and economic crisis, became increasingly unable to fulfil the caring, maternal roles which the revolutionary government had so valorised in the campaign against the *contras*. Yet moral identities and religious and political ideologies are fluid and changeable processes rather than fixed states of being and understanding. The religious sphere was a key site for the operation of these changing processes of identification and the 1990 change in government both reflected and indicated a shift in rational and common sense understandings of morality.

In looking at the *olla*, I explored gender questions through talking with the women about a number of issues including: their relations with men, motivations for participation, and the lack of male involvement in projects like the *olla* These perspectives were gendered, but gendered in particular ways. The character of these women's outlooks depended on a wider set of factors including: their relationship to the Catholic church, the economic situation and the level of politicisation around gender interests in the society as a whole. Perhaps the gender dimension of CEBs has not often been explored in any great detail because it has rarely been seen as an issue by women CEB participants themselves, as my research has confirmed. The distinction between strategic and practical gender interests (Molyneux, 1984) was important here because, in the *olla*, it was clear that certain gender interests (i.e. providing food and health care for children and pregnant women) were being articulated and organised around - interests that were not recognised as gender interests *per se*.

Significantly, the pursuit of strategic gender interests within the CEB framework was limited as a consequence of both hierarchical and popular church resistance to abortion and contraception. It is unlikely that CEBs, especially given the context of their relationship to the Catholic church, would be key sites for the advancement of strategic gender interests. After all the *conscientization* process had been around 'class' rather than 'gender'. However the lack of activity around strategic gender interests in CEBs could change if these issues become more prominent in Nicaraguan society in general. Further, the possibility, however unlikely, exists for pastoral agents working with these communities to engage in education around these issues.

In linking the practice of the *olla* to feminist liberation theology, the concept of 'doing theology' (Tamez, 1989), elaborated in the literature review, comes to the fore. Feminist liberation theology is often focused on practice both because of the positioning of women theologians within the Catholic church and because many more women theologians are engaged in grassroots work than their male counterparts. Ivone Gebara remarks on the gendered division of labour within the church whereby women do pastoral work and men reflect on it (Gebara, 1989). This division of labour between male and female liberation theologians was replicated in the gendered division of labour within CEBs where work such as that carried out in the *olla* was women's work whilst leadership positions within the CEB structure were often held by men. In effect women 'did', men 'thought'.

In asking the women in the *olla* about their relationship with or connection to politics and religion, I aimed to establish a link between this and what liberation theologians say about praxis and religion and how the women themselves conceived of their praxis. My study confirmed that the connection between religion and commitment to a revolutionary project had been severely weakened by the collapse of the FSLN's hegemony, a conclusion to which I will return below.

The relationship between Christianity and Marxism has been a central concern of liberation theology (e.g. Miranda, 1974; Gutiérrez, 1987, 1973). According to this tradition, the two discourses have been posited as distinct. Yet in Nicaragua, in the work of liberation theologians (Girardi, 1987) and avowed Marxists alike (Borge, 1985) there was an attempt to achieve some measure of integration between the two, particularly in their theorisation of practice. My fieldwork has helped to deepen analytical understanding of the relationship between 'Marxism' and 'Christianity', positing it not simply as unity in practice but as a symbiotic relationship in which each discourse informed and shaped the other. Thus, in the context of the CEB activities, the *olla* and popular religious festivals, it was often difficult to untangle the threads of these intertwined discourses.

3 Popular religion

Although I use the distinct categories of popular church, hierarchical church and popular religion, there was some overlap between these classifications and this was particularly true in how people recognised themselves in relation to them. Nevertheless, popular religious festivals were sites of religious practice distinct from the institutional sites offered by the popular church. Significantly, popular religion helped to create the values that underlie commitment to particular political projects. For example, the levelling feature of La Purísima instilled, through practice, the conviction that surplus should be redistributed and material wealth equalised (Lancaster, 1988).

During the years of revolutionary government, it was upon these popular understandings that class consciousness was built and a particular version of socialism came to make 'common sense'. But within this normative framework there can be very traditional conceptions of gender, so that while popular religion may serve to strengthen class-based identities, it may also serve to reinforce norms around gender and sexuality that may also make 'common sense'. In this way, popular religion may enhance class interests at the expense of women's strategic gender interests. For example, the levelling features

229

of La Purísima may promote the notion of equality and intra-class solidarity while at the same time entrenching the existing gendered division of labour. This is an issue that Lancaster does not consider in his study of popular religion, and in highlighting questions of gender, I have sought to deepen and build upon Lancaster's positive assessment of Nicaraguan popular religion (Lancaster, 1988).

However, the meanings attached to popular religious practices were fluid. In the absence of a dominant discourse, popular religious practices may take on new meanings or may generate new values and understandings. My research showed that despite the use of popular religion by both the Left and the Right, it retained an autonomous character. Popular religion was never controlled or contained in the way, for example, that the popular church took the lead in the articulation and practical expression of liberation theology. So one cannot say that the FSLN 'had popular religion on their side'. Rather they successfully drew on values and notions that had been inculcated through popular religion. In contrast, popular religion did not have an organised constituency. Yet, in providing the normative basis for class consciousness, popular religious practice helped to make sense of the revolution.

The popular church had a praxis-oriented discourse which inspired and legitimised CEB practices. Popular religion embraced people who were not necessarily 'working for the revolution'. Yet, partly through their participation in popular religious practices, they underwent a process of politicisation, enhanced by the discourse of the popular church, which broadened the revolutionary consensus to the hitherto apolitical.

During the time of the revolutionary government, all productive activity was geared towards supporting sectors of the economy which would in turn sustain the war effort and contribute to the survival of the revolution. The popular church equated the revolutionary process with 'building the kingdom of God on earth' and this powerful linkage gave religious meaning to almost all productive activity. Thus actions were made sense of through a matrix of religiously inspired and politicised understandings of praxis.

The distinctions between popular religion, the discourse of the popular church and the FSLN's use of these discourses are not clear cut. Popular religious festivals like Santo Domingo and La Purísima in and of themselves transmitted particular values that underlie the common sense understanding and acceptance of the revolution. In other words, in participating in popular religious festivals, the discourse of the time (i.e. religious/revolutionary) made people recognise their practice in a certain way. This matrix changed the meaning of seemingly apolitical religious and secular activities.

Different religious understandings can become a part of common sense which can be harnessed to political projects of both the Left and the Right. In looking at the alliance of political and religious groupings, it could be said that the left was broadly allied with the popular church, CEB and progressive and mainline Protestant denominations grouped together in CEPAD. The Right was supported by the hierarchical church and some Pentecostal sects. Yet the hierarchical Catholic church and Pentecostals are not the most 'natural' of partners, particularly given the hierarchy's worries about the encroachment of Pentecostalism. As a consequence, the hierarchical church has remained unwilling to cede any of its power to define Nicaraguan religiosity, even to potentially politically sympathetic allies. The Chamorro government's less than helpful posture in relation to the Pentecostals (including both the imposition of taxes and broadcasting restrictions) demonstrated the paradox whereby Pentecostals were harnessed to a right-wing project yet did not receive the legitimacy and support of the state they enjoy elsewhere in Latin America.

In Nicaragua, the popular church linked pre-Christian indigenous discourse with a modern Christian discourse, i.e. liberation theology, but did so in a country where indigenous identity was generally much weaker than in other parts of Latin America. In looking at popular religious festivals, it was apparent that indigenous religious practices and beliefs had been retained and recast through popular religion. In Chapters 6 and 7, I drew out and unpacked the indigenous elements of Nicaraguan popular religious practices and beliefs and the way in which indigenous identity has been a point of organisation for both the popular church and the FSLN. In their discourses around the 500 years commemorations, there was an interesting synthesis of the 'modern' and the 'pre-modern'. Here, the 'pre-modern' or indigenous was used to attack one version of Christianity (the discourse of the hierarchical church) as oppressive and complicit in the conquest and to validate another as liberating and opposed to the conquest (liberation theology).

4 Moral identities

There is a link between the notion of practical and strategic interests with respect to gender and the concept of practical and strategic interests in relation to political consciousness and practice more generally. As Chapter 5 demonstrated, in the *olla*, the older women saw their commitment to the revolution as originating in concern over the

231

consequences of Somoza's repressive policies on their own families and neighbourhoods. Thus, for these women, a commitment to the FSLN and the revolution was rooted in a nexus between their practical interests and the strategy proposed by the FSLN. Molyneux's distinction between practical and strategic gender interests can also be used to explore political consciousness around issues other than gender. In Nicaragua, the popular church helped to politicise the practical interests of its constituents in the insurrection and in the subsequent years of revolutionary government. Ironically, the involvement of the popular church in this politicisation of practical class interests was actually a limitation of this same process with respect to gender.

Identification has been a key area of concern for this book and I have concentrated in particular on how processes of identification are shaped by gender. Projects which focused on women's roles as mothers generated a wide degree of neighbourhood participation. In this way, the *olla* was a 'motherist' rather than a 'feminist' project. Carol Gilligan's suggestion that women's basis of moral judgement is an ethic of care was borne out in the way that the women who worked in the *olla* described their motivations (Gilligan, 1977, 1982). This does not prove that women and men have essentially different processes of moral judgement. However, the *olla* was a project which was defined not in terms of justice, which Gilligan designates as the basis of male moral judgement, but rather unambiguously in terms of care for children and women in their maternal roles. In post-1990 period, identification for both men and women increasingly became more practical.

Yet the articulation of strategic gender interests has also become more pronounced since 1990. I demonstrated in my analysis that the greater autonomy of the women's movement has resulted in the space to articulate strategic gender interests. One of the ways that this can be measured is in the changing attitudes towards contraception, which I have argued was linked to the proliferation of feminist organising around women's health care. The lack of a strong revolutionary state has meant an end to the connection previously made between, on the one hand, productive activities and the revolutionary project, and, on the other, the freedom from the imperative to defend the revolution and hence to organise around sectoral interests.

Despite the low rates of participation in popular church activities in Nicaragua, CEBs had an influence above and beyond their absolute numerical significance. During the years of revolutionary government, the popular church's influence stemmed from its ability to focus religious discourse on support for the revolution. But the hegemony of the FSLN was not just based on a core of committed FSLN and popular church supporters; it also rested on the tacit support of those who were not active supporters. In this period the discourse of the FSLN and the popular church served to re-inscribe both formal and organised religious expression as well as popular religious practices. This recasting of religious expression reinforced an identification with the revolutionary project for the committed and helped to inspire a more tacit acceptance by the seemingly apolitical or unaffiliated.

In the post-1990 period, my research demonstrated that even amongst the most committed of popular church participants there was significant ambiguity with respect to the link between religious commitment and political affiliation. This ambiguity rested in part on the increasingly unstable political and economic situation and the apparent inability of either Left or Right to come to grips with it.

Gramsci made a distinction between ideology merely as a body of ideas and ideology as it becomes inscribed in social practices which are conditioned by and on social position. In Gramscian terms, hegemony is political power whereby one class has managed to achieve political dominance through its leadership skills and its willingness to incorporate or co-opt the demands of the allied classes. Hegemony is won, lost and maintained through struggles on the terrain of ideology. However, 'the popular classes' were not just the province of one bloc or the other. They negotiated their way through a complex web of political, economic and religious discourses. The FSLN utilised religious discourse in order to achieve a hegemonic consensus. The Chamorro government has tried to harness a different set of discourses in its struggle to achieve hegemony and has yet to achieve full hegemony in Nicaragua, it has certainly initiated a shift in common sense away from the politicised and religiously inspired understandings that made up the revolutionary matrix.

The analysis of such political developments in Nicaragua suggests a possible reappraisal of Gramsci's concept of hegemony itself. In particular, the relationship between hegemony and coercion is difficult to conceptualise in part because at some junctures Gramsci posited them as separate but operating in tandem whilst at others he designated coercion as one of the functions of hegemony (Gramsci, 1971, p.239 and Gramsci in Joll, 1977, p.99, respectively). Thus Gramsci presents seemingly contradictory conceptualisations of the role that force plays in hegemony. Building upon Doug Brown's notion of a continuum between democratic and authoritarian hegemony in the Nicaraguan revolution, I have argued for a concept of hegemony that includes both coercion and consent. Although it primarily employed democratic means, the FSLN built and maintained its hegemonic bloc through both authoritarian and democratic efforts. To acknowledge the force component of hegemony is not to valorise the coercive aspects of political power but rather to recognise and interrogate them.

Moral identities appear, on the face of it, to be part of the construction of hegemony based on persuasion rather than 'force'. However, the processes of constructing moral identities have changed with changing political conditions. The ability of a group or bloc to shape moral identities is often partly contingent upon access to formal political power, and with it coercion. Coercion is thus often part of the process of legitimation which helps to construct moral identities.

Ideologies are capable of being reshaped and ultimately transformed and this is what happened in Nicaragua with the recasting of Catholicism into a revolutionary theology of liberation. Of course, transformations of this order are often partial and contested and this was certainly the case in Nicaragua during the years of revolutionary government. Gramsci did not account for the possibility of such a transformation in his explicit rejection of a revolutionary role for Catholicism (Gramsci, 1971, pp.332-3). In contrast to his analysis of ideology more generally, Gramsci took to be a universal what was in fact a historically specific expression of Catholicism. Yet in other respects Gramsci argues for historical specific analyses and the possibility of shifts around what constitutes a revolutionary consciousness at any given moment in time. Thus, the Nicaraguan example challenges Gramsci's contention that the Catholic church cannot be a space for the development of a revolutionary common sense. It was evident that what prompted people to ally themselves to the revolution was in part made up of the analogies that they drew between the revolution and Christianity.

In Nicaragua, particular moral identities generated action for social change in the revolutionary period. These were rooted not only in an ethical imperative but also in this transformation of the practical into the strategic. There were two types of moral identities in support of the revolution. The first was an active one, which could be seen in the practice of the popular church. The second was a more passive, tacit one that was inculcated partly through popular religious practice and through the matrix of religiously inspired popular discourse that was *Sandinismo*.

At an 'everyday' level, religious custom actually drew on political custom, and vice versa. The values of what appeared distinct spheres, the political and the religious, were mutually reinforced through their shared practices and customs and the ways in which these were experienced. People may have been living and experiencing different spheres but actually they were familiar because both the practices and customs of these spheres overlapped. Here the examples of the CEB

234

mass, the homily-dialogue and the fifteenth anniversary celebration of the revolution illustrated the merging of these spheres. Thus, at some points, being at church might have felt like being at a political rally and being at a political rally might have felt like being at church. There was a symmetry in the cross-over of religious and political practices which helped to foster a continuity of experience.

Yet as my interviews in the *olla* demonstrated and as Danilo Silva's comments suggest, even the most committed are failing to see post-1990 Nicaragua through the revolutionary lens which had once filtered most experience (Silva, 1993). In this way, interests were being perceived as more practical than strategic and as such moral identities were shifting. These identities were characterised by greater fluidity and locality where resistance to the sweeping back of the gains of the revolution was often the priority. For some, moral identities based on a collective ideology of national transformation were displaced by individualised identities increasingly concerned with survival.

During the time of the revolutionary government, *Sandinismo* had pervaded all surfaces of Nicaraguan culture. With the collapse of the FSLN's hegemony, people no longer made sense of their actions within the political/religious framework of *Sandinismo*. In the post-1990 period no overarching framework has emerged to replace *Sandinismo*. In effect, in post-1990 Nicaragua the absence of a coherent hegemonic consensus or ruling ideology has made for a very unstable society. The FSLN has aimed to reconstruct its hegemony, but in vastly changed circumstances. In the 1990s, they lack the legitimacy of state power, the recourse to armed struggle, and a central dictatorial figure like Somoza to organise against. Further, the apparent transcendence of Marxism, both in Nicaragua and elsewhere, has forced the FSLN to devise a new language without losing what is essential to *Sandinismo*. Most importantly perhaps, the FSLN are working within a context in which international support (i.e. the USSR) for governments pursuing alternative development strategies is no longer available. Hence, the FSLN is attempting to re-articulate *Sandinismo* in a transformed national-political and global context, one in which people in Nicaragua no longer make 'common sense' of their lives in the way they did during the period of revolutionary government.

Finally, popular organisations in post -1990 Nicaragua are now playing a more oppositional role in relation to the state and thus fit more neatly into the framework developed by many theorists of new social movements. Popular organisations have developed a degree of autonomy that they did not have in their collaboration with the revolutionary government. Women's organisations, in particular, are no longer subject to pressure to subordinate their sectoral interests in deference to the revolution. The greater autonomy of organisations like AMNLAE will mean that sectoral interests may be better articulated and defended. There has been a real growth in popular movements in Nicaragua as the dramatic expansion of the Nicaraguan Community Movement (MCN), an outgrowth of the CDS structure, demonstrates (Nicaragua Solidarity Campaign, 1993). Despite the unstable situation in Nicaragua, popular organisations are filling the power vacuum to some degree. The MCN is a growing organisation, linking popular movements and taking over some of the functions of the shrinking social security structure. It remains to be seen what role religious discourses will play in shaping future moral identities and hegemonic configurations in Nicaragua.

Bibliography

Acosta, Gladys (1994), 'Feminism and the New World Order' in Gaby Küppers (ed.), *Compañeras: Voices from the Latin American Women's Movement*, Latin America Bureau: London.

Adriance, Madeline (1991), 'Agents of Change: The Roles of Priests, Sisters, and Lay Workers in the Grass Roots Catholic Church in Brazil', *Journal for the Scientific Study of Religion*, 30(3), September.

Alemán, Verónica (1993), 'Sexist Laws Scorched', *Barricada Internacional*, 13 (395), March.

Altman, Lori (1991), 'Exodus: The Symbolic Strength of Women' *LADOC*, 22, September/October.

Alvarez Calero, Manuel, 'Daniel: Hay crisis Etica y Moral en el Sandinismo', *Barricada*, 25 September 1992.

Amin, S. (1974), *Accumulation on a World Scale*, Monthly Review Press: NY.

Andersson, Susanne and Fernández, Guillermo (1994), 'Defining the FSLN', *Barricada Internacional*, 14(371), March.

Angel, Adriana and Macintosh, Fiona (1987), *The Tiger's Milk: Women of Nicaragua*, Virago Press:London.

Angell, Alan (1986), 'Party Systems in Latin America', in Claudio Véliz (ed.), *Latin America and the Caribbean: A Handbook*, Anthony Blond: London.

Aragón, Omar Cárdenas (1992), 'El Dogma de La Inmaculada Concepción', *Barricada*, 5 December.

Arce, B. (1991), 'Pinning the Tail on the Donkey!' in *Barricada Internacional*, 11(341), September.

Arellano, Luz Beatriz (1987), 'El Aporte de la Mujer a la Transformación de la Sociedad y de la Iglesia en Nicaragua' in G. Girardi, B.Forcano, and J. Mª Vigil, (eds), *Nicaragua Trinchera Teologica*, Nuevos Textos: Managua and Madrid.

Arellano, Luz Beatriz (1994), 'Women's Experience of God in Emerging Spirituality' in Ursula King (ed.), *Feminist Theology from the Third World: A Reader*, SPCK: London.

Argüello, José (1987), 'Azarías H. Pallais: Profeta de la Iglesia de los Pobres', in G. Girardi, B.Forcano, and J. Mª Vigil, (eds), *Nicaragua Trinchera Teologica*, Nuevos Textos: Managua and Madrid.

Argüello, José (1992), Presentation at CEB 500 Years Conference, Managua, 5 September.

Aricó, Jose (1978) (selección y prólogo), *Mariategui y Los Orígenes del Marxismo Latinamericano*, Siglo Veintiuno Editores: México, D.F.

Astelli, Nancy and Henríquez, Eduardo (1992), 'Organizarse Para Sobrevivir: Otra Cara del Capitalismo en Chile', *Esta Tierra Nuestra: Diálogos Latinoamericanos*, 5, Primero trimestre de 1992.

Babbie, Earl (1983), *The Practice of Social Research*, Wadsworth: Belmont, CA.

Badone, Ellen (ed.) (1990), *Religious Orthodoxy and Popular Faith in European Society*, Princeton University Press: Princeton, NJ.

Bahr, Donald, Gregorio, J, Lopez, D.I. and Alvarez, A. (1974), *Piman Shamanism and Staying Sickness*, University of Arizona Press: Tuscon.

Bamat, Thomas (1992), 'Will Latin America Become Protestant?', *Maryknoll*, 86(7), July.

Barberena, Edgard (1992), 'La Homosexualidad Regresa al Tapete de la Polémica!', *El Neuevo Diario*, 13 November.

Barricada, (1992), 'Padre Hergueta Renunció a Mayordomía de Minguito', 27 July.

Barricada (Gente) (1992), 'La Cultura Madre: El Mundo Náhuatl', 25 September.

Barricada, (1992) AMNLAE Anouncement, 28 September.

Barricada, (1992), 'Obando: FSLN Podría Volver al Poder', 26 October.

Barricada, (1992), 'Carta Abierta a Gladys Báez', 4 November.

Barricada, (1992), 'Purísima en La Verde Sonrisa', 6 December.

Barricada Internacional, (1991), 'Peru: Wave of Fake Miracles', 11(338), June.

Barricada Internacional, (1992a), 'Letter From Shepherds... Or From Wolves?', 12(355-6), November/December.

Barricada Internacional, (1992b), 'The Indigenous Medical System', 12(355-6), November/December.

Barricada Internacional, (1992c), 'Virgin Mary in Politics', 12(355-6), November/December.

Barricada Internacional, (1993), 'Cardinal Obando Rebukes President', 13(358), February.

Barricada Internacional, (1993a), 'Good-bye to Free Education', 13(359), March.

Barricada Internacional, (1993b), 'In the Name of the Heroes', 13(359), March.

Barricada Internacional, (1993a), 'Education', 13(360), April.

Barricada Internacional, (1993b), 'Politics and the Military', 13(360), April.

Barricada Internacional, (1993c), 'Women's Commission Formed', 13(360), April.

Barricada Internacional, (1993), 'The Challenges of Non-Hierarchical Organisation', 13(362), June.

Barricada Internacional, (1993), 'A Country of Children', 13(364), August.

Barricada Internacional, (1993), 'Church Denies Asking for UN Peacekeeping Forces', 13(365), September.

Barricada Internacional, (1993), 'Finally...Cardinal Obando Inaugurates Cathedral', 13(366), October.

Barricada Internacional, (1993), 'The Highest Infant Mortality Rate in Central America', 13(367-8), November/December.

Barricada Internacional, (1994), 'Women Use Contraceptives without Permission', 14(369), January.

Barricada Internacional, (1994), 'Attack on Secular Education', 14(374), June.

Barthes, Roland (1967), *Elements of Semiology*, Jonathan Cape: London.

Bastian, Jean-Pierre (1993), 'The Metamorphosis of Latin American Protestant Groups: A Sociohistorical Perspective', *Latin American Research Review*, 28(2).

Behar, Ruth (1990), 'The Struggle for Church: Popular Anti-clericalism and Religiosity in Post-Franco Spain' in Ellen Badone (ed.), *Religious Orthodoxy and Popular Faith in European Society*, Princeton University Press: Princeton, NJ.

Behrman, J.R. and Wolfe, B.L. (1989), 'Does More Schooling Make Women Better Nourished and Healthier?: Adult Sibling Random and Fixed Effects Estimates for Nicaragua', *Journal of Human Resources*, 24, Fall.

239

Belli, Gioconda (1992), 'El FSLN y Los Peligros de la Ambigüedad', *Barricada*,1 August.

Belli, Humberto (1985), *Breaking Faith*, Crossway Books: Westchester, IL.

Bennett, Jon with George, Susan (1987), *The Hunger Machine*, Polity Press: Cambridge.

Berryman, Philip (1987), *Liberation Theology*, I.B. Tauris & Co Ltd, London.

Bethke Elshtain, Jean (1981), *Public Man, Private Woman: Women in Social and Political Thought*, Princeton University Press: Princeton, NJ.

Betto, Frei (1987), *Fidel and Religion: Castro Talks on Revolution and Religion with Frei Betto*, Simon & Schuster: NY.

Bhabha, Homi (1990), Interview: 'The Third Space', in Jonathan Rutherford (ed.), *Identity, Community, Culture, Difference*, Lawrence & Wishart: London.

Bianchi, Enzo (1987), 'The Centrality of the Word of God' in Giuseppe Alberigo, Jean-Pierre Jossua, and Komonchak (eds), *The Reception of Vatican II*, Burns & Oates Tunbridge Wells, Kent, England.

Bidegain, Ana María (1989), 'Women and the Theology of Liberation' in Elsa Tamez (ed.), *Through Her Eyes: Women's Theology from Latin America*, Orbis: Maryknoll, NY.

Bingemer, María Clara (1994), 'Women in the Future of the Theology of Liberation' in Ursula King (ed.), *Feminist Theology from the Third World: A Reader*, SPCK: London.

Blandón, María Teresa (1994), 'The Impact of the Sandinista Defeat on Nicaraguan Feminism', in Gabby Küppers (ed.), *Compañeras: Voices from the Latin American Women's Movement*, Latin America Bureau: London.

Boff, Leonardo (1985), *Church Charism and Power: Liberation Theology and the Institutional Church*, SMC Press: London.

Boff, Leonardo (1986), *Ecclesiogenesis: The Base Communities Reinvent the Church*, Collins Liturgical Publications: London.

Boff, Leonardo and Boff, Clodovis (1985), *Salvation and Liberation: In Search of a Balance Between Faith and Politics*, Orbis Books: Maryknoll, NY.

Bonino, José Míguez (1975), *Revolutionary Theology Comes of Age*, SPCK: London.

Borge, Tomás (1982), excerpts from speach printed in *Amancer*, 7-8, March-April.

Borge, Tomás (1985), 'Cristianismo Y Sandinismo', *Nicaráuac*, Año VI, No.11, Managua, Nicaragua, May.

Bradstock, Andrew (1987), *Saints and Sandinistas: The Catholic Church in Nicaragua and its Response to the Revolution*, Epworth Press: London.

Bragg, Wayne (ed.) (1991), *Sandino in the Streets*, University of Indiana Press: Bloomington.

Brockman, James R. (1989), *Romero: A Life*, Orbis Books: Maryknoll, NY.

Brosnahan, Tom, Keller, Nancy and Rachowiecki, Rob (1992), *Central America*, Lonley Planet Publications: Hawthorn, Australia.

Brown, Doug (1990), 'Sandinismo and the Problem of Democratic Hegemony', *Latin American Perspectives*, 65, (17), No. 2, Spring.

Bruneau, Thomas C. (1986), 'Brazil: The Catholic Church and Basic Christian Communities' in Daniel H. Levine (ed.), *Religion and Political Conflict in Latin America*, University of North Carolina Press: Chapel Hill and London.

Burbach, Roger and Nuñéz (1987), Orlando, *Fire in the Americas*, Verso: London.

Buel, Rebecca (1994), (Talk given on current situation in Nicaragua by regional director for Oxfam Central America), Birmingham,18 June.

Burgos-Debray, Elisabeth (1984), *I... Rigoberta Menchu an Indian Woman in Guatemala*, translated by Ann Wright, Verso: London.

Cabestero, Teofilo (1983), *Ministers of God, Ministers of the People*, Translated by Robert R. Barr, Zed Press: London.

Cabezas, Omar (1985), *Fire from the Mountain: The Making of a Sansinista*, Crown Publishers: NY.

Cadorette, Curt (1988), *From the Heart of the People: The Theology of Gustavo Gutierrez*, Myer Stone Books: Oak Park, IL.

Cardenal, Ernesto (1976), *El Evangelio en Solentiname*, Ediciones Sigueme: Salamanca.

Cardenal, P. Fernando (1992), Open letter to *Barricada*, 10 December.

Cardoso, Fernando H. and Faletto, Enzo (1969), *Dependencia y desarrollo en América Latina*, Siglo XXI: Mexico City.

Carías, Rafael (1991), 'The Santo Domingo Preliminary Document: The Culture' (translated from SIC, 527, August 1990) in *LADOC*, 21(3), January/February.

Caribbean and Central America Report, (1993), 'Sandinista Joins Chamorro Government', RC-93-0225, February.

Carrasco, David (1990), *Religions of Mesoamerica*, Harper: San Francisco.

Castells, Manuel (1983), *The City and the Grassroots: a Cross-Cultural Theory of Urban Social Movements*, University of California Press: Berkeley, CA.

Castillo M., Ernesto (1992), 'Otro congresso no es solución mágica', *Barricada*, 6 September.

Castillo, Fernando (1976), 'El Problema de la Praxis en la Teologia de la Liberación', inaugural-dissertation, Fachbereich Katholische Theologie der Westfälischen Wilhelms-Universität, Münster in Westfalen.

Castillo, María Dolores Castillo (1993), 'Betting on the Noras', *Barricada Internacional*, 13(360), April.

Castro, Fidel (1990), 'Revolution: Socialism and Independence', *Fight Racism! Fight Imperialism!* (Revolutionary Communist Group newspaper), 92, January.

Chilcote, Ronald H. (1990), 'Post-Marxism and the Retreat from Class in Latin America', *Latin American Perspectives*, 17, (65), No. 2, Spring.

Chinchilla, Norma (1985-86), 'Women in the Nicaragun Revolution', *Nicaraguan Perspective*, 11, Winter.

Chomsky, Noam (1885), *Turning the Tide: US Intervention in Central America and the Struggle for Peace*, South End Press: Boston, MA.

Chopp, Rebecca S. (1986), *The Praxis of Suffering: An Interpretation of Liberation and Political Theologies*, Orbis Books: Maryknoll, NY.

Chow, Napoleon H. (1992), 'Latin American Liberation Theology: Religion, Poetry, and Revolution in Nicaragua', The Florida State University, PhD.

Christian Jr., William A. (1981), *Local Religion in Sixteenth-Century Spain*, Princeton University Press: Princeton, NJ.

Ciurczak, Gary Andrew (1992), 'Nicaraguans' Human Rights and the US-Nicaraguan Relationship in the 20th Century: Views from Modernization and Dependency Theories', PhD, State University of NY at Buffalo, PhD.

Clifford, James (1988), *The Predicament of Culture: Twentieth-Century Ethnography, Literature and Art*, Harvard University Press: Cambridge, MA.

Cochran III, Agustus and Scott, Catherine V. (1992), 'Class, State and Popular Organizations in Mozambique and Nicaragua', *Latin American Perspectives*, 73, (19), No. 2, Spring.

Collins, Joseph, with Moore Lappé, Frances, Allen, Nick and Rice, Paul (1985), *Nicaragua: What a Difference a Revolution Could Make?*, Institute for Food and Development Policy, San Francisco.

Collinson, Helen (ed.) (1990), *Women and the Revolution in Nicaragua*, Zed Books: London.

Comblin, José (1989), *The Holy Spirit and Liberation*, Burns/Oates Press: Tunbridge Wells, Kent.

Coraggio, José Luis (1985), 'Social Movements and Revolution: The Case of Nicaragua', in David Slater (ed.), *New Social Movements and the State in Latin America*, Foris Publications: Dordrecht-Holland.

Cotter, Joseph Donald (1993), 'Keeping the Faith: An Analysis of Ideological Continuity in the FSLN's Revolutionary Leadership in Transition to Revolutionary Rulership in Nicaragua (1979-1989)' PhD, George Mason University.

Crahan, Margaret E. (1989), 'Religion and Revolutionary Politics in Nicaragua', in Scott Mainwaring and Alexander Wilde (eds), *The Progressive Church in Latin America*, University of Notre Dame Press, Notre Dame, IN.

Crahan, Margaret E. (1989), 'Religion and Revolutionary Politics in Nicaragua', in Scott Mainwaring and Alexander Wilde (eds), *The Progressive Church in Latin America*, University of Notre Dame Press, Notre Dame, IN.

Cuadra, Scarlet (1992), Fernández, Guillermo and Lurya Ubeda, Francis, 'Nicaragua's Women's Conference: Seeking Unity and Diversity' *Barricada Internacional*, 12(347), March.

Cuadra, Scarlet (1994a), 'PLC Electoral Victory vs. Sandinista Political Victorty', *Barricada Internacional*, 14(371), March.

Cuadra, Scarlet (1994b), 'Baking Their Own Bread' in *Barricada Internacional*, 14(373), May.

Deere, Carmen Diana; Marchetti, Peter and Reinhardt, Nola (1985), 'The Peasantry and Development of Sandinista Agrarian Policy: 1979-1984', *Latin American Research Review*, Fall.

De La Torre, Carlos (1992), 'The Ambiguous Meanings of Latin American Populisms', *Social Research*, 59(2), Summer.

Denzin, Norman (1978), *The Research Act in Sociology*, Butterworths: London.

De Pury, Silvan (1992), *Human Rights in Nicaragua*, Benjamin Linder Talk, Managua, Nicaragua, 27 August.

Díaz Lacayo, Aldo (1992), 'Still Lost in the Storm', *Barricada Internacional*, 12(347), March.

Di Tella, Torcuato (1973), *Populismo y Condicciones de Clase en Latinoamérica*, Editorial ERA: Mexico.

Dodson, Michael (1986), 'The Struggle for the Church', in Daniel H. Levine (ed.), *Religion and Political Conflict in Latin America*, University of North Carolina Press: Chapel Hill and London.

Dodson, Michael and Nuzzi O'Shaughnessy, Laura (1985), 'Religion and Politics', in Thomas Walker (ed.), *Nicaragua: The First Five Years*, Praeger: NY.

Dodson, Michael and Nuzzi O'Shaughnessy, Laura (1990), *Nicaragua's Other Revolution: Religious Faith and Political Struggle*, University of North Carolina Press: Chapel Hill and London.

Dueñas, Frederico (1992), 'La Comisión Etica del FSLN', *La Prensa*,1 October.

Dunkerley, James (1988), *Power in the Isthmus*, Verso: London.

Dunkerley, James (1990), 'Reflections on the Nicaraguan Election' in *New Left Review*, 182, July/August.

Duquoc, Christian (1987), 'Clerical Reform', in *The Reception of Vatican II*, Giuseppe Alberigo, Jean-Pierre Jossua and Komonchak, Burns & Oates Tunbribge Wells, Kent.

Ekern, Stener (1987), *Street Power: Culture and Politics in a Nicaraguan Neighbourhood*, Department of Anthropology, University of Bergen, Norway.

El Tayacán (a collective) (1987), *Historia de la Iglesia de los Pobres en Nicaragua*, El Tayacán: Managua.

Ely, Margot with Anzul, Margaret, Friedman, Teri, Garner, Diane and McCormack Steinmetz, Ann (1991), *Doing Qualitive Research: Circles Within Circles*, Falmer Press: Bristol, PA

Emmanuel, A. (1972), *Unequal Exchange*, New Left Books: London.

Enriquez, Laura J. (1985), 'The Dilemmas of Agro-Export Planning in Revolutionary Nicaragua', in Thomas Walker (ed.), *Nicaragua: The First Five Years*, Praeger: NY.

Enriquez, Laura J. and Spalding, Rose (1987), 'Banking Systems and Revolutionary Change: The Politics of Agricultural Credit in Nicaragua', in Rose Spanding (ed.), *The Political Economy of Revolutionary Nicaragua*, Allen & Unwin: London.

Envio, (1987), 'Church-State Relations: A Chronology-Part II', 6(78), December.

Envio, (1988), 'Nicaragua's First Opinion Poll', 7(89), December.

Envio, (1989), 'Poll of Youth in Managua: Strong Believers, Diverging Directions', 8 (92), March.

Envio, (1991), 'Women in Nicaragua: The Revolution on Hold', 10, (119), June.

Envio, (1993), 'Nicaragua's Children', 12(145), August.

Envio, (1994), 'The Case Against Mayor Alemán', 12(150), January.

Envio, (1995), 'UN Report on Nicaragua', 14(162), January.

Epstein Jayaratne, Toby (1993), 'The Value of Quantitative Methodology for Feminist Research', in Martyn Hammersley (ed.), *Social Research: Philosophy, Politics and Practice*, Sage Publications: London.

Everingham, Mark Warren (1993), 'Dictatorship, Development, and Revolutionary Coalitions: The Case of Nicaragua', PhD, The George Washington University.

Ezcurra, Ana María (1987), 'Hacia un Nuevo Pensamiento Social Latinoamericano: Bases Ideológicas de una Teología de la Liberación en Nicaragua', in G. Girardi, B.Forcano, and J. Mª Vigil, (eds) , *Nicaragua Trinchera Teologica*, Nuevos Textos: Managua and Madrid.

Fabella, Virginia and Oduyoye, Mercy Amba (eds) (1988), *With Passion and Compassion: Third World Women Doing Theology*, Orbis: Maryknoll, NY.

Fernández Arellano, Francisco de Asís (1992), 'El FSLN que tenemos', *Barricada,* 6 September.

Fernández de Oviedo y Valdés, Gonzalo (1992), '1528: Nicaragua Indígena', *El Semanario.*

Fernández, Raquel (1993), 'Hope in Lechecuagos', *Envio*, 12, (147), October.

Ferrari, Sergio (1992), 'La Confessión de Leonardo Boff' in *Nuevo Diario*, 3 October.

Fielding, Nick and Fielding, J. (1986), *Linking Data: The Articulation of Quantative and Qualitative Methods in Social Research*, Sage Publications: London.

Flota, Enrique (1994), 'Chiapas and the Crisis of Mexican "Democracy"', in *Envio*, 13(154), May.

Flores, Juan, Franco, Jean and Yúdice (1992), George, *On Edge: The Crisis of Contemporary Latin American Culture*, (Cultural Politics, Volume 4), University of Minnesota Press: Minneapolis and London.

Foroohar, Manzar (1989), *The Catholic Church and Social Change in Nicaragua,* State University of NY Press, Albany, NY.

Franco, Jean (1989), *Plotting Women: Gender and Representation in Mexico*, Verso: London.

Franco, Jean (1992), 'Going Public Reinhabiting the Private', in George Yúdice, Jean Franco and Juan Flores (eds), *On Edge: The Crisis of Contemporary Latin American Culture*, University of Minnesota Press: Minneapolis and London.

Frank, A.G. (1970), *Capitalism and Underdevelopment in Latin America*, Monthly Review Press: NY.

Fraser, Nancy, 'What's Critical About Critical Theory' in Seyla Benhabib and Drucilla Cornell (eds), *Feminism as Critique: On the Politics of Gender*, University of Minnesota Press: Minneapolis, Minnesota.

Freire, Paulo (1972), *The Pedagogy of the Oppressed*, Penguin Books: London.

Freire, Paulo (1985), *The Politics of Education: Culture, Power, and Liberation*, Macmillan: NY.

Friedman, Michael (1992), 'The Counterrevolution in Nicaraguan Education', *Monthly Review*, 43(9), February.

Gabriel, Leo (1992), 'Las Ollas Comunales en los Barrios de Managua', *Esta Tierra Nuestra: Diálogos Latinoamericanos*, 5, Primero trimestre de 1992.

Galeano, Eduardo (1973), *Open Veins of Latin America: Five Centuries of the Pillage of a Continent*, Monthly Review Press: NY.

Galilea, Segundo (1987), 'Latin America in the Medellín and Puebla Conferences: An Example of Selective and Creative Reception of Vatican II', in Giuseppe Alberigo, Jean-Pierre Jossua, and Komonchak (eds), *The Reception of Vatican II*, Burns & Oates Tunbridge Wells, Kent, England.

García Canclini, Nestor (1992), 'Cultural Reconversion' in George Yúdice, Jean Franco and Juan Flores (eds), *On Edge: The Crisis of Contemporary Latin American Culture*, University of Minnesota Press: Minneapolis and London.

Gebara, Ivone (1989), 'Women Doing Theology in Latin America', in Elsa Tamez (ed.), *Through Her Eyes: Women's Theology from Latin America*, Orbis: Maryknoll, NY.

Gebara, Ivone (1994), 'Women and Theology' in Ursula King (ed.), *Feminist Theology from the Third World: A Reader*, SPCK: London.

George, Susan (1984), *Ill Fares the Land: Essays on Food Hunger and Development*, Writers and Readers: London.

Germani, Gino (1971), *Política y Sociedad en una Epoca de Transición*, Editorial Paidos: Buenos Aires.

Germani, Gino (1978), *Authoritarianism, Fascism and National Populism*, Transaction Books: New Brunswick, NJ.

Gerth, H. H. and Mills, C. Wright (eds) (1974), *From Max Weber: Essays in Sociology*, Routledge & Kegan Paul: London.

Gilligan, Carol (1977), 'Concepts of the Self and of Morality', *Harvard Education Review*, 47.

Gilligan, Carol (1982), *In a Different Voice: Psychological Theory and Women's Development*, Harvard University Press: Cambridge, MA.

Girardi, Giulio (1987), *Sandinismo, Marxismo, Cristianismo: La Confluencia*, 2nd edn, Centro Ecuménico Antonio Valdivieso: Managua, Nicaragua.

Girardi, G., Forcano, B. and Vigil, J. Mª (eds.) (1987), *Nicaragua Trinchera Teologica*, Nuevos Textos: Managua and Madrid.

Gismondi, Michael Anthony (1990), 'Religion and Revolution in Nicaragua: An Historical Perspective', PhD, York University, Canada.

Glaser, Barney and Strauss, Anselm (1967), *The Discovery of Grounded Theory*, Aldine: Chicago.

Gonzalez, Mike (1990), *Nicaragua: What Went Wrong?*, Bookmarks: London.

Goodman, David and Redclift, Michael (1991), *Refashioning Nature: Food, Ecology and Culture*, Routledge: London.

Gordon, Deborah A. (1993), 'Words of Consequence: Feminist Ethnography as Social Action', *Critique of Anthropology*, 13(4), December.

Gramci, Antonio (1971), *Selections from the Prision Notebooks*, Lawrence & Wishart, London.

Granada (1992), Dorothy Women's Health Projects, Benjamin Linder Talk, 6th August.

Guardian, (1995), 'General Ortega Steps Down', 21 February.

Gugelberger, Georg and Kearney, Michael (1991), 'Voices of the Voiceless: Testimonial Literature in Latin America', *Latin American Perspectives*, 70, (18), No. 3, Summer.

Gutiérrez, Gustavo (1973), *A Theology of Liberation*, translated and edited by Sister Caridad Inda and John Eagleson, Orbis Books: Maryknoll, NY.

Gutiérrez, Gustavo (1983), *The Power of the Poor in History*, SCM Press: London.

Gutiérrez, Gustavo (1987), 'The Church and the Poor: A Latin American Perspective', in Giuseppe Alberigo, Jean-Pierre Jossua, and Komonchak (eds), *The Reception of Vatican II*, Burns & Oates Tunbridge Wells, Kent, England.

Hakim, Catherine (1987), *Research Design: Strategies and Choices in the Design of Social Science Research*, Unwin Hyman: London.

Hall, Stuart (1991a), 'The Local and the Global: Globalization and Ethnicity' in Anthony King (ed.), *Culture, Globalization and the World System*, Macmillan: London.

Hall, Stuart (1991b), 'Old and New Identities: Old and New Ethnicities' in Anthony King (ed.), *Culture, Globalization and the World System*, Macmillan: London.

Hammersley, Martyn and Atkinson, Paul (1983), *Ethnography: Principles in Practice*, Tavistock:London.

Harding, Sandra (1991), *Whose Science? Whose Knowledge? Thinking From Women's Lives*, Cornell University Press: Ithaca, NY.

Harding, Sandra (1992), 'Subjectivity, Experience and Knowledge: An Epistemology from/for Rainbow Coalition Politics', in *Development and Change*, 23(3).

Harris, Hermione (1987), 'Introduction' in Angel, Adriana and Macintosh, Fiona, *The Tiger's Milk: Women of Nicaragua*, Virago Press, Ltd.:London.

Hayter, Teresa (1981), *The Creation of World Poverty: An Alternative to the Brandt Report*, Pluto Press: London.

Hebblethwaite, Peter (1978), *The Runaway Church*, Collins: Glasgow.

Hebblethwaite, Peter (1984), *John XXIII, Pope of the Council*, Geoffrey Chapman: London.

Hebblethwaite, Peter (1990), 'The Vatican's Latin American Policy' in Dermot Keogh (ed.), *Church and Politics in Latin America*, Macmillan: London and Basingstoke.

Herrera, Ruth (1992), 'Diverse, Yes... but United?' interview in *Barricada Internacional*, 12(347), March.

Hewitt, W.E. (1988), 'Christian Base Communities (CEBs)', *Thought*, 63(249), June.

Heyck, Denis Lynn Daly (1990), *Life Stories of the Nicaraguan Revolution*, Routledge, Chapman and Hall: NY.

Hinkelammert, Franz (1972), *Dialéctica del Desarrollo Desigual*, Ediciones Universitarias de Valparaiso: Valparaiso.

Hinkelammert, Franz (1987), 'Economía y Teología: El Dios de la Vida y la Vida Humana', in G. Girardi, B.Forcano, and J. Mª Vigil, (eds), *Nicaragua Trinchera Teologica*, Nuevos Textos: Managua and Madrid.

Hinkelammert, Franz (1992), 'Nuevo Orden Mundial y Tercer Mundo', talk given at the VIII Semana Teologia held in Managua, Nicaragua, 1 September.

Hodges, Donald (1986), *Intellectual Foundations of the Nicaraguan Revolution*, University of Texas Press: Austin.

Holler, Stephen C. (1992), 'Responses of the Church to Marian Popular Religion', PhD, Saint Louis University.

hooks, bell (1984), *Feminist Theory: From Margin to Center*, South End Press: Boston, MA.

hooks, bell (1991), *Yearning: Race, Gender and Cultural Politics*, Turnaround: London.

Hösle, Vittorio (1992), 'The Third World as a Philosophical Problem', *Social Research*, 59(2), Summer.

Houtart, François and Lemercinier, Geneviève (1989), *La Cultura Religiosa de las Comunidaded Eclesiales de Base en Nicaragua*, Centro de Análisis Socio-Cultural, UCA: Managua.

Houtart, François (1990), 'CELAM: The Forgetting of Origins' in Dermot Keogh (ed.), *Church and Politics in Latin America*, Macmillan: London and Basingstoke.

Hulme, Alan, Krekel, Steve and O'Reilly, Shannon (1990), *Not Just Another Nicaragua Travel Guide*, Mango Publications: Chico, CA.

Ingham, J. (1986), *Mary, Michael and Lucifer: Folk Catholicism in Central Mexico*, University of Austin Press: Austin, TX.

Jiménez, Felix (1987), 'La Parroquia San Pablo, Germen de Las Communidades de Base en Nicaragua', in G. Girardi, B.Forcano, and J. Mª Vigil, (eds), *Nicaragua Trinchera Teologica*, Nuevos Textos: Managua and Madrid.

Joll, James (1977), *Gramsci*, Fontana: Glasgow.

Jonas, Susan and Stein, Nancy (1990), 'The Construction of Democracy in Nicaragua', *Latin American Perspectives*, 66(7), No. 3, Summer.

Jordan, Glenn and Weedon, Chris (1995), *Cultural Politics: Class, Gender, Race and the Postmodern World*, Blackwell: Oxford.

Kattenberg, David (1991), 'Criole Stew', *Border/Lines*, 22, Summer.

Kee, Alistair (1990), *Marx and the Failure of Liberation Theology*, SMC Press:London.

Keller, Nancy, Brosnahan, Tom and Rachowiecki, Rob (1992), *Central Ameria*, Lonely Planet Publications: Berkeley, CA.

Keogh, Dermot (ed.) (1990), *Church and Politics in Latin America*, Macmillan: London and Basingstoke.

King, Ursula (ed.) (1994), *Feminist Theology from the Third World: A Reader*, SPCK:London.

Kselman, Thomas A. (1986), 'Ambivalence and Assumption in the Concept of Popular Religion', in Daniel H. Levine (ed.), *Religion and Political Conflict in Latin America*, University of North Carolina Press: Chapel Hill and London.

Küppers, Gabby (ed.) (1994), *Compañeras: Voices from the Latin American Women's Movement*, Latin America Bureau: London.

Lacayo, Juan José (1992), 'Critican a Comisión Etica', *Barricada*, 24 September.

Laclau, Ernesto (1977), *Politics and Ideology in Marxist Theory*, Verso: London.

Laclau, Ernesto (1985), 'New Social Movements and the Plurality of the Social' in David Slater (ed.), *New Social Movements and the State in Latin America*, Foris Publications: Dordrecht-Holland.

Laclau, Ernesto (1988), 'Populism y Transformación del Imaginario Político en América Latina', in *Cuadernos de la Realidad*, 3, CIRE: Quito.

Laclau, Ernesto (1992), 'Beyond Emancipation', *Development and Change*, 23, July.

Laclau, Ernesto and Mouffe, Chantal (1985), *Hegemony and Socialist Strategy: Towards a Radical Democratic Politics*, Verso: London.

La Feber, Walter (1984), *Inevitable Revolutions: The United States in Central America*, W. W. Norton: NY.

Lancaster, Roger (1988), *Thanks to God and the Revolution: Popular Religion and Class Consciousness in the New Nicaragua*, Columbia University Press: NY.

Lancaster, Roger (1992), *Life is Hard: Machismo, Danger, and the Intimacy of Power in Nicaragua*, University of California Press, Berkeley.

Largaespada, Mildred (1992), 'Virginidad en el Cielo...Violación en la Tierra: El Caso de los Peloteros', *Barricada* (Gente), 4 December.

Larrain, Jorge (1979), *The Concept of Ideology*, Hutchinson: London.

Larrain, Jorge (1983), *Marxism and Ideology*, Macmillan Publishers Ltd., London.

Larrain, Jorge (1986), *A Reconstruction of Historical Materialism*, Allen & Unwin: London.

Larrain, Jorge (1989), *Theories of Development: Capitalism, Colonialism and Dependency*, Polity Press: Cambridge.

Larrain, Jorge (1994), *Ideology and Cultural Identity: Modernity and the Third World Presence*, Polity Press: London.

Latin American Weekly Report, (1993), 'Now FSLN Wants "Piñata" Solved', WR-93-09, 4 March.

Léon-Portilla, Miguel (ed.) (1980), translations by Miguel Léon-Portilla, J.O. Anderson, Charles E. Dibble and Munro S. Edmonson, with foreword, introduction and notes by Miguel Léon-Portilla, *Native Mesoamerican Spirituality, Ancient Myths, Discourses, Stories, Doctrines, Hymns, Poems from the Aztec, Yucatec, Quiche-Maya and Other Sacred Traditions*, SPCK: London.

Lernoux, Penny (1980), *Cry of the People: US Involvement in the Rise of Fascism, Torture, Murder and the Persecution of the Catholic Church in Latin America*, Doubleday: NY.

Lernoux, Penny (1989), *People of God: The Struggle for World Catholicism*, Viking: NY.

Lernoux, Penny, with Jones, Arthur and Ellsberg, Robert (1994), *Hearts on Fire*, Orbis: Maryknoll, N.Y.

Leví, Lillián (1992), 'Del Grito y la Gritería', *Barricada* (Gente), 11 December.

Levine, Daniel H. (ed.) (1986), *Religion and Political Conflict in Latin America*, The University of North Carolina Press: Chapel Hill and London.

Levine, Daniel H. (1990), 'The Catholic Church and Politics in Latin America: Basic Trends and Likely Futures', in Dermot Keogh (ed.),

Church and Politics in Latin America, Macmillan: London and Basingstoke.

Linden, Ian (1993), 'Reflections on Santo Domingo', *The Month*, CIIR, January.

Longino, Helen (1993), 'Feminist Standpoint Theory and the Problems of Knowledge', *Signs: Journal of Women in Culture and Society*, 19(1).

Luciak, Ilja (1990), 'Democracy in the Nicaraguan Countryside: A Comparative Analysis of Sandinista Grassroots Movements' in *Latin American Perspectives*, 66, (17) No. 3, Summer.

McConnell, R., Pacheco-Anton, A.F. and Magnotti, R. (1990), 'Crop Duster Aviation Mechanics: High Risk for Pesticide Poisoning', *American Journal of Public Health*, 80, October.

McDonagh, Francis (1991), 'Accents in Theology', *New Blackfriarss*, 72 (853), October.

McDonagh, Francis (1993), 'The Santo Domingo Conference', in Gustavo Gutiérrez, Francis McDonagh, Cândido Padin OSB and Jon Sobrino, *Santo Domingo and After: The Challenges for the Latin American Church*, CIIR: London.

Mainwaring, Scott and Viola, E. (1984), 'New Social Movements Political Culture and Democracy: Brazil and Argentina', *Telos*, 61, Fall.

Mainwaring, Scott and Wilde, Alexander (1989), 'The Progressive Church in Latin America: An Interpretation', in Scott Mainwaring and Alexander Wilde (eds), *The Progressive Church in Latin America*, University of Notre Dame Press: Notre Dame, IN.

Malessa, Falko (1994), 'Christian Base Communities in Monimbó: Hope in the Desert', *Barricada Internacional*, 14(376), August.

Malloy, James (1987), 'The Politics of Transition in Latin America' in James Mallory and Mitchell Selligson (eds), *Authoritarians and Democrats: Regime Transition in Latin America*, University of Pittsburgh Press: Pittsburgh, PA.

Majnep, Ian and Blumer, Ralph (1977), *Birds of My Kalam Country*, Oxford University Press: Auckland.

March, Robert H. (1978), *Physics for Poets*, Contemporary Books: Chicago.

Maríategui, José Carlos (1958), *7 Ensayos de Interpretacion de la Realidad Peruana*, Empresa Editora Amauta: Lima, Peru.

Marín, Linda (1991), 'Speaking Out Together: Testimonials of Latin American Women', *Latin American Perspectives*, 70(18), No. 3, Summer.

Martin, David (1985), *Religious Vision and Political Reality*, (Pamphlet Library no. 7), Centre for the Study of Religion and Society, University of Kent at Canterbury: Canterbury.

Martin, Randy (1992), 'Theater after the Revolution: Refiguring the Political in Cuba and Nicaragua', in George Yúdice, Jean Franco and Juan Flores (eds), *On Edge: The Crisis of Contemporary Latin American Culture*, University of Minnesota Press: Minneapolis, MN.

Marx, Karl (1970), *The German Ideology*, Lawrence and Wishart: London.

Mayoux, Linda (1992), 'From Idealism to Realism: Women, Feminism and Empowerment in Nicaraguan Tailoring Cooperative', *Development and Change*, 23(2), April.

Medvedev, P.N. and Bakhtin, Mikhail (1978), *The Formal Method of Literary Scholarship: A Critical Introduction to Sociological Poetics*, Johns Hopkins University Press: Baltimore.

Melrose, Dianna (1985), *Nicaragua: The Threat of a Good Example?*, Oxfam: Oxford.

Melucci, Alberto (1980), 'The New Social Movements: A Theoretical Approach', *Social Science Information*, 19(2).

Mies, Maria (1993), 'Towards a Methodology for Feminist Research', in Martyn Hammersley (ed.), *Social Research: Philosophy, Politics and Practice*, Sage Publications: London.

Miller, William D. (1973), *A Harsh and Dreadful Love*, Liveright: NY.

Miranda, José Porfirio (1974), *Marx and the Bible: A Critique of the Philosophy of Oppression*, Orbis Books: Maryknoll, NY.

Mistral, Gabriela (1992), 'Ahora', *Amanecer*, 77, March-May.

Moghadam, Valentine (1987), 'Socialism or Anti-Imperialism?: The Left and the Revolution in Iran', *New Left Review*, November/December.

Molina Oliú, Uriel (1987), 'Novedad y Conflictividad en las Comunidades Cristianas Revolucionarias', in G. Girardi, B.Forcano, and J. Mª Vigil, (eds), *Nicaragua Trinchera Teologica*, Nuevos Textos: Managua and Madrid.

Molyneux, Maxine (1981), 'Socialist Societies Old and New: Progress towards Women's Emancipation?' *Feminist Review*, 8, Summer.

Molyneux, Maxine (1984), 'Mobilisation without Emancipation? Women's Interests, State and Revolution in Nicaragua', *Critical Social Policy*, 10(4), No. 1.

Molyneux, Maxine (1988), The Politics of Abortion in Nicaragua: Revolutionary Pragmatism - or Feminism in the Realm of Necessity?' *Feminist Review*, 29, Spring.

Montenegro, Sofía (1992), 'La Gritería: La Otro Cara del Culto a la Inmaculada Concepción', *Barricada (Gente)*, 4 December.

Montenegro, Sofía, 'The Future From a Female Point of View', in Gabby Küppers (ed.), *Compañeras: Voices from the Latin American Women's Movement*, Latin America Bureau: London, 1994.

Moore Lappé and Joseph Collins with Cray Fowler, *Food First: Beyond the Myth of Scarcity*, Ballantine Books: NY, 1978.

Munck, Rolando (1990), 'Farewell to Socialism?: A Comment on Recent Debates', *Latin American Perspectives*, 65(17), no. 2, Spring.

Munck, Rolando (1989), *Latin America: The Transition to Democracy*, Zed Books: London.

Nash, June and Safa, Helen (eds.) (1985), *Women and Change in Latin America*, Bergin & Garvey: MA.

Nicaragua Solidarity Campaign (1993), 'Community Movement', in *Nicaragua Special Report*,

Nicaragua Solidarity Campaign (1994), *Current Situation Briefing: FSLN Holds Extraordinary Party Congress*, 13 June.

Nichols, OP, Aidan (1991), 'The Rise and Fall of Liberation Theology? An Evaluative Chronicle', *New Blackfriars*, 72(853), October.

Nord, Cristina (1994), 'Unemployed and Under-Employed Women: No Exit?', in *Barricada Internacional*, 14(371), March.

Norsworthy, Kent with Barry, Tom (1990), *Nicaragua: A Country Guide*, The Inter-Hemispheric Education Resource Center: Albuquerque, NM.

Nuevo Diario (1992), 'Chávez Quiere Colgar los Guantes', 31 July.

O'Brien, Conor Cruise (1990), 'God and Man in Church and Politics in Latin America' in Dermot Keogh (ed.), *Church and Politics in Latin America*, Macmillan, Basingstoke and London.

O'Campo, José Antonio (1990), 'New Economic Thinking in Latin America', *Journal of Latin American Studies*, 22(1), February.

O'Connor, James (1984), *Accumulation Crisis*, Basil Backwell: Oxford.

O'Connor, James (1987), *The Meaning of Crisis: A Theoretical Introduction*, Basil Backwell Ltd: Oxford.

O'Connor, James (1988), class notes for 'Capitalism and Nature', University of California Santa Cruz.

O'Donnell, Guillermo (1973), *Modernization and Bureaucratic Authoritarianism*: Studies in South American Politics, Institute of International Studies, University of California: Berkeley.

Ormrod, David (1988), *Nicaragua: The Theology and Political Economy of Liberation*, (Pamphlet Library no.19), Centre for the Study of Religion and Society, Pamphlet Library, University of Kent: Canterbury.

O'Shaughnessy, Hugh (1993), 'Nicaragua Vies with Haiti as West's Nightmare', in *Observer*, 12 September.

Palma, G. (1981), 'Dependency and Development: A Critical Overview' in D. Seers (ed.), *Dependency Theory a Critical Reassessment*, Francis Pinter: London.

Parker, Christian (1993), *Otra Lógica en América Latina: Religión Popular y Modernización Capitalista*, Fundo de Cultura Económica: Chile.

Parmar, Pratibha (1990), 'Black Feminism: the Politics of Articulation', in Jonathan Rutherford (ed.), *Identity, Community, Culture, Difference*, Lawrence & Wishart: London.

Parpart, Jane, L. (1993), 'Who Is the 'Other': A Postmodern Feminist Critique of Women and Developemnt Theory and Practice', *Development and Change*, 24(3), July.

Paz, Octavio (1961), *The Labyrinth of Solitude: Life and Thought in Mexico*, Grove Press: NY.

Peralta, Marta (1993), *Psychology and Health in Nicaragua*, Birmingham, 9 June.

Perry, Nicholas and Echeverría, Loreto (1988), *Under the Heel of Mary*, Routledge: London.

Poulat, Emile (1990), 'The Path of Latin American Catholicism', in Dermot Keogh, (ed.), *Church and Politics in Latin America*, Macmillan:London and Basingstoke.

Pui-lan, Kwok and Russell, Letty (eds) (1988), *Inheriting Our Mothers' Gardens: Feminist Theology in Third World Perspective*, Westminister Press: Philadelphia.

Quintero M., Armando (1992), 'Traditición Viene desde Tiempos Coloniales: Léon Listo Para Gritería', *La Prensa*, 5 December.

Quintero, Rafael (1980), *El Mito del Populismo en el Ecuador*, FLACSO: Quito.

Radcliffe, Sarah (1990), 'Multiple Identities and Negotiation over Gender: Female Peasant Union Leaders in Peru', *Bulletin of Latin American Research*, 9(2).

Ramírez, Maria (1992), *Education in Nicaragua*, Benjamin Linder Talk, Managua, Nicaragua, 13 August.

Randall, Margaret (1981), *Sandino's Daughters: Testimonies of Nicaraguan Women in Struggle*, ed. Lynda Yanz, Zed Press: London.

Randall, Margaret (1983), *Christians in the Nicaraguan Revolution*, translated by Mariana Valverde, New Star Books: Vancouver.

Recinos, Harold Joseph (1993), 'The Politics of Salvadoran Refugee Religion', PhD, The American University.

Reilly, Charles (1986), 'Latin America's Religious Populists', in Daniel H. Levine (ed.), *Religion and Political Conflict in Latin*

America, University of North Carolina Press: Chapel Hill and London.

Rice, Paul (1987), 'Growing with Experience. Eight Years of Agrarian Reform', *Nicaraguan Perspectives*, Fall.

Richard, Pablo (1987), 'Nicaragua en la Teología de la Liberación Latinoamerica', in G. Girardi, B. Forcano, and J. Mª Vigil, (eds), *Nicaragua Trinchera Teologica*, Nuevos Textos: Managua and Madrid.

Richard, Pablo (1993), 'Liberation Theology: Theology of the South', in *Envio*, 12(143), June.

Rosaldo, Renato (1993), *Culture and Truth: The Remaking of Social Analysis*, Routledge: London.

Rosengarten, Frank (1968), *The Italian Anti-Fascist Press (1919-1945)*, The Press of Case Western Reserve University: Cleveland, OH.

Rowe, William and Schelling, Vivian (1991), *Memory and Modernity: Popular Culture in Latin America*, Verso: London.

Roxborough, Ian (1984), 'Unity and Diversity in Latin American History', *Journal of Latin American Studies*, 16.

Ruchwarger, Gary (1985), 'The Sandinista Mass Orginizations and the Revolutionary Process', in Richard Harris and Carlos Vilas (eds), *Nicaragua: A Revolution under Siege*, Zed Books: London.

Ruchwarger, Gary (1987), *People in Power: Forging a Grassroots Democracy in Nicaragua*, Bergin and Garvery: Boston.

Runciman, W.G. (1978), *Weber: Selections in Translation*, translated by Eric Matthews, Cambridge University Press: Cambridge.

Sabet, Amir (1990), 'Religion and Social Transformation: A Liberative Approach', PhD, University of Calgary.

Said, Edward (1978), *Orientalism*, Random House: NY.

Samandu, Luis (1988), 'El pentacostalismo en Nicaragua y sus raíses religiosas populares', *Pasos*, 17, (published in San José, Costa Rica), May-June.

Sánchez, Mario (1992), 'Se Inaugura Primera Radio Para la Mujer', *Nuevo Diario*, 4 December.

Sandino, Arturo (1992), Nicaragua since the FSLN's Electoral Loss, Benjamin Linder Talk, Managua, Nicaragua, 23 July.

Sandoval, Moses (1991), 'Stumbling over a Milestone', in *Maryknoll*, 85(4), April.

Saporta Sternbach, Nancy (1991), 'Re-membering the Dead: Latin American Women's 'Testimonal' Discourse', *Latin American Perspectives*, 70(18), No. 3, Summer.

Sassoon, Anne Showstack (1978), 'Hegemony and Political Intervention', in Sally Hibbin (ed.) *Politics, Ideology and the State*, Lawrence & Wishart: London.

Sassoon, Anne Showstack (1982), 'Hegemony, War of Position and Political Intervention', in Sally Hibbin (ed.), *Approaches to Gramsci*, Writers and Readers Publishing Cooperative: London.

Schirmer, Jennifer (1993), 'The Seeking of Truth and the Gendering of Consciousness: The Comadres of El Salvador and the Conavigua Widows of Guatemala', in Radcliffe, Sarah and Westwood (eds), Sallie, *Viva: Women and Popular Protest in Latin America*, Routledge: London.

Schneider, Jane (1990), 'Spirits and the Spirit of Capitalism', in Ellen Badone (ed.), *Religious Orthodoxy and Popular Faith in European Society*, Princeton University Press: Princeton, NJ.

Segundo, Juan Luis (1975), *The Liberation of Theology*, Orbis Books: Maryknoll, NY.

Serra, Luis Héctor (1985a), 'The Grass-Roots Organizations', in Thomas Walker (ed.), *Nicaragua: The First Five Years*, Praeger: NY.

Serra, Luis Héctor (1985b), 'Ideology, Religion and the Class Struggle in the Nicaraguan Revolution', in Richard Harris and Carlos M. Vilas (eds), *Nicaragua: A Revolution under Siege*, Zed Books: London.

Silva, Danilo (1993), 'Need to Talk Clearly', *Barricada Internacional*, 13(367-8), November/December.

Slater, David (ed.) (1985), *New Social Movements and the State in Latin America*, Foris: Dordrecht.

Smith, Dorothy (1990), *Texts, Facts, and Femininity: Exploring the Relations of Ruling*, Routledge: London.

Snitow, Ann (1990), 'A Gender Diary', in Marianne Hirsch and Evelyn Fox Keller (eds), *Conflicts in Feminism*, Routledge: London.

Sobrino, Jon (1984), *The True Church and the Poor*, SMC Press: London.

Sommer, Doris (1991), 'Rigoberta's Secrets', *Latin American Perspectives*, 70(18), No. 3, Summer.

Spalding, Rose (ed.) (1987), *The Political Economy of Revolutionary Nicaragua*, Allen & Unwin: London.

Spivak, Gayatri Chakravorty, *Outside in the Teaching Machine*, Routledge: London, 1993.

Stacey, Judith (1990), 'On Resistance, Ambivalence and Feminist Theory: A Response to Carol Gilligan', *Michigan Quaterly Review*, 29(4).

Stanley, Liz (ed.), *Feminist Praxis: Research, Theory and Epistemology in Feminist Sociology*, Routledge: London, 1990.

Stanley, Liz and Wise, Sue (1993), *Breaking Out Again: Feminist Ontology and Epistemology*, Routledge: London.

Stavenhagen, Rodolfo (1993), 'Decolonializing Applied Social Sciences', in Martyn Hammersley, (ed.), *Social Research: Philosophy, Politics and Practice*, Sage Publications Ltd.: London.

Stein, Steve (1980), *Populism in Peru*, University of Wisconsin Press: Madison.

Stephens, Beth (1990), 'Developing a Legal System Graples with an Ancient Problem: Rape in Nicaragua' in *Women's Rights Law Reporter* 12, No. 2.

Stoll, David (1990), *Is Latin America Turning Protestant?: The Politics of Evangelical Growth*, Berkeley and Los Angeles: University of California Press.

Suarez, Wagner (1991), 'The Santo Domingo Preliminary Document The Social Reality' (translated from SIC, 527, August 1990) in *LADOC*, 21(3), January/February.

Talavera, María Alicia (1992), 'Mingo "Sube" sin el Relajo de la "Bajada"', *Barricada*, 11 August.

Tamez, Elsa (1982), *Bible of the Oppressed*, Orbis: Maryknoll, NY.

Tamez, Elsa (ed.) (1989), *Through Her Eyes: Women's Theology from Latin America*, Orbis: Maryknoll, NY.

Taussig, Michael T. (1980), *The Devil and Commodity Fetishism in South America*, University of North Carolina Press: Chapel Hill, SC.

Taylor, Lawrence J. (1990), 'Stories of Power, Powerful Stories: The Drunken Priest in Donegal', in Ellen Badone (ed.), *Religious Orthodoxy and Popular Faith in European Society*, Princeton University Press: Princeton, NJ.

Teles, Maria Amélia (1994), 'A Feminist Perspective on Power and Population Control', in Gabby Küppers (ed.), *Compañeras: Voices from the Latin American Women's Movement*, Latin America Bureau: London.

Thompson, Carol B. (1988), 'War by Another Name: Destabilisation in Nicaragua and Mozambique', *Race and Class*, 29, Spring.

Tomlinson, John (1991), *Cultural Imperialism*, Pinter Publishers: London.

Touraine, Alain (1989), *América Latina Política y Sociedad*, Espasa-Calpe: Madrid.

Trejos Ubau, Brenda (1992), 'Todos a Traer a Minguio', *Barricada*, 1 August.

Ubeda Bravo, Cesar (1992), 'Piedad Popular' in *La Prensa*, 19 de August.

Utting, Peter (1987), 'Domestic Supply and Food Shortages' in Rose Spalding (ed.), *The Political Economy of Revolutionary Nicaragua*, Allen & Unwin: London.

Valiverde, Luis (1992), 'Daniel: Ajustes Incrementan Analfabetismo y Mortalidad', *Barricada*, 24 August.

Vanden, Harry (1982a), 'The Ideology of the Nicaraguan Revolution', *Monthly Review*, 34(2), June.

Vanden, Harry (1982b), 'The Ideology of the Insurrection', in Thomas Walker (ed.), *Nicaragua in Revolution*, Westview Press: Boulder, CO.

Van Vught, Johannes (1989), 'Democratic Organization for Social Transformation: a Case Study of Nicaragua's Christian Base Communities in the Revolutionary Process', Draft working copy of PhD dissertation, Social Sciences, University of California Irvine.

Vargas, Virginia (1992), 'The Feminist Movement in Latin America: Between Hope and Disenchantment', *Development and Change*, 23(3).

Vasconi, Tomás A. (1990), (translated by Susan Casal Sánchez) 'Democracy and Socialism in South America', *Latin American Perspectives*, 65(17), No. 2, Spring.

Vilas, Carlos M. (1990), 'Nicaragua: Haunted by the Past', *NACLA, Report on the Americas*, 24, June.

Vilas, Carlos M. (1992), 'Family Affairs: Class, Lineage and Politics in Contemporary Nicaragua', *Journal of Latin American Studies*, 24(2), May.

Vilas, Carlos (1992-93), 'Latin American Populism: A Structural Approach', *Science and Society*, 56(4), Winter.

Villavicencio, José Luis (1992), '¿Para qué un congreso extraordinario?', *Barricada*, 11 September.

Villavicencio, Maritza (1994), 'The Feminist Movement and the Social Movement: Willing Partners?' in Gabby Küppers (ed.), *Compañeras: Voices from the Latin American Women's Movement*, Latin America Bureau: London.

Vindell Matus, Pedro José (1992), 'Policía: No hay Denuncio Sobre Saqueo a Panaloya', *Barricada*, 11 September.

Vink, Nico (1985), 'Base Communities and Urban Social Movements: A Case Study of the Metal Workers Strike 1980 - São Bernardo, Brazil' in David Slater (ed.), *New Social Movements and the State in Latin America*, Foris Publications: Dordrecht.

Virtuoso, S.J., José (1993), 'Insurrection in Chiapas... Revolution in Mexico', in *Envio*, 13(153), April.

Walker, Thomas (ed.) (1982), *Nicaragua in Revolution*, Westview Press: Boulder, CO.

Walker, Thomas (ed.) (1985), *Nicaragua: The First Five Years*, Praeger: NY.

Wallerstein, I. (1974), *The Modern World System*, Academic Press: NY.

Warne, Randi R. (1989), 'Toward a Brave New Paradigm: The Impact of Women's Studies on Religious Studies', *Religious Studies and Theology*, Vol. 9, Nos. 2 & 3.

Warner, Marina (1985), *Alone of All Her Sex: The Myth and Cult of the Virgin Mary*, Picador: London.

Warnock, J. W., *The Politics of Hunger*, Methuen: Toronto.

Weedon, Chris (1987), *Feminist Practice and Poststructuralist Theory*, Basil Blackwell: Oxford.

Weinberg, Bill (1991), *War on the Land: Ecology and Politics in Central America*, Zed Books: London.

Welch, Sharon D. (1985), *Communities of Resistance and Solidarity: A Feminist Theology of Liberation*, Orbis Books: Maryknoll, NY.

Wessel, Lois (1991), 'Reproductive Rights in Nicaragua: From the Sandinistas to the Governmnt of Violeta Chamorro', *Feminist Studies*, 17(3), Fall.

Williams, Peter (1989), *Popular Religion in America: Symbolic Change and the Modernization Process in Historical Perspective*, University of Illinois Press: Urbana and Chicago.

Williams, Philip J. (1989a), *The Catholic Church and Politics in Nicaragua and Costa Rica*, MacMillan: Basingstoke.

Williams, Philip J. (1989b), 'The Catholic Church in the Nicaraguan Revolution: Differing Responses and New Challenges', in Scott Mainwaring and Alexander Wilde (eds), *The Progressive Church in Latin America*, University of Notre Dame Press: Notre Dame, IN.

Williams, Raymond (1983), *Towards 2000*, Chatto & Windus: London, 1983.

Woodford Bray, Marjory and Dugan Abbassi, Jennifer (1990), Introduction to a collection of articles entitled 'The Sandinista Legacy: The Construction of Democracy', *Latin American Perspectives*, 17(66), No.3, Summer.

Woodward, Kenneth L. (1991), 'Blessings on the Market', *Newsweek*, 117(19), 13 May.

Yúdice, George (1991), 'Testimonio and Postmodernism', *Latin American Perspectives*, 70(18), No. 3, Summer .

Yúdice, George, Franco, Jean and Flores, Juan (eds) (1992), *On Edge: The Crisis of Contemporary Latin American Culture*, University of Minnesota Press: Minneapolis and London.

Zenteno, SJ, Arnaldo (1992), *Nicaragua: Hambre, Confusion Y Violencia...*, Casa CEB: Managua.

Index

abortion 55, 79-79, 96-98
Adriance, Madeline 56
Adorno, Theodor 174
Amin, S 44
AMNLAE (Association of
Nicaraguan Women, Luisa
Amanda Espinosa) 77, 78, 80,
81, 83, 94-98, 116-117, 161
anarcho-communism 72
anthropology 28, 32
anti-imperialism 72
Antonio Valdivieso
Ecumenical
Centre 31, 182
Arce, Bayardo 68 85
Arellano, Luz Beatriz 55, 66
Arias, José 119
Atlantic Coast 183, 184
autobiographies 25, 35

Báez, Gladys 95
Baltodano, Monica 91, 124
Barbie, Dominique 58
Barthes, Roland 30
Basatian, Jean-Pierre 167, 175-
177

Belli, Gioconda 90
Belli, Humberto 93, 212-213
Bianchi, Enzo 62
Bidegain, Ana María 52, 53
Bingemer, María Clara 53
Boff, Leonardo15, 42, 45, 46,
47, 50-52, 56, 58, 59, 208
Borge, Tomás 91, 184, 197, 215
Bradstock, Andrew 13
Brown, Doug 11
Bruneau, Thomas 171
Burbach, Roger and Nuñéz,
Orlando 69, 112-117

Cabezas, Omar 36
Cabrales, Bertha Inés 80
Cardenal, Ernesto 9, 60, 63
Cardenal, Fenando 87-88
Cardoso, F. H. and Faletto, E.
44
Carrión, Luis 91-92
Carter, Jimmy 11
Catholic Action 110
Catholic church 12, 16, 17, 39,
46, 50, 51, 59, 61, 64

Kselman, Thomas 171

Laclau, Ernesto 74-75
Laclau, Ernesto and Mouffe,
Chantal 113
Lancaster, Roger 3, 82-83, 156,
188, 189, 198, 199, 202, 206,
207, 210, 215, 217-218, 223
Larrain, Jorge 5
Latin American Episcopal
Conference (CELAM) 17, 171,
178
   conservatives 17, 59, 171,
   186
   Medellín 17, 171
   progressives 17, 59, 171,
   186
   Puebla 17, 171
   Santo Domingo 17, 171,
   172- 174, 180
Law between Mothers,
Fathers and Children 77
Left 30, 174, 188, 210, 211, 218,
169, 170, 198, 210, 211, 213,
214, 217
Lernoux, Penny 45, 104
Leví, Lillian 194, 195
liberation theology 2, 3,7,
12,14, 15, 16-20, 36, 37, 43-51,
59, 62, 64, 66, 72, 76, 107, 170,
169, 198, 210-214, 217
'little groups' 111
Locke, John 5

machismo 76
Mainwaring, Scott and Wilde,
Alexander 61, 63
Mainwaring, Scott and Viola,
E. 114
Majorities 90, 91

Maríategui, Jose 14, 126, 214,
211
Marín, Lynda 36
Marx, Karl 8, 44, 64, 126
Marxism13, 14, 43, 45, 46, 47,
49, 50, 59, 61, 63, 66, 72, 141,
213, 215

Maynoux, Linda 163, 164
Mazzi, Don Enzo 111
Medvedev, P.N. and Bakhtin,
Mikhail 30
Menchú, Rigoberta 46
Mendiola, Benigna 91
methodology 24-37
Mies, Maria 26
   conscious partiality 26
Miranda, José 2 47
MOs (Mass Organisations) 99,
105-106, 123-124, 127
Moghadam, Valentine 75
Molyneux, Maxine 21, 159,
164
   strategic gender interests,
   21, 38, 68, 79, 80-82, 94, 95,
   158- 164
   practical gender interests,
   21, 23, 79, 68, 81, 94, 97, 98,
   158- 164
Montenegro, Sofía 100, 208,
193, 194
Moral identities 4, 7, 83, 106,
107, 115, 137, 141-142, 143,
168, 232-236
Moran, Lucy 164
Motherism, motherist
organisations 20, 150-158, 232
multi-method research 29, 32
myth 189, 190, 211, 214, 215,
217-219, 221, 222
Mulukukú Women's Clinic 97

National Directorate 81, 85, 124
National Guard 89, 217
Nationalism 72-73, 208, 209
neo-liberalism 1, 20, 31, 130, 158, 199
'New Man' 125, 211
New Social Movements
  See social movements
Nicaraguan Catholic church 16, 39, 60, 61, 68, 92-94, 80, 104
hierarchical church,
traditional church 39, 92-94, 119-120, 121, 124
popular church, church of the poor 2,3, 4,7, 13, 14, 15,16-20, 28, 30, 34, 37,38, 39, 55, 61, 93, 94, 170, 172, 175, 176, 177, 179, 181, 182, 184-185, 213
Nicaraguan Revolution 1, 2, 3, 4, 5, 7, 8, 9, 11, 14, 17, 18, 19, 20, 22, 29, 36, 38, 40, 55, 74, 100, 103-106, 121, 129, 141
The Nora Astorga Front 98
Norsworthy, Kent 100

Obando y Bravo, Miguel 60, 92-93, 130, 131, 171
O'Connor, Jim 10
olla , communal kitchen 14, 19, 20, 22, 26, 27, 28, 29, 31, 33, 34, 35, 38, 39, 107, 108, 127, 130, 139, 140-166, 185, 228-229
oral histories 25
Ortega, Daniel 82, 86, 87, 91, 153, 184, 213
Ortega, Humberto 70-71, 89
'the other' 22, 27
Ormrod, David 43

parallel magisterium 2, 12, 18
Parmar, Pratibha 6

participant observation 32- 34
Paz, Octavio 180
Peralta, Marta 159
piñata 83-88
pluralism 70
Pope John XXIII 16
Pope John Paul II 17, 60, 122, 211
Popol Vuh 133
popular religion 3, 4, 7, 15, 19, 20, 24, 28, 31, 37, 38-40, 166-185, 198, 208-211, 229-232
popular religious festivals 2, 15, 31, 39, 107
La Purísima 2, 33, 39, 107, 188, 191-199
Santo Domingo 2,33, 39, 107, 188, 199-208
population control 55
populism 72, 73-75
postmodernism 5
Protestantism 175-178
Pui-lan, Kwok and Russell, Letty 53

Quincentenary 133, 134, 136, 137, 178-189

Race 54
Radcliffe, Sarah 79
Radio Mujer 96
Ramírez, Gladys 99
Ramírez, Sergio 86, 91
Right 7, 30, 38, 86, 93, 89, 175, 182, 184, 197, 210, 210-213, 218, 220-223, 226
Rosaldo, Renato 32, 35
Rowe, William and Schelling, Vivian 74, 75
Ruiz, Henry 184

Samandu, Luis, 176